THE SECRET SOCIETIES

OF ALL AGES AND COUNTRIES

Volume I

Dalla straordinarietà degli effetti certo può indursi la straordinarietà, la grandezza, l' insistenza delle cagioni; ma l' intreccio e l' alterno prevalere di queste, l' attrazione che esercitano, sfuggono all' analisi. Il mistero precinge la notturna fecondazione. Dai più disparati sentimenti trae vigore la setta. Le materie più preziose ed insieme le meno elette concorrono a formare questo gigante, rifusione ciclopica e tetra di quanto s' agita, ribolle e schiuma nelle viscere sociali.—G. DE CASTRO.

From the extraordinary nature of the effects we may infer the extraordinary nature, grandeur, and permanency of the causes; hnt their connection, varying predominance, and mutual attraction, escape all analysis. Mystery surrounds the obscure fecundation. Sects draw vigour from the most opposite sentiments. The most exalted as well as the meanest elements concur in forming this giant, a cyclopean and hlack fusion of all that seethes, boils, and ferments in the social viscera.

THE SECRET SOCIETIES
OF ALL AGES AND COUNTRIES

Volume I

BY
Charles William Heckethorn

Athens ‡ Manchester

The Secret Societies of all Ages and Countries

Volume I

Old Book Publishing Ltd

Book Cover Design: Old Book Publishing Ltd

Copyright © 2018 Old Book Publishing Ltd
All rights reserved.

Title of original: The Secret Societies of all Ages and Countries. Volume I

Originally published in 1875

Cover Image: Ismail lion calligram symbolising the lion of God.

ISBN–10: 1-78107-200-0 **volume I**
ISBN–10: 1-78107-201-9 volume II
ISBN–10: 1-78107-202-7 set

ISBN–13: 978-1-78107-200-4 **volume I**
ISBN–13: 978-1-78107-201-1 volume II
ISBN–13: 978-1-78107-202-8 set

Editor's Note

Old Book Publishing Ltd takes care in preserving the wording and images of the original books. For this reason we have invested in technology that enables us to enhance the quality of such reproduction. This investment helps overcome problems encountered when reproducing old books, such as stains, coloured paper, discolouration of ink, yellowed pages, see-through and onion skin type paper.

This reproduction book, produced from digital images of the original, may contain occasional defects such as missing pages or blemishes due to the original source content or were introduced by the scanning process.

These are scanned pages and the quality of print represents accurately the print quality of the original book, though we may have been able to enhance it.

As this book has been scanned and reformatted from the original we cannot guarantee that it is error-free or contains the full content of the original.

However, we believe that this work is culturally important, and despite its imperfections, have elected to bring it back into print as part of our commitment to the preservation of printed works.

The small number of corrections indicated in the errata list of the original edition have been entered into the text of the current edition and as a result the errata page has been omitted. A few minor errors in the Hebrew text have been corrected and some omitted closing quote marks restored.

Old Book Publishing

THE SECRET SOCIETIES

OF ALL AGES AND COUNTRIES.

BY

CHARLES WILLIAM HECKETHORN.

IN TWO VOLUMES.

VOL. I.

LONDON:
RICHARD BENTLEY AND SON,
Publishers in Ordinary to Her Majesty,
NEW BURLINGTON STREET.
1875.

ANALYTICAL TABLE OF CONTENTS.

The numbers refer to the §.

VOLUME I.

PREFACE xiii

INTRODUCTION.

1. Intelligibility and nature of Secret Societies. 2. Classification of Secret Societies. 3. Religious Societies. 4. Political Societies. 5. Aims of Political Societies. 6. Religious Secret Societies. 7. Most perfect human Type. 8. Causes of high mental Development. 9. Primitive Culture. 10. True Doctrines of Nature and Being. 11. Fundamental Principles of true Knowledge possessed by the Ancients; the Seven Properties of Eternal Nature. 12. Key to Mystic Teaching. 13. Mystic Teaching summarized. 14. How true Knowledge came to be lost. 15. Original Spirit of the Mysteries and Results of their Decay. 16. The Mysteries under their Astronomical Aspect. 17. Astronomical Aspects continued. 18. Uniformity of Dogmas. 19. Secret Societies no longer needed.

Book I.

ANCIENT MYSTERIES.

I. MAGI.—20. Derivation of term Magus. 21. Antiquity of the Magi. 22. Zoroaster. 23. Doctrine of Zoroaster. 24. The Light worshipped. 25. Origin of the word *Deus*. 26. Mode of Initiation. 27. Myth of Rustam.

II. MITHRAICS.—28. Mysteries of Mithras. 29. Origin of Mithraic worship. 30. Dogmas. 31. Rites of Initiation. 32. Rites derived from Magism.

III. BRAHMINS AND GYMNOSOPHISTS.—33. Vulgar creed of India. 34. Secret Doctrines. 35. Brahma and Buddha. 36. Asceticism. 37. Gymnosophists. 38. Places for Celebrating Mysteries. 39. Initiation. 39A. *Brahm and Brahma*. 40. Ineffable Name *Aum*. 41. The Lingam. 42. The Lotos.

IV. EGYPTIAN MYSTERIES.—43. Antiquity of Egyptian Civilization. 44. Temples of Ancient Egypt. 45. Egyptian Priests and Kings. 46. Exoteric and Esoteric Doctrines. 47. Egyptian Mythology. 48. The Phœnix. 49. The Cross. 50. Places of Initiation. 51. Process of Initiation. 52. Mysteries of Serapis. 53. Mysteries of Osiris. 54. Isis.

V. METAMORPHOSES OF THE LEGEND OF ISIS.—55. Spread of Egyptian Mysteries. 56. Dionysiaca or Bacchic Mysteries. 57. Sabazian Mysteries. 58. Mysteries of the Cabiri. 59. Eleusinian Mysteries. 60. Doors of Horn and Ivory. 61. Suppression of Eleusinian Mysteries. 62. Thesmophoria. 63. Aim of Grecian Mysteries more moral than religious.

VI. CHINESE AND JAPANESE MYSTERIES.—64. Chinese Metaphysics. 65. Introduction of Chinese Mysteries. 66. Parallel between Buddhism and Roman Catholicism. 67.

Lau-Tze. 68. Modern Chinese Societies. 69. Japanese Mysteries. 70. Japanese Doctrines. 71. The Lama.
VII. MEXICAN AND PERUVIAN MYSTERIES.—72. American Aborigines. 73. Mexican Deities. 74. Cruelty of Mexican Worship. 75. Initiation into Mysteries. 76. The Greater Mysteries. 77. Human Sacrifices. 78. Clothing in Bloody Skin. 79. Peruvian Mysteries.
VIII. DRUIDS.—80. The Druids the Magi of the West. 81. Temples. 82. Places of Initiation. 83. Rites. 84. Doctrines. 85. Political and Judicial Power. 86. Priestesses. 87. Abolition.
IX. SCANDINAVIAN MYSTERIES.—88. Drottes. 89. Ritual. 90. Astronomical Meaning.

Book II.

EMANATIONISTS.

I. CABALA.—91. Its Origin. 92. Its Progress. 93. Its Date. 94. Book of the Creation. 95. Different Kinds of Cabala. 96. Visions of Ezekiel. 97. The Creation out of Nothing. 98. Diffusion of Cabalistic Ideas.
II. THE GNOSTICS.—99. Character of Gnosticism. 100. Doctrines. 101. Development of Gnosticism. 102. Spirit of Gnosticism.

Book III.

RELIGION OF LOVE.

I. SONS OF THE WIDOW.—103. Origin of Religion of Love. 104. Manes. 105. Manichæism. 106. Life of Manes. 107. Progress of Manichæism. 108. Doctrines. 109. Spread of Religion of Love.

II. THE GAY SCIENCE.—110. Transition from Ancient to Modern Initiations. 111. Spirit of Ancient Secret Societies. 112. Spirit of Modern Secret Societies. 113. Cause and Progress of Heresy. 114. Efforts and Influence of Heretics. 115. The Albigenses. 116. Tenets of Albigenses. 117. Aims of Albigenses. 118. Religion of the Troubadours. 119. Difficulty to understand the Troubadours. 120. Poetry of Troubadours. 121. Degrees among Troubadours. 122. Courts of Love.

III. THE CONSOLATION.—123. Historical Notices. 124. Doctrines and Tenets.

IV. CHIVALRY.—125. Original Aim. 126. Knights the Military Apostles of the Religion of Love. 127. Tenets and Doctrines.

BOOK IV.

ISHMAELITES.

I. LODGE OF WISDOM.—128. Various Sects sprung from Manichæism. 129. Secret Doctrines of Islamism. 130. Candidati. 131. Cruelty of Babeck the Gay. 132. Ishmaelites. 133. Teaching of the Lodge of Cairo. 134. Progress of Doctrines.

II. ASSASSINS.—135. Foundation of Order. 136. Influence of Hassan. 137. Catechism of the Order. 138. Devotion of Followers. 139. The Imaginary Paradise. 140. Sanguinary Character of Hassan. 141. Further Instances of Devotion in Followers. 142. Christian Princes in League with Assassins. 143. Extinction of Sect.

III. DRUSES.—144. Origin of Sect. 145. Doctrines. 146. Recent Events.

Book V.

KNIGHTS TEMPLARS.

147. Foundation of Order. 148. Its Progress. 149. Account of Commanderies. 150. Imputations against the Order. 151. Plots against the Order. 152. Attentions paid to Grand Master Molay. 153. Charges against Templars. 154. Burning of Knights. 155. James de Molay burnt. 156. Mysteries of the Knights Templars. 157. The Temple and the Church. 158. The Temple the Symbol of the Holy Spirit. 159. Doctrines. 160. Initiation. 161. Cursing and Spitting on the Cross. 162. The Templars the Opponents of the Pope. 163. Baphomet. 164. Effects of the Downfall of the Knights of the Temple. 165. Connexion with Freemasonry.

Book VI.

FREE JUDGES.

I. HOLY VEHM.—166. Origin and Objects of Institution. 167. Officers and Organization. 168. Language and Rules of Initiated. 169. Procedure. 170. Execution of Sentences. 171. Decay of the Institution. 172. Kissing the Virgin.

II. BEATI PAOLI.—173. Character of the Society. 174. Tendencies and Tenets. 175. Account of Sicilian writer.

Book VII.

ALCHYMISTS.

I. ALCHYMISTS.—176. Astrology perhaps secret Heresy. 177. Process by which Astrology degenerated. 178.

Scientific Value of Alchymy. 179. The Tincture. 180. Aims of Alchymy. 181. History of Alchymy. 182. Specimen of Alchymistic Language. 183. Personal Fate of the Alchymists.

II. ROSICRUCIANS.—184. Merits of the Rosicrucians. 185. Origin of Society doubtful. 186. Origin of Name. 187. Statements concerning themselves. 188. Poetical Fictions of Rosicrucians. 189. Progress and Extinction of Rosicrucians. 190. Transition to Freemasons.

Book VIII.

FREEMASONS.

I. LEGEND OF THE TEMPLE.—191. Ancestry of Hiram Abiff. 192. Hiram, Solomon, and the Queen of Sheba.

II. ORIGIN.—TRADITIONS.—193. The First Masons. 194. Periods of Freemasonry. 195. Freemasonry derived from many sources.

III. RITES AND CUSTOMS.—196. List of Rites. 197. Masonic Customs. 198. Masonic Alphabet.

IV. THE LODGE.—199. Interior Arrangement of Lodge. 200. Modern Lodge. 201. Officers. 202. Opening the Lodge.

V. GENUINE AND SPURIOUS MASONRY.—203. Distinction between Genuine and Spurious Masonry. 204. Some Rites only deserve special mention.

VI. CEREMONIES OF INITIATION.—205. The Apprentice. 206. Fellow-craft. 207. Master. Ceremony of Initiation and Story of Hiram's Murder. 208. The Legend Explained. 209. The Raising of Osiris. 210. Blazing Star.

VII. HOLY ROYAL ARCH.—211. Officers. 212. Ceremonies. 213. Passing the Veils.

VIII. GRAND ELECTED KNIGHT OF KADOSH.—214. The Term

Kadosh. 215. Reception into the Degree. 216. The Mysterious Ladder. 217. The Seven Steps.

IX. PRINCE OF ROSE-CROIX.—218. Distinct from Rosicrucian, and has various names. 219. Officers and Lodge. 220. Reception in the First Apartment. 221. Second Apartment. 222. Reception in the Third Apartment.

X. RITES OF MISRAIM AND MEMPHIS.—223. Anomalies of Rite of Misraim. 224. Organization. 225. History and Constitution. 226. Rites and Ceremonies. 227. Rite of Memphis.

XI. MODERN KNIGHTS TEMPLARS.—228. Origin. 229. Supposititious List of Grand Masters. 230. Revival of the Order. 231. The Leviticon. 232. Ceremonies of Initiation.

XII. FREEMASONRY IN ENGLAND AND SCOTLAND.—233. Freemasonry in England. 234. Freemasonry in Scotland. 235. Modern Freemasonry.

XIII. FREEMASONRY IN FRANCE.—236. Introduction of Freemasonry into France. 237. Chevalier Ramsay. 238. Philosophical Rites. 239. The Duke de Chartres.

XIV. CHAPTER OF CLERMONT AND THE STRICT OBSERVANCE. —240. Jesuitical Influence. 241. The Strict Observance.

XV. RELAXED OBSERVANCE.—242. Organization of Relaxed Observance. 243. Disputes in German Lodges. 244. Rite of Zinnendorf. 245. African Architects.

XVI. CONGRESS OF WILHELMSBAD.—246. Various Congresses. 247. Discussions at Wilhelmsbad. 248. Result of Convention.

XVII. FREEMASONRY AND NAPOLEONISM.—249. Masonry protected by Napoleon. 250. Spread of Masonry. 251. Obsequiousness of Freemasonry. 252. Anti-Napoleonic Freemasonry.

XVIII. FREEMASONRY, THE RESTORATION OF THE SECOND EMPIRE.—253. The Society of "France Regenerated." 254. Priestly Opposition to Masonry. 255. Political Insignificance of Masonry. 256. Freemasonry and Napoleon III. 257. Jesuitical Manœuvres.

XIX. FREEMASONRY IN ITALY.—258. Whimsical Societies. 259. Illuminati in Italy. 260. Freemasonry at Naples. 261. Details of Document. 262. Freemasonry at Venice. 263. Abasement of Masonry under Napoleon. 264. The Freemasonry of the Present in Italy. 265. Reform needed.

XX. CAGLIOSTRO AND EGYPTIAN MASONRY.—266. Life of Cagliostro. 267. Egyptian Rite. 268. Cagliostro's Hydromancy.

XXI. ADOPTIVE MASONRY.—269. Historical Notice. 270. Organization. 271. Jesuit Degrees.

XXII. ANDROGYNOUS MASONRY.—272. Origin and Tendency. 273. Earliest Androgynous Societies. 274. Other Androgynous Societies. 275. Vicious Androgynous Societies. 276. Knights and Nymphs of the Rose. 277. Mason's Daughter.

XXIII. PERSECUTIONS OF FREEMASONRY.—278. Causes of Persecution. 279. Instances of Persecution. 280. Anti-Masonic Publications.

XXIV. SCHISMATIC RITES AND SECTS.—281. Schismatic Rites and Sects. 282. Ludicrous Degree.

XXV. DIFFUSION OF THE ORDER.—283. Freemasonry in Spain and Portugal. 284. Freemasonry in Russia. 285. Freemasonry in Switzerland. 286. Freemasonry in Sweden and Poland. 287. Freemasonry in Holland and Germany. 288. Freemasonry in Turkey, Asia, Africa, Oceania. 289. Freemasonry in America.

XXVI. FUTILITY OF MODERN FREEMASONRY.—290. Vain Pretensions of Modern Masonry. 291. Vanity of Masonic Ceremonial. 292. Masonry Diffuses no Knowledge. 293. Is unfitted for the Task. 294. Decay of Freemasonry. 295. Masonic Literature.

PREFACE.

FOR many years the fascinating subject of Secret Societies had engaged my attention, and it had long been my intention to collect in a comprehensive work all the information that could be gathered from numerous, often remote, and sometimes almost inaccessible sources, concerning one of the most curious phases of the history of mankind—those secret organizations, religious, political, and social, which have existed from the most remote ages down to the present time. Before, however, I had arranged and digested my materials, a review in the "Athenæum" (No. 2196), directed my attention to the Italian work "Il Mondo Secreto," by Signor De Castro, whom I have since then had the pleasure of meeting at Milan. I procured the book, and intended at first to give a translation of it, but though I began as a translator, my labours speedily assumed a more independent form. Much, I found, had to be omitted from an original coloured by a certain political bias, and somewhat too indulgent to various Italian political sects, who, in many instances, were scarcely more than hordes of brigands. Much, on the other hand, had to be added from sources, chiefly English and German, unknown to the Italian author; much had to be placed on a different basis and in another light; and again, many societies not mentioned by Signor De Castro had to be introduced to the reader, such as the Garduna, the Chauffeurs, Fenians, International, O-Kee-Pa, Ku-Klux, Inquisition, Wahábees; so that, with these additions, and the amplifications of sections in the original Italian, forming frequently entirely new articles, the work, as it now is presented to the English public, though in its framework retaining much of its foreign prototype, may yet claim the merit of being not only essentially original, but the most comprehensive account of Secret Societies extant in English, French, German, or Italian, the leading languages of Europe; for whatever has been written on the subject in any one of them has been consulted and put under contribution. In English there is no work that can at all compete with it, for the small book published in 1836 by Charles Knight, and entitled, "Secret Societies of the Middle Ages," embraces four societies only.

Anxious to utilize my latest memoranda, I have taken advantage of the MS. having for some time been in the publisher's hands, before the second volume went to press, to insert several additional sections, though at the expense of methodical arrangement; or to give supplemental details from information collected during my recent twelve months' wanderings in Italy, the country *par excellence* of secret societies.

The student who wishes for more ample information will have to consult the lists of authorities given at the head of each Book, as it was thought best not to encumber the text with foot-notes, which would have swelled the work to at least twice its present extent. The reader may rest satisfied that few statements are made which could not be supported by numerous and weighty authorities; though dealing as we do here with societies whose very existence depended on secrecy, and which, therefore, as a matter of policy, left behind them as little documentary evidence as possible, the old distich applies with peculiar force :—

> "What is hits is history,
> And what is mist is mystery."

Again, bearing in mind that the imperative compass of the work exacted a concise setting forth of facts—ranging as the subject does over a surface so vast—I have been careful to interrupt the narrative only by such comments and reflections as would seem almost indispensable for clearing up obscurities or supplying missing historical links.

It may at first appear as if some societies had improperly been inserted in this work as "secret" societies; the Freemasons, for instance. Members of secret associations, it might be objected, are not in the habit of proclaiming their membership to the world, but no Freemason is ashamed or afraid of avowing himself such; nay, he is rather proud of the fact, and given to proclaim it somewhat obtrusively; yet the most rabid Celt, who wishes to have a hand in the regeneration of his native land by joining the Fenian brotherhood, has sense enough to keep his affiliation a profound secret from the uninitiated. But the rule I have followed in adopting societies as "secret," was to include in my collection all such as had or have "secret rites and ceremonies" kept from the outer world, though the existence of the society itself be no secret at all. In fact, no association of men can for any length of time remain a secret, since however anxious the members may be to shroud themselves in darkness, and remain personally unknown, the purpose for which they band together must always betray itself by some overt acts; and wherever there is an act, the world surmises an agent; and if none that is visible can be found, a secret one is suspected. The Thugs, for instance, had every desire to remain unknown; yet the fact of the existence of such a society was suspected long before any of its members were discovered. On the principle also of their being the propounders of secret doctrines, or doctrines clothed in language understood by the adepts alone, Alchymists and Mystics have found places in this work; and the Inquisition, though a state tribunal, had its secret agents and secret procedure, and may therefore justly be included in the category of Secret Societies.

Secret Societies, religious and political, are again springing up on many sides: the religious may be dismissed without comment, as they are generally without any novelty or significance, but those that have political objects ought not to be disregarded as without importance. The International, Fenians, Communists, Nihilists, Wahábees, are secretly aiming at the overthrow of existing governments and the present order of things. The murders of Englishmen perpetrated by native Indians point to the machinations of secret societies in British India. Before the outbreak of the great Indian mutiny, English newspaper correspondents spoke rather contemptuously of some religious ceremony observed throughout British India of carrying small loaves from village to village, but this ceremony was the summons to the people to prepare for the general rising; hence the proceedings of the natives should be closely watched.

The first volume and a portion of the second having passed through the press while the author was in Italy, the revisal of the last proofs had to be confided to another hand; hence some *errata* will be found in those portions of the work, an evil almost unavoidable, under the circumstances, in a text so full of proper names, whose correct spelling frequently is scarcely fixed, and containing numerous quotations which could only be verified by reference to the originals whence they were taken, which in this case was clearly impossible. A list of the more important *errata* with their corrections has been appended at the end of vol. ii.

For the sake of clearness and of facilitating reference, the text has been divided throughout into short sections with appropriate headings, and numbered continuously.

November, 1874.

INTRODUCTION.

"The cause which I knew not, I searched out."
Job xxix. 16.

"Ignis ubique latet, naturam amplectitur omnem;
Cuncta parit, renovat, dividit, urit, alit."

INTRODUCTION.

1.

INTELLIGIBILITY *and Nature of Secret Societies.*—For those true thinkers who look upon history as a tissue of wondrous design, there is nothing accidental in the life of the world. For them the appearance and action of secret societies are no singular and inexplicable phenomenon, no transitory form, no unexpected and fugitive effect, but the intelligible and foreseen result of known causes.

Secret societies once were as necessary as open societies; the tree presupposes a root. Beside the empire of Might, the idols of fortune, the fetishes of superstition, there must in every age and state have existed a place where the empire of Might was at an end, where the idols were no longer worshipped, where the fetishes were derided. Such a place was the closet of the philosopher, the temple of the priest, the subterranean cave of the sectary.

2. *Classification of Secret Societies.*—Secret societies may be classed under the following heads: 1. Religious: such as the Egyptian or Eleusinian Mysteries.—2. Military: Knights Templars.—3. Judiciary: Vehmgerichte.—4. Scientific: Alchymists.—5. Civil: Freemasons.—6. Political: Carbonari. But the line of division is not always strictly defined; some that had scientific objects combined theological dogmas therewith—as the Rosicrucians, for instance; and political societies must necessarily influence civil life. We may therefore more conveniently range secret societies in the two comprehensive divisions of religious and political.

3. *Religious Societies.*—Religion has had its secret societies from the most ancient times; they date, in fact, from the period when the true religious knowledge—which, be it understood, consisted in the knowledge of the constitution of the universe and the Eternal Power that had produced, and the laws that maintained it—possessed by the first men, began to decay among the general mass of mankind. The genuine knowledge was to a great extent preserved in the ancient "Mysteries," though even these were already a degree removed from the first primeval native wisdom, since they represented only the type, instead of the archetype; namely, the phenomena of outward temporal nature, instead of the realities of the inward eternal nature,

of which this visible universe is the outward manifestation. Since the definition of this now recovered genuine knowledge is necessary for understanding much that was taught in the religious societies of antiquity, we shall, further on, enter into fuller details concerning it.

4. *Political Societies.*—Politically secret societies were the provident temperers and safety-valves of the present and the powerful levers of the future. Without them the monologue of absolutism alone would occupy the drama of history, appearing moreover without an aim, and producing no effect, if it had not exercised the will of man by inducing reaction and provoking resistance.

Every secret society is an act of reflection, therefore of conscience. For reflection, accumulated and fixed, is conscience. In so far, secret societies are in a certain manner the expression of conscience in history. For every man has in himself a Something which belongs to him, and which yet seems as if it were not a thing within him, but, so to speak, without him. This obscure Something is stronger than he, and he cannot rebel against its dominion nor withdraw himself or fly from its search. This part of us is intangible; the assassin's steel, the executioner's axe cannot reach it; allurements cannot seduce, prayers cannot soften, threats cannot terrify it. It creates in us a dualism, which makes itself felt as remorse. When man is virtuous, he feels himself one, at peace with himself; that obscure Something does neither oppress nor torture him: just as in physical nature the powers of man's body, when working in harmony, are unfelt (11); but when his actions are evil, his better part rebels. Now secret societies are the expression of this dualism reproduced on a grand scale in nations; they are that obscure Something of politics acting in the public conscience, and producing a remorse, which shows itself as "secret society," an avenging and purifying remorse. It regenerates through death, and brings forth light through fire, out of darkness, according to eternal laws. No one discerns it, yet every man may feel it. It may be compared to an invisible star, whose light, however, reaches us; to the heat coming from a region where no human foot will ever be placed, but which we feel, and can demonstrate with the thermometer.

Indeed, one of the most obvious sentiments that gives rise to secret societies is that of revenge, but good and wise revenge, different from personal rancour, unknown where popular interests are in question; that desires to punish institutions and not individuals, to strike ideas and not men—the grand collective revenge, the inheritance that fathers transmit to their children, a pious legacy of love, that sanctifies hatred and enlarges the responsibility and character of man. For there is a legitimate and necessary hatred, that of evil, which forms the salvation of nations. Woe to the people that knows not how to hate, because evil is intolerance, hypocrisy, superstition, slavery!

5. *Aims of Political Societies.*—The aim of the sectaries is the erection of the ideal temple of progress; to fecundate in the bosom of sleeping or enslaved peoples the germs of a future liberty. This glorious edifice, it is true, is not yet finished, and perhaps never will be, but the attempt itself invests secret societies with a moral grandeur; whereas, without such aim, their struggle would be debased into a paltry egotistical party-fight. It also explains the existence of secret societies, though it does not perhaps justify it. For if I am asked to give my honest opinion, I do not think that secret societies will ever accomplish what they promise. As a lover of justice, I cannot but approve of the *theoretical* striving after liberty and equality; but as a thinking being, judging by the experience of the past and the nature of things, in which good and evil must exist for ever, and for ever be at war, such striving must also for ever remain without any adequate *practical* result. The cause of liberty, indeed, may be, and often has been—nay, is daily being—benefited; but if universal, social, and political equality were established to-day, it would scarcely last till to-morrow. It is undeniable, that as long as men have unequal gifts and unequal passions, so long will equality among men

remain a dream. And it would be difficult to name any country that derived substantial and permanent benefit from the operation of any secret political society. In fact, neither of the two states enjoying the greatest freedom, political and social, viz. England and Switzerland, ever had any secret societies of national comprehensiveness or historical importance. It is true, when the Swiss in 1308 made themselves free from the Austrian yoke, thirty men had formed a pact to effect that deliverance; they were conspirators, and even then their plans were greatly modified by the conduct and death of Gessler. And Tell did not kill the latter because he (Tell) was a member of a secret society, and was bound to do so, but because the Austrian governor had done him a personal wrong, by aiming at his child's life.

6. *Religious Secret Societies.*—But the earliest secret societies were not formed for political, so much as for religious purposes, embracing every art and science; wherefore religion has truly been called the archæology of human knowledge. Comparative mythology reduces all the apparently contradictory and opposite creeds to one primeval, fundamental, and true comprehension of nature and her laws; all the metamorphoses, appositions, and conversations of one or more gods, recorded in the sacred books of the Hindoos, Parsees, and other nations, are indeed founded on simple physical facts, disfigured and misrepresented, intentionally

or accidentally. The true comprehension of nature was the prerogative of the most highly developed of all races of men (10), viz. the Aryan races, whose seat was on the highest point of the mountain region of Asia, to the north of the Himalayas. South of these lies the Vale of Cashmere, whose eternal spring, wonderful wealth of vegetation, and general natural features, best adapt it to represent the earthly paradise and the blissful residence of the most highly favoured human beings.

7. *Most perfect human Type.*—So highly favoured precisely because nature in so favoured a spot could only produce a superior type; which being, as it were, the quintessence of that copious nature, was one with it, and therefore able to apprehend it and its fulness. For as the powers of nature have brought forth plants and animals of different degrees of development and perfection, so they have produced various types of men in various stages of development; the most perfect being, as already mentioned, the Aryan or Caucasian type, the only one that has a history, and the only one that deserves our attention, when inquiring into the mental history of mankind. For even where the Caucasian comes in contact and intermingles with a dark race, as in India and Egypt, it is the white man with whom the higher and historical development begins.

8. *Causes of high Mental Development.*—I have already stated that climatic and other outward circumstances are favourable to high development. This is universally known to be true of plants: but man is only a plant endowed with consciousness and mobility, and therefore it must be true of him; and, in fact, experience proves it. His organs, and especially his brain, attain to the highest perfection, and therefore he is most fully able to apprehend nature and understand its working; hence he can never be an ignorant barbarian, and hence he must from the very first have possessed a knowledge superior even to that he is now so proud of. For, as I have shown elsewhere,[1] all barbarism among white races is only the sequel of a perished civilization. In the same publication[2] I have also demonstrated what this knowledge was, and how it came to be partly lost or perverted. But as this work would be incomplete without at least a portion of the explanations given in that publication, I must quote so much from those articles as will suffice to show that man once possessed a true knowledge of nature and her working, and that this is the reason why the mysteries of the most distant nations had so much in common dogmatically and ritually, and why in all so much importance was attached to certain figures

---

[1] "Rectangular Review," vol. i. p. 404.
[2] Ibid. p. 446.

and ideas, and why all were funereal. The sanctity attributed in all ages and all countries to the number seven has not been correctly explained by any known writer;[1] the elucidations I shall offer on this point will show that the conformity with each other of the religious and scientific doctrines of nations far apart must be due to their transmission from one common source, though the enigmatical and mystical forms in which this knowledge was preserved were gradually taken for the facts themselves.

The reader will now see that these remarks, the object of which he may not have perceived at first, are not irrelevant; we cannot understand the origin and meaning of what was taught in the mysteries without a clear apprehension of man's primitive culture and knowledge.

9. *Primitive Culture.* — From what precedes it will be evident that I am no disciple of the school that holds that man has raised himself from a state of barbarism to his present civilization. No, I belong to those who, at a distance of time which startles thought, discern the light of a high mental culture and transcendent powers. As a rule, prehistoric ages seem obscure, and men fancy that at every retrogressive step they must enter into greater darkness. But if we proceed with our eyes

---

[1] Except, of course, the one from whom I derive my information, Jacob Böhme, concerning whom, see *post*.

open, the darkness recedes like the horizon as we seem to approach it; new light is added to our light, new suns are lit up, new auroras arise before us; the darkness, which is only light compacted, is dissolved into its original, viz. light; and as outwardness implies multiplicity, and inwardness unity—there are many branches, but only one root —so all religious creeds, even those most disguised in absurd and debasing rites and superstitions, the nearer we trace them to their source, appear in greater and greater purity and nobility, with more exalted views, doctrines and aims. For as Tegner says:

" . . . känslan's grundton är ändå densamma."
The fundamental tone of feeling is ever the same.

And as the same poet expresses it, antiquity is

" . . . det Atlantis som gick nnder
Med högre kraft, med ädlare begär."
. . . That Atlantis, that perished
With higher powers and higher aims.

Thus the ethic odes of Buddha and Zoroaster have been regarded as anticipations of the teaching of Christianity; so that even St. Augustin remarked: "What is now called the Christian religion existed among the ancients, and was not absent from the beginning of the human race until Christ came, from which time the true religion which existed already began to be called Christian."

Again, through all the more elevated creeds there were certain fundamental ideas which, differing and even sometimes distorted in form, may yet in a certain sense be regarded as common to all. Such were the belief in a Trinity; the dogma that the "Logos," or omnific Word, created all things by making the Nothing manifest; the worship of light; the doctrine of regeneration by passing through the fire, and others.

10. *The true Doctrines of Nature and Being.*— But what was the knowledge on which the teaching of the mysteries was founded? It was no less than that of the ground and geniture of all things; the whole state, the rise, the workings, and the progress of all nature (16), together with the unity that pervades heaven and earth. A few years ago this was proclaimed with great sound of trumpets as a new discovery, although so ancient an author as Homer speaks, in the 8th book of the "Iliad," of the *golden chain* connecting heaven and earth; the golden chain of sympathy, the occult, all-pervading, all-uniting influence, called by a variety of names, such as *anima mundi, mercurius philosophorum, Jacob's ladder,* the *vital magnetic series,* the *magician's fire,* etc. This knowledge, in course of time, and through man's love of change, was gradually distorted by perverse interpretations,

and overlaid or embroidered, as it were, with fanciful creations of man's own brain; and thus arose superstitious systems, which became the creed of the unthinking crowd, and have not lost their hold on the public mind, even to this day, keeping in spiritual thraldom myriads who tremble at a thousand phantoms conjured up by priestcraft and their own ignorance, whilst

> "Felix qui potuit rerum cognoscere causas;
> Atque metus omnes et inexorabile fatum
> Subjecit pedibus, strepitumque Acherontis avari."

11. *Fundamental Principles of true Knowledge possessed by the Ancients.*—From what was taught in the mysteries, we are justified in believing that the first men knew what follows; though the knowledge is already dimmed and perverted in the mysteries, the phenomena of outward nature only being presented in them, instead of the inward spiritual truths symbolized.

i. All around us we behold the evidences of a life permeating all things; we must needs, therefore, admit that there is a universal, all-powerful, all-sustaining life.

ii. Behind or above the primeval life which is the basis of this system, may be beheld the "Unmoved Mover," the only supernatural *ens*, who, by the Word, or "Logos," has spoken forth all things out of himself; which does not imply any pantheism, for the words of the speaker, though proceeding from him, are not the speaker himself.

iii. The universal life is eternal.

iv. Matter is eternal.

v. That matter is light.

vi. Whatsoever is outwardly manifest must have existed ideally, from all eternity, in an archetypal figure, reflected in what Indian mythology calls the mirror *Maja*, whence are derived the terms "magus," "magia," "magic," "image," "imagination," all implying the fixing of the primeval, structureless, living matter, in a form, figure, or creature. In modern theosophy, the mirror Maja is called the Eternal Mirror of Wonders, the Virgin Sophia, ever bringing forth, yet ever a virgin—the analogue of the Virgin Mary.

vii. The eternal life which thus manifests itself in matter is an intelligent life, and this visible universe is ruled by the same laws that rule the invisible world of forces.

viii. These laws, according to which the life manifests itself, are the seven properties of eternal nature, six working properties, and the seventh, in which the six, as it were, rest, or are combined into perfect balance or harmony, *i. e.* paradise. These seven properties, the foundation of all the septenary numbers running through natural phenomena and all ancient and modern knowledge, are—1. Attraction; 2. Re-action or Repulsion; 3. Circulation;

4. Fire; 5. Light; 6. Sound; 7. Body, or comprisal of all.

ix. This septenary is divisible into two ternaries or poles, with the fire—symbolized by a cross—in the middle. These two poles constitute the eternal dualism or antagonism in nature—the first three forming matter or darkness, and producing pain and anguish, *i. e.* hell, cosmically winter; the last three being filled with light and delight, *i. e.* paradise, cosmically summer.

x. The fire is the great chymist, or purifier and transmuter of nature, turning darkness into light. Hence the excessive veneration and universal worship paid to it by ancient nations; the priests of Zoroaster wearing a veil over their mouths for fear of polluting the fire with their breath. By the fire here of course is meant the empyrean, electric fire, whose existence and nature were tolerably well known to the ancients. They distinguished the moving principle from the thing moved, and called the former the igneous ether or spirit, the principle of life, the Deity, You-piter, Vulcan, Phtha, Kneph (18, 24).

xi. All light is born out of darkness, and must pass through the fire to arrive at the light; there is no other way but through darkness, or death, or hell—an idea which we find enunciated and represented in all the mysteries. As little as a plant can come forth into the beauty of blossoms, leaves, and fruit, without having passed through the dark state of the seed and being buried in the earth, where it is chymically transmuted by the fire, so little can the mind arrive at the fulness of knowledge and enlightenment without having passed through a stage of self-darkening and imprisonment, in which it suffered torment, anguish—in which it was as in a furnace, in the throes of generation.

12. *Key to Mystic Teaching.*—That the first men possessed the knowledge of the foregoing facts is certain, not only from the positive and inferential teachings of the mysteries, but also from the monuments of antiquity, which in grandeur of conception and singleness of ideal aim, excel all that modern art or industry, or even faith, has accomplished. By bearing this in mind, the reader will get a deeper insight into the true meaning of the dogmas of initiation, than was attainable by the epopts themselves. He will also understand that the reason why there was so much uniformity in the teaching of the mysteries, was the fact that the dogmas enunciated were explanations of universal natural phenomena, alike in all parts of the earth. In describing the ceremonies of initiation, I shall therefore abstain from appending to them a commentary or exegesis, but simply refer to the paragraphs of this introduction, as to a key.

13. *Mystic Teaching summarized.*—It was theo-

logical, moral, and scientific. Theologically the initiated were shown the error of vulgar polytheism and taught the doctrine of the Unity and of a future state of reward and punishment; morally, the precepts were summed up in the words of Christ: "Love thy neighbour as thyself," and in those of Confucius: "If thou be doubtful whether an action be right or wrong, abstain from it altogether;" scientifically, the principles were such as we have detailed above (11), with their natural and necessary deductions, consequences and results.

14. *How true Knowledge came to be lost.*—Though I have already on several occasions (*e. g.* 10), alluded to the fact that the true knowledge of nature possessed by the first men had in course of time become corrupted and intermixed with error, it will not be amiss to show the process by which this came to pass. It is well known that the oldest religious rites of which we have any written records were Sabæan or Helio-Arkite. The sun, moon and stars, however, to the true original epopts were merely the outward manifestations and symbols of the inward powers of the Eternal Life. But such abstract truths could not be rendered intelligible to the vulgar mind of the increasing multitudes, necessarily more occupied with the satisfaction of material wants; and hence arose the personification of the heavenly bodies and terrestrial seasons depending on them. Gradually, what in the

first instance had been a mere human figure of a symbol came to be looked upon as the representation of an individual being that had actually lived on earth. Thus the sun to the primitive men was the outward manifestation of the Eternal, all-sustaining, all-saving Life; in different countries and ages this power was personified under the names of Chrisna, Fo, Osiris, Hermes, Hercules, and so on; and eventually these latter were supposed to have been men that really existed, and had been deified on account of the benefits they had conferred on mankind. The tombs of these supposed gods were shown, such as the Great Pyramid, said to be the tomb of Osiris; feasts were celebrated, the object of which seemed to be to renew every year the grief occasioned by their loss.. The passing of the sun through the signs of the Zodiac gave rise to the myths of the incantations of Vishnu, the labours of Hercules, &c., his apparent loss of power during the winter season, and the restoration thereof at the winter solstice, to the story of the death, descent into hell, and resurrection of Osiris, and of Mithras. In fact, what was pure nature-wisdom in one age became mythology in the next, and romance in the third, taking its characteristics from the country where it prevailed. The number seven being found everywhere, and the knowledge that its prevalence was the necessary consequence of the seven properties of nature being lost, it was supposed to have reference only to the seven planets then known.

15. *Original Spirit of the Mysteries and Results of their Decay.*—In the mysteries all was astronomical, but a deeper meaning lay hid under the astromical symbols. While bewailing the loss of the sun the epopts were in reality mourning the loss of that light whose influence is life; whilst the working of the elements according to the laws of elective affinity produces only phenomena of decay and death. The initiated strove to pass from under the dominion of the bond-woman Night into the glorious liberty of the free-woman Sophia; to be mentally absorbed into the Deity, *i.e.* into the Light. The dogmas of ancient nature-wisdom were set before the pupil, but their understanding had to arise as inspiration in his soul. It was not the dead body of science that was surrendered to the epopt, leaving it to chance whether it quickened or not, but the living spirit itself was infused into him. But for this reason, because more had to be apprehended from within by inspiration than from without by oral instruction, the Mysteries gradually decayed; the ideal yielded to the realistic, and the merely physical elements—Sabæism and Arkism—became their leading features. The frequent emblems and mementos in the sanctuary of death and resurrection, pointing to the mystery that the moments of highest psychical enjoyment are the

most destructive to bodily existence—*i. e.* that the most intense delight is a glimpse of paradise—these emblems and mementos eventually were applied to outward nature only, and their misapprehension led to all the creeds or superstitions that have filled the earth with crime and woe, sanguinary wars, internecine cruelty, and persecution of every kind. Blood-thirsty fanatics, disputing about words, whose meaning they did not understand, maintaining antagonistic dogmas, false on both sides, have invented the most fiendish tortures to compel their opponents to adopt their own views. While the two Mahommedan sects of Omar and Ali will fight each other to decide whether ablution ought to commence at the wrist or the elbow, they will unite to slay or to convert the Christians. Nay, even these latter, divided into sects without number, have distinguished themselves by persecutions as cruel as any ever practised by so-called pagan nations. Not satisfied with attempting to exterminate by fire and sword Turks and Jews, one Christian sect established such a tribunal as the Inquisition; whilst its opponents, scarcely less cruel, when they had the power, deprived the Roman Catholics of their civil rights, and occasionally executed them. Their mutual hatred even attends them in their missionary efforts—very poor in their results, in spite of the sensational reports manufactured by the societies at home for extracting money from the public. To mention but one instance: a leading missionary endeavoured to prejudice the Polynesians in advance against some expected Roman Catholic missionaries by translating Foxe's "Book of Martyrs" into their language, and illustrating its scenes by the aid of a magic-lantern.

16. *The Mysteries under their Astronomical Aspect.*—But seeing that the mysteries, as they have come down to us, and are still perpetuated, in a corrupted and aimless manner, in Freemasonry, have chiefly an astronomical bearing, a few general remarks on the leading principles of all will save a deal of needless repetition in describing them separately.

In the most ancient Indian creed we have the story of the fall of mankind by tasting of the fruit of the tree of knowledge and their consequent expulsion from Paradise. And, read in its mysterious and astronomical aspect, the narrative of the Fall, as given in the Book of Genesis, would assume some such form as the following. Adam, which does not mean an individual, but the universal man, mankind, and his companion Eve, which means life, having passed spring and summer in the Garden of Eden, necessarily reached the season when the serpent, Typhon (47), the symbol of winter, points out on the celestial sphere that the reign of Evil, of winter, is approaching. Allegorical science, which insinuated itself everywhere, caused *malum,* "evil," also to mean an "apple," the produce of autumn, which indicates that the harvest is over, and that man in the sweat of his brow must again till the earth. The cold season comes, and he must cover himself with the allegorical fig-leaf. The sphere revolves, the man of the constellation Boötes, the same as Adam, preceded by the woman, the Virgin, carrying in her hand the autumnal branch laden with fruit, seems to be allured or beguiled by her. A sacred bough or plant is introduced into all the mysteries. We have the Indian and Egyptian lotus, the fig-tree of Atys, the myrtle of Venus, the mistletoe of the Druids, the golden bough of Virgil, the rose-tree of Isis;—in the "Golden Ass" Apuleius is restored to his natural form by eating roses—the box of Palm-Sunday, and the acacia of freemasonry. The bough in the opera "Roberto il Diavolo" is the mystic bough of the mysteries.

17. *Astronomical Aspects continued.*—*The Mysteries funereal.*—In all the mysteries we encounter a god, a superior being, or an extraordinary man suffering death to recommence a more glorious existence; everywhere the remembrance of a grand and mournful event plunges the nations into grief and mourning, immediately followed by the most lively joy. Osiris is slain by Typhon, Uranus by Saturn, Sousarman by Sudra, Adonis by a wild boar; Ormuzd is conquered by Ahrimanes; Atys and Mithras and Hercules kill themselves; Abel is slain by Cain, Balder by Loke, Bacchus by the giants;

the Assyrians mourn the death of Thammuz, the Scythians and Phœnicians that of Acmon, all nature that of the great Pan, the Freemasons that of Hiram, and so on. The origin of this universal belief has already been pointed out.

18. *Uniformity of Dogmas.*—The doctrine of the Unity and Trinity was inculcated in all the mysteries. In many religious creeds we meet with a kind of travesty of the Christian dogma, in which a virgin is seen bringing forth a saviour, and yet ever remaining a virgin (11). In the more outward sense, that virgin is the Virgo of the zodiac, and the saviour brought forth is the sun (17); in the most inward sense, it is the eternal ideal, wherein the eternal life and intelligence, the power of electricity, and the virtue of the tincture, the first the sustainer, the latter the beautifier of apprehensible existence, are, as it were, corporified in the countless creatures that fill this universe—yea, in the universe itself. And the virgin remains a virgin, and her own nature is not affected by it, just as the air brings forth sounds, the light colours, the mind ideas, without any of them being intrinsically altered by the production. We certainly do not find these principles so fully and distinctly enunciated in the teaching of the ancient mystagogues, but a primitive knowledge of them may be inferred from what they *did* teach.

In all the mysteries, light was represented as

born out of darkness. Thus reappears the Deity called now Maja Bhawani, now Kâli, Isis, Ceres, Proserpina; Persephone, the Queen of Heaven, is the night from whose bosom issues life, into which the life returns, a secret reunion of life and death. She is, moreover, called the Rosy, and in the German myths the Rosy is called the restoring principle of life. She is not only the night, but, as mother of the sun, she is also the aurora, behind whom the stars are shining. When she symbolizes the earth as Ceres, she is represented with ears of corn. Like the sad Proserpina, she is beautiful and lustrous, but also melancholy and black. Thus she joins night with day, joy with sadness, the sun with the moon, heat with humidity, the divine with the human. The ancient Egyptians often represented the Deity by a black stone, and the black stone Kaábah, worshipped by the Arabs, and which is described as having originally been whiter than snow, and more brilliant than the sun, embodies the same idea, with the additional hint that light was anterior to darkness. In all the mysteries we meet with the cross (49) as a symbol of purification and salvation; the numbers three, four, and seven were sacred; in most of the mythologies we meet with two pillars; mystic banquets were common to all, as also the trials by fire, water, and air; the circle and triangle, single and double, everywhere represented the dualism or polarity of nature; in all the initiations, the aspirant represented the good principle, the light, overcome by evil, the darkness ; and his task was to regain his former supremacy, to be born again or regenerated, by passing through death and hell and their terrors, that were scenically enacted during the neophyte's passage through seven caves, or ascent of seven steps. All this, in its deepest meaning, represented the eternal struggle of light to free itself from the encumbrance of materiality it has put on in its passage through the seven properties of eternal nature (11) ; and in its secondary meaning, when the deeper one was lost to mankind, the progress of the sun through the seven signs of the zodiac, from Aries to Libra, as shown in Royal Arch Masonry, and also in the ladder with seven steps of the Knight of Kadosh. In all the mysteries the officers were the same, and personified astronomical or cosmical phenomena; in all, the initiated recognized each other by signs and passwords; in all, the conditions for initiation were the same—maturity of age and purity of conduct. Nero, on this account, did not dare, when in Greece, to offer himself as a candidate for initiation into the Eleusinian mysteries. In many, the chief hierophant was compelled to lead a retired life of perpetual celibacy, that he might be entirely at liberty to devote himself to the study and contemplation of celestial things. And to accomplish this abstraction, it was customary for the priests, in the earlier periods of their history, to mortify the flesh by the use of certain herbs, which were reputed to possess the virtue of repelling all passionate excitements; to guard against which they even occasionally adopted severer and more decided precautions. In all countries where mysteries existed, initiation came to be looked upon as much a necessity as afterwards baptism among Christians; which ceremony, indeed, is one that had been practised in all the mysteries. The initiated were called epopts, *i. e.* those that see things as they are; whilst before they were called "mystes," meaning quite the contrary. In all we find greater and less mysteries, an exoteric and an esoteric doctrine, and three degrees. To betray the mysteries was everywhere considered infamous, and the heaviest penalties were attached to it; hence also, in all initiations, the candidate had to take the most terrible oaths that he would keep the secrets entrusted to him. Alcibiades was banished and consigned to the Furies for having revealed the mysteries of Ceres; Prometheus, Tantalus, Œdipus, Orpheus, suffered various punishments for the same reason.

19. *Secret Societies no longer needed.*—Thanks to secret societies themselves, they are now no longer needed, at least not in the realms of thought. In politics, however, circumstances will arise in every age to call them into existence; and though they

seldom attain their direct object, yet are they not without influence on the relations between ruler and ruled, advantageously for the latter in the long run, though not immediately. But thought, religious, philosophical and political, is free—if not as yet in every country, it is so certainly in the lands inhabited by the Saxon races. And though the bigot and the fool would crush it, the former because it undermines his absolutism, and the latter because it interferes with his ease, yet shall it only grow stronger by the opposition. Science becomes the strong bulwark against the invasion of dogmatic absurdities; and there is growing up a scientific church, wherein knowledge, and not humility, labour, and not penance and fasting, are considered essentials. Various phenomena in modern life are proofs of this. But if man during ages of intellectual gloom annihilated himself in behalf of the great deified All, he will not, in better times, deny God what he owes Him; in his homage to God he studies and respects himself, destroys the fetishes, and combats for truth, which is the word of God. He could not deny the divine without denying himself.

In ancient times the mind rose from religion to philosophy; in our times, by a violent re-action, it will ascend from philosophy to religion. And the men whose religion is so arrived at, whose universal sympathy has cast out fear—such men are the true regenerators of mankind, and need neither secret signs nor pass-words to recognize each other; in fact they are opposed to all such devices, because they know that liberty consists in publicity. Wherever liberty rules, secresy is no longer necessary to effect any good and useful work; once it needed secret societies in order to triumph, now it wants open union to maintain itself. Not that the time is come when every truth may be uttered without fear of calumny and cavil and opposition, especially in religious matters; far from it, as some recent notable instances have shown. The words of Faust still have their application:—

> " Who dare call the child by its right name ?
> The few that knew something of it,
> And foolishly opened their hearts,
> Revealing to the vulgar crowd their views,
> Were ever crucified or burnt."

Certes, bodily crucifying or burning are out of the question now, but statecraft, and especially priestcraft, still have a few thumbscrews and red-hot irons to hold a man's hands or sear his reputation; wherefore, though I doubt the policy, and in most cases the success, of secret association, yet I cannot withhold my tribute of admiration for those who have acted or do act up to the words of the poet Lowell:

> " They are slaves who dare not speak
> For the fallen and the weak;
> They are slaves who will not choose
> Hatred, scoffing, and abuse,

Rather than in silence shrink
From the truth they needs must think;
They are the slaves who dare not be
In the right with two or three."

BOOK I.

ANCIENT MYSTERIES.

Of man's original relation to nature, whence we start, in order to render the essentials of physical science and nature comprehensible in their inmost depth, we find but obscure hints. In the mysteries and the holy initiations of those nations that as yet were nearest to the primeval people, the mind apprehends a few scarcely intelligible sounds, which, arising deep from the nature of our being, move it mightily. How our hearts are wrung by the mournful sounds of the first human race and of nature; how they are stirred by an exalted nature-worship, and penetrated by the breath of an eternal inspiration! We shall hear that suppressed sound from the temple of Isis, from the speaking pillars of Ihot, in the hymns of the Egyptian priests. On the lonely coast under the black rocks of Iceland the Edda will convey to us a sound from the graves, and fancy shall bring us face to face with those priests who by a stern silence have concealed from future ages the holy science of their worship. Yea, the eye shall yet discover the lost features of the noble past in the altars of Mexico, and on the pyramid which saw the blood and tears of thousands of human victims.

v. Schubert.

AUTHORITIES.

Hyde. De Religione Veterum Persarum. Oxford, 1700.
Anquetil. Zend-Avesta; ouvrage de Zoroastre traduit. Paris, 1771.
J. G. Rhode. Die heilige Sage. Frankfort on the Maine, 1820.
Wullers. Fragmente über die Religion Zoroasters. Bonn, 1831.
Cattaneo, C. Le Origini Italiche illustrate coi libri sacri dell' antica Persia.
De Hammer. Mém. sur le Culte de Mithra. Paris, 1833.
Müller. Mithras. Wiesbaden, 1833.
Eichhorn. De Deo Sole Invicto Mithra.
Payne Knight. Inquiry into the Symbol Language.
Ch. Lassen. Gymnosophista. Bonn, 1832.
Windischmann. De Theologumenis Vedanticorum. Bonn, 1833.
Colebrooke. Essay on the Philosophy of India. 1853.
Jones. Extracts from the Vedas.
Iamblichus. De Mysteriis Ægypt.
Saint-Victor. Mysteries of Antiquity. Ispahan, 1788.
Creuzer. Symbolik. Leipsic.
Pritchard. Analysis of Egyptian Mythology.
Ritter. History of Ancient Philosophy.
Stuhr. Religions-Systeme der Hellenen.
Taylor. Dissertation on Eleusinian and Bacchic Mysteries. London, 1770.
Schelling. Ueber die Götter von Samothrace.
Diogenes Laërtius.
Robin. Recherches sur les Initiations Anciennes et Modernes. Paris, 1779.
Ouwaroff. Essais sur les Mystères d'Eleusis. Paris, 1816.

D

Marconis et Moultet. L'Hiérophante. Paris, 1839.
Barth. Ueber die Druiden. Erlau, 1826.
Frickius. Commentatio de Druidis. Ulm, 1744.
Forcito. Prose Letterarie, vol. ii.
Higgins. Celtic Druids. London, 1829.
Lewis. Antiquities of the Hebrew Republic. London, 1724.
Jennings. Jewish Antiquities. London, 1766.
Meyer. Der Tempel Solomons. Berlin, 1830.
Fellows. The Mysteries of Freemasonry. London, 1860.
Oliver. Theocratic Philosophy. London, 1840.
Oliver. History of Initiation. London, 1829.
Mackey. Lexicon of Freemasonry, 1867.
Bredow. Handbuch der alten Geschichte. Altona, 1837.
Schubert. Nachtseite der Naturwissenschaft. Leipzig, 1850.
Lesley. Man's Origin. Philadelphia, 1868.
Faber. Mysteries of the Cabiri. Oxford, 1803.
Faber. Horæ Mosaicæ. Oxford, 1801.
Brasseur. Collection de Documents, &c. Paris, 1861.
Volney. Ruins of Empires.
Ragon. Cours Philosophique des Initiations Anciennes et Modernes. Paris, 1841.
Fabre d'Olivet. La Langue Hébraïque Restituée. Paris, 1815.
Tylor. Primitive Culture. London, 1871.

I.

THE MAGI.

20.

DERIVATION *of the term Magus.*—Magus is derived from *Maja,* the mirror (11) wherein Brahm, according to Indian mythology, from all eternity beholds himself and all his power and wonders. Hence also our terms magia, magic, image, imagination, all implying the fixing in a form, figure or creature—these words being synonymous—of the potencies of the primeval, structureless, living matter. The Magus therefore is one that makes the operations of the Eternal Life his study.

21. *Antiquity of the Magi.*—The Magi, as the ancient priests of Persia were called, did not constitute a doctrine or religion only; they constituted a monarchy—their power truly was that of kings. And this fact is still commemorated by the circum-

stance that the Magi recorded to have been led by the star to the cradle of Jesus are just as frequently called kings as Magi. As sages, they were kings in the sense of Horace:

> "Ad summam, sapiens uno minor est Jove, dives,
> Liber, honoratus, pulcher, rex denique regum."

Their pontifical reign preceded the ascendancy of Assyria, Media, and Persia. Aristotle asserts it to have been more ancient than the foundation of the kingdom of Egypt; Plato, unable to reckon it by years, computes it by myriads. At the present day most writers agree in dating the rise of the reign of the Magi five thousand years before the Trojan war.

22. *Zoroaster.*—The founder of the order was Zoroaster, who was not, as some will have it, a contemporary of Darius, but lived nearly seventy centuries before our era. Nor was his home in India, but in Bactriana, which lies more to the east, beyond the Caspian Sea, close to the mountains of India, along the great rivers Oxus and Iaxartes; so that the Brahmins, or priests of India, may be called the descendants of the Magi.

23. *Doctrine of Zoroaster.*—His doctrine was the most perfect and rational of all those that in ancient times were the objects of initiation, and has more or less survived in all successive theosophies. Traces of it may be found in the ancient Zendavesta—not the book now passing by that name, which is merely

a kind of breviary—which entered into all the details of nature.

This doctrine is not the creed of the two opposite, but equally powerful principles, as has been asserted; for Ahrimanes, the principle of evil, is not equal with Oromazes, which is good. Evil is not uncreated and eternal; it is rather transitory and limited in power. And Plutarch records an opinion, which anon we shall see confirmed, that Ahrimanes and his angels shall be annihilated—that dualism is not eternal; its life is in time, of which it constitutes the grand drama, and in which it is the perennial cause of motion and transformation. This is true philosophy, and fully in accordance with the fundamental principles of nature (11).

The Supreme Being, or Eternal Life, is elsewhere called *Time without limits*, for no origin can be assigned to him; enshrined in his glory, and possessing properties and attributes inapprehensible by our understanding, to him belongs silent adoration.

Creation had a beginning by means of emanation. The first emanation from the Eternal was the light, whence issued the King of Light, Oromazes. By means of speech Oromazes created the pure world, of which he is the preserver and judge. Oromazes is a holy and celestial being, intelligence and knowledge.

Oromazes, the first-born of Time without limits, began by creating after his image and likeness, six genii, called *amshaspands*, that surround his throne, and are his messengers to the inferior spirits and to men, being also to the latter types of purity and perfection.

The second series of creations by Oromazes was that of the twenty-eight *izads*, that watch over the happiness, innocence and preservation of the world; models of virtue, interpreters of the prayers of men.

The third host of pure spirits is more numerous, and forms that of the *farohars*, the thoughts of Oromazes, or the ideas conceived by him before proceeding to the creation of things. Not only the *farohars* of holy men and innocent infants stand before Oromazes, but this latter himself has his *farohar*, the personification of his wisdom and beneficent idea, his reason, his logos. These spirits hover over the head of every man; and this idea passed over to the Greeks and Romans, and we meet with it again in the familiar spirit of Socrates, the evil genius of Brutus, and the *genius comes* of Horace.

The threefold creation of good spirits was the necessary consequence of the contemporaneous development of the principle of evil. The second-born of the Eternal, Ahrimanes, emanated like Oromazes from the primitive light, and was pure like it, but being ambitious and haughty, he became jealous. To punish him, the Supreme Being condemned him to dwell for twelve thousand years in the region of darkness, a time which was to be sufficient to end the strife between good and evil; but Ahrimanes created countless evil genii, that filled the earth with misery, disease and guilt. The evil spirits are impurity, violence, covetousness, cruelty; the demons of cold, hunger, poverty, leanness, sterility, ignorance; and the most perverse of all, *Peetash*, the demon of calumny.[1]

Oromazes, after a reign of three thousand years, created the material world in six periods, in the same order as they are found in Genesis, successively calling into existence the terrestrial light (not to be confounded with the celestial), the water, the earth, plants, animals and man.[2] Ahrimanes assisted in the formation of earth and water, because the darkness had already invaded those elements, and Oromazes could not conceal them. Ahrimanes also took part in the creation and subsequent corruption and destruction of man, whom Oromazes had produced by an act of his will and by the Word. Out of the seed of that being Oromazes afterwards drew the first human pair, *Meshia* and *Meshiane*; but Ahrimanes first seduced the woman and then the man, leading them into evil chiefly by the eating of certain fruits. And

---

[1] All these traditions show already a very great departure from, and decay of, the original knowledge possessed by the primitive men. See "Introduction."

[2] Or rather a being compounded of a man and a bull.

not only did he alter the nature of man, but also that of animals, opposing insects, serpents, wolves, and all kinds of vermin to the good animals, thus spreading corruption over the face of the earth. But Ahrimanes and his evil spirits are eventually to be overcome and cast out from every place; and in the stern combat just and industrious men have nothing to fear; for according to Zoroaster, labour is the exterminator of evil, and that man best obeys the righteous judge of all who assiduously tills the earth and causes it to bring forth harvests and fruit-bearing trees. At the end of twelve thousand years, when the earth shall cease to be afflicted by the evils brought upon it by the spirits of darkness, three prophets shall appear and assist man with their power and knowledge, restoring the earth to its pristine beauty, judging the good and the evil, and conducting the first into a region of ineffable bliss. Ahrimanes, and the captive demons and men, shall be purified in a sea of liquid metal, and the law of Oromazes shall rule everywhere.

It is scarcely necessary to point out to the reader the astronomical bearing of the theogony of Zoroaster. The six good genii represent the six summer months, while the evil genii stand for the winter months. The twenty-eight *izads* are the days of a lunar month. But theosophically, the six periods during which the universe was created refer to the six working properties of nature.

24. *The Light worshipped.*—We have seen that Zoroaster taught light to be the first emanation of the Eternal Life; hence in the Parsee writings, light, the perennial flame, is the symbol of the Deity or uncreated Life. Hence the Magi and Parsees have been called fire-worshippers. But the former saw and the latter see in the fire not a divinity, but simply the cause of heat and motion, thus anticipating the most recent discoveries of physical science, or rather, remembering some of the lost knowledge. The Parsees did not form any God, to call him the one true God; they did not invoke any authority extrinsic to life; they did not rely on any uncertain tradition; but amidst all the recondite forces of nature, they chose the one that governs them all, that reveals itself by the most tremendous effects.

25. *Origin of the word Deus, God.*—In this sense the Magi, as well as the Chinese, had no theology, or they had one that is distinguished from all others. Those Magi that gave their name to occult science (magic) performed no sorcery and believed in no miracles. In the bosom of Asiatic immobility they did not condemn motion, but rather considered it as the glorious symbol of the Eternal Cause. Other castes aimed at impoverishing the people and subjecting it to the yoke of ignorance and superstition; but thanks to the Magi, the Indian Olympus, peopled with monstrous creatures, gave place to the conception of the unity of God, which always indicates progress in the history of thought. The text of the most ancient Zend literature acknowledges but one creative *ens* of all things, and his name, *Dao*, signifies "light" and "wisdom," and is explained by the root *daer*, "to shine," whence are derived all such words as *deus*, *dies*, &c. The conception of Deity indeed was primarily that of the "bright one," whence also the Sanskrit *dyáus*, "sky," which led to so many mythological fables. But the original idea was founded on a correct perception of the origin and nature of things, for light is truly the substance of all things; all matter is only a compaction of light. Thus the Magi founded a moral system and an empire; they had a literature, a science and a poetry. Five thousand years before the "Iliad," they put forth the "Zendavesta," three grand poems, the first ethical, the second military, and the third scientific.

26. *Mode of Initiation.*—The candidate for initiation was prepared by numerous lustrations with fire, water, and honey. The number of probations he had to pass through was very great, and ended with a fast of fifty days' continuance. These trials had to be endured in a subterranean cave, where he was condemned to perpetual silence and total solitude. This novitiate in some instances was attended with fatal effects, in others the candidate became par-

tially or wholly deranged; those who surmounted the trials were eligible to the highest honours. At the expiration of the novitiate, the candidate was brought forth into the cavern of initiation, where he was armed with enchanted armour by his guide, who was the representative of Simorgh, a monstrous griffin (27), and an important agent in the machinery of Persian mythology, and furnished with talismans, that he might be ready to encounter all the hideous monsters raised up by the evil spirits to impede his progress. Introduced into an inner apartment, he was purified with fire and water, and put through the seven stages of initiation. First, he beheld a deep and dangerous vault from the precipice where he stood, into which a single false step might throw him down to the "throne of dreadful necessity,"—the first three properties of nature. Groping his way through the mazes of the gloomy cavern, he soon beheld the sacred fire at intervals flash through its recesses and illuminate his path; he also heard the distant yelling of ravenous beasts—the roaring of lions, the howling of wolves, the fierce and threatening bark of dogs. But his attendant, who maintained a profound silence, hurried him forward towards the quarter whence these sounds proceeded, and at the sudden opening of a door he found himself in a den of wild beasts, dimly lighted with a single lamp. He was immediately attacked by the initiated in the forms of lions, tigers, wolves, griffins, and other monstrous beasts, from whom he seldom escaped unhurt. Thence he passed into another cavern, shrouded in darkness, where he heard the terrific roaring of thunder and saw vivid and continuous flashes of lightning, which in streaming sheets of fire rendered visible the flitting shades of avenging genii, resenting his intrusion into their chosen abodes. To restore the candidate a little, he was next conducted into another apartment, where his excited feelings were soothed with melodious music and the flavour of grateful perfumes. On his expressing his readiness to proceed through the remaining ceremonies, a signal was given by his conductor, and three priests immediately made their appearance, one of whom cast a living serpent into his bosom as a token of regeneration (57); and, a private door having been opened, there issued forth such howlings and cries of lamentation and dismay, as struck him with new and indescribable emotions of terror. On turning his eyes to the place whence these noises proceeded, he beheld exhibited in every appalling form the torments of the wicked in Hades. Thus he was passed through the devious labyrinth consisting of seven spacious vaults, connected by winding galleries, each opening with a narrow stone portal, the scene of some perilous adventure, until he reached the Sacellum, or Holy of Holies, which was brilliantly illuminated, and which sparkled with gold and precious stones. A splendid sun and starry system moved in accordance with delicious music. The archimagus sat in the east on a throne of burnished gold, crowned with a rich diadem decorated with myrtle-boughs, and habited in a tunic of bright cerulean hue; round him were assembled the præsules and dispensers of the mysteries. By these the novice was received with congratulations, and after having entered into the usual engagements for keeping secret the rites of Zoroaster, the sacred words were entrusted to him, of which the Tetractys, or name of God, was the chief. The Tetractys of Pythagoras is analogous to the Jewish Tetragrammaton, or name of the Deity in four letters. The number four was considered the most perfect, because in the first four properties of nature (11) are comprised and implied all the rest; wherefore also the first four numbers summed up make up the decad, after which all is only repetition.

27. *Myth of Rustam.*—This progress was denominated ascending the ladder of perfection, and from it has arisen the tale of Rustam, the Persian Hercules, who, mounted on the monster Rakshi, which is the Arabic name of Simorgh, undertakes the conquest of Mazendaraun, celebrated as a perfect earthly paradise. Having amidst many dangers fought his way along a road of seven stages, he reaches the cavern of the White Giant, who smites

all that assail him with blindness. But Rustam overcomes him, and with three drops of the giant's blood restores sight to all his captives. The symbolical three drops of blood had their counterparts in all the mysteries of the ancient world. In Britain the emblem was three drops of water; in Mexico, as in this legend, three drops of blood; in India, a belt composed of three triple threads; in China, the three strokes of the letter Y, &c. The blindness with which those who seek the giant are smitten, of course refers to the emblematic mental blindness of the aspirant to initiation.

II.

THE MITHRAICS.

28.

MYSTERIES *of Mithras.*—Upon the trunk of a religion so spiritual and hostile to idolatry, which undertook iconoclastic expeditions into Babylonia, Assyria, Syria, and Lybia, which vindicated the pure worship of God, destroying by means of the sword of Cambyses the Egyptian priesthood, which overthrew the temples and idols of Greece, which gave to the Israelites the Pharisees, which appears so simple and pure as to have bestowed on the Parsees the appellation of the Puritans of antiquity, and on Cyrus that of the Anointed of the Lord—on this trunk there were afterwards ingrafted idolatrous branches, as perhaps the Brahminic, and certainly the Mithraic worship, the origin of which latter Dupuis places at 4,500 years before Christ.

29. *Origin of Mithraic Worship.*—Mithras is a beneficent genius presiding over the sun, the most powerful *izad*, invoked together with the sun, and not at first confounded with it; the chief mediator and intercessor between Oromazes and man. But in course of time the conception of this Mithras became perverted, and he usurped the attributes of divinity. Such usurpation of the rank of the superior Deity on the part of the inferior is of frequent occurrence in mythology; it suffices to refer to Siva and Vishnu in India, Serapis in Egypt, Jupiter in Greece. The perversion was rendered easy by confounding the symbol with the thing symbolized, the genius of the sun with the sun itself, which alone remained in the language, since the modern Persian name of the sun (*mihr*) represents the regular modification of the Zend *Mithras*.

The Persian Mithras must not be confounded with that of India, for it is undoubted that another Mithras, different from the Zendic, from the most ancient times was the object of a special mysterious worship, and that the initiated knew him as the sun. Taking the letters of the Greek word "Meithras" at their numerical value, we obtain the number 365, the days of the year. The same holds good of "Abraxas," the name which Basilides gave to the Deity, and further of "Belenos," the name given to the sun in Gaul.

30. *Dogmas, &c.*—On the Mithraic monuments

we find representations of the globe of the sun, the club and bull, symbols of the highest truth, the highest creative activity, the highest vital power. Such a trinity agrees with that of Plato, which consists of the Supreme Good, the Word, and the Soul of the World; with that of Hermes Trismegistus, consisting of Light, Intelligence, and Soul; with that of Porphyry, which consists of Father, Word, and Supreme Soul.

According to Herodotus, Mithras became the Mylitta of Babylon, the Assyrian Venus, to whom was paid an obscene worship as to the female principle of creation, the goddess of fecundity, of life; one perhaps with Anaitis, the Armenian goddess.

The worship of the Persian Mithras, or Apollo, spread over Italy,[1] Gaul, Germany, Britain; and expiring polytheism opposed to the sun Christ, the sun Mithras.

31. *Rites of Initiation.*—The sanctuaries of this worship were always subterranean, and in each sanctuary was placed a ladder with seven steps, by which one ascended to the mansions of felicity.

---

[1] Underneath the church of St. Clement, at Rome, a singularly well-preserved temple of Mithras was discovered some years ago. When the monk who had, on my visit to Rome, shown me the church above, said that he would now take me down to the pagan temple of Mithras, I could not help saying to myself, "If you but knew it, Mithras is above as well as below!"

The initiations into this degree were similar to those detailed in the foregoing section, but, if possible, more severe than into any other, and few passed through all the tests. The festival of the god was held towards the middle of the month of Mihr (October), and the probationer had to undergo long and severe trials before he was admitted to the full knowledge of the mysteries.

The first degree was inaugurated with purifying lustrations, and a sign was set on the neophyte's brow, whilst he offered to the god a loaf and a cup of water. A crown was presented to him on the point of a sword, and he put it on his head saying, "Mithras is my crown."

In the second degree the aspirant put on armour to meet giants and monsters, and a wild chase took place in the subterranean caves. The priests and officers of the temple, disguised as lions, tigers, leopards, bears, wolves, and other wild beasts, attacked the candidate with fierce howlings. In these sham fights the aspirant ran great personal danger, though sometimes the priests caught a Tartar. Thus we are told that the Emperor Commodus on his initiation carried the joke too far, and slew one of the priests who had assailed him in the form of a wild beast.

In the next degree he put on a mantle on which were painted the signs of the zodiac. A curtain then concealed him from the sight of all; but this being withdrawn, he appeared surrounded by frightful griffins. After passing through other trials, if his courage did not fail him, he was hailed as a "Lion of Mithras," in allusion to the zodiacal sign in which the sun attained his greatest power. We meet with the same idea in the degree of Master Mason. The grand secret was then imparted. What was it? At this distance of time it is difficult to decide, but we may assume that the priests communicated to him the most authentic sacerdotal traditions, the best accredited theories concerning the origin of the universe, and the attributes, perfections, and works of Oromazes. In fact, the Mithraic mysteries represent the progress of darkness to light. According to Guignault, Mithras is love; with regard to the Eternal, he is the son of mercy; with regard to Oromazes and Ahrimanes, the fire of love.

32. *Rites derived from Magism.*—This was not the sole heresy, the only secret society that issued from the womb of Magism; and its rites gradually became so corrupt as to serve as a cloak for the most licentious practices, which were at length sanctioned and even encouraged in the mysteries. Further, it became an axiom in religion that the offspring of a son and a mother was the best calculated for the office of a priest. Traces of Magism are also found in the speculations of Manes, the Religion of Love, and the secret history of the Templars.

III.

BRAHMINS AND GYMNOSOPHISTS.

33.

VULGAR Creed of India.—The Indian religion, whether we look on it as an adulteration of Magism, or as the common trunk of all Asiatic theosophy, offers so boundless a wealth of deities, that no other in this respect can approach it. This wealth is an infallible sign of the mental poverty and grossness of the people, who, ignorant of the laws of nature, and terrified at its phenomena, acknowledged as many supernatural beings as there were mysteries for them. The Brahmins reckon up 300,000 gods —a frightful host, that have kept Indian life servile and stagnant, perpetuated the divisions of caste, upheld ignorance, and weighed like an incubus on the breasts of their deluded dupes, and turned existence into a nightmare of grief and servitude.

34. *Secret Doctrines.*—But in the secret sanctuary these vain phantoms disappear, and the initiated are taught to look upon them as countless accidents and outward manifestations of the First Cause. The Brahmins did not consider the people fit to apprehend and preserve in its purity the religion of the spirit, hence they veiled it in these figures, and also invented a language incomprehensible to the vulgar, but which the investigations of Oriental scholars have enabled us to read, and to perceive that the creed of India is one of the purest ever known to man. Thus in the second chapter of the first part of the "Vishnu Purana," it is written: " God is without form, epithet, definition, or description; free from defect, incapable of annihilation, change, grief, or pain. We can only say that he, that is, the Eternal Being, is God. Vulgar men think that God is in the water; the more enlightened, in celestial bodies; the ignorant, in wood and stone; but the wise, in the universal mind." The " Mahanirvana," says:—" Numerous figures, corresponding with the nature of divers powers and quality, were invented for the benefit of those who are wanting in sufficient understanding." Again, "We have no notion of how the Eternal Being is to be described; he is above all the mind can apprehend, above nature. . . . That Only One that was never defined by any language, and gave to language all its meaning, he is the Supreme Being . . and no partial thing that man worships. . . This Being extends over all things. He is mere spirit without corporeal form; without extension of any size, unimpressionable, and without any organs; he is pure, perfect, omniscient, omnipresent, the ruler of the intellect . . . he is the soul of the whole universe."

35. *Brahma and Buddha.*—The polytheism of India branched off into two great sects,—Buddhists and Brahminists,—each possessing distinctive characteristics. Allusions to this separation are found in the Legend of the Temple; and there are other divisions in theological nomenclature which respectively refer to the traditions of those grand sections. The Indians, the Greeks (except Pythagoras, who was to some extent a Buddhist), and the Britons, were Brahminists; whilst the Chinese, Japanese, Persians, and Saxons, were Buddhists. The Buddhists were Magians, the Brahminists Sabæans. The famous Buddhist doctrine of Nirvâna or Nihilism—so totally misapprehended, as long as it was supposed to mean total annihilation—is profoundly theosophical, and really means the perfect absorption into the Deity, though Buddha does not allow of a personal god or creator. By the Deity he means the light, the eternal liberty, and therefore calls Nirvâna the highest stage of spiritual liberty and bliss. The individual soul, on leaving the body in which it was imprisoned, returns into the universal soul; just as the solar light,

imprisoned in a piece of wood, when this is burnt, returns into the universal ocean of light. On this doctrine was afterwards engrafted the false belief in the metempsychosis, or transmigration of souls, and the misanthropic system of self-renunciation, which, in India, led to the self-torturings of fakirs and other fanatics; and which finds its analogies in Christian communities in the asceticism of fasts, penances, macerations, solitude, flagellation, and all the mad practices of monks, anchorets, and other religious zealots.

36. *Asceticism.*—This asceticism, founded on the above notion, viz. that the Absolute or All is the real existence, and that individual phenomena, especially matter in all its forms, are really nothing, *i. e.* mere phantasms, and to be avoided, as increasing the distance from the Absolute, and that absorption into the Deity is to be obtained, even in this life, by the maceration of the body, was and even now is prevalent in India, where it was carried, in thousands of instances, further than mere self-torture, even to death. When, at the festival of the dread goddess Bhovani, the wife of Siva, her ponderous image was borne on a car, with cutting wheels, to the Ganges, a crowd of frantic beings, wreathed with flowers, joyous as if they went to the nuptial altar, would cast themselves under the wheels of the car, offering themselves, amidst the sounding of trumpets, as voluntary sacrifices, to be cut to pieces

by the wheels. And in various sects asceticism has led to the adoption of many strange practices. In the "Contes de la Reine de Navarre" there is a passage which at some length refers to a special mode adopted by monks and other men for the mortification of the flesh. Of such persons the queen says:—"*Ils disent qu'il faut s'habituer à la chasteté, et pour éprouver leurs forces ils parlent aux plus belles, et à celles qu'ils aiment le plus, et en baisant et touchant, ils éprouvent qu'ils sont dans une entière mortification. Quand ils sentent que ce plaisir les émeut, ils vivent dans la retraite, jeûnent et se disciplinent, et quand ils ont mâté leur chair en sorte que ni la conversation ni le baiser leur causent point d'émotion, ils essayent la sotte tentation de coucher ensemble, et de s'embrasser sans aucun désir de volupté.*"

37. *Gymnosophists.*—We have very few notices of the Gymnosophists, the Magi of Brahminism, the most severe custodians of the primitive law, and originally most free from imposture. They spread over Africa; and in Ethiopia they lived as solitaires, and revived on the banks of the Nile many phases of Asiatic theosophy. Priests-errant, they were reported to carry with them a secret doctrine, of which the simplicity of their lives and the purity of their morals might be considered as the outward manifestation; though in after times they became one of the most debauched and immoral sects in India.

They went almost naked (hence their name— γυμνὸς, naked; σοφὸς, wise), and lived on herbs; but their own austerity did not render them harsh towards other men, nor unjust as regarded other common conditions of life. They believed in one only God, the immortality of the soul and its transmigration, and when old age or disease prostrated them, they ascended the funeral pile, deeming it ignominious to let years or evils afflict them. Alexander saw one of them close his life in this manner.

The priestly colleges of Ethiopia and Egypt maintained constant relations. Osiris is an Ethiopian divinity. Every year the two families of priests met on the boundaries of the two countries to offer common sacrifices to Ammon,—another name for Jupiter,—and celebrate the festival which the Greeks called *heliotrapeza*, or Table of the Sun. Amidst the predominant fetishism of Africa, produced partly by climate and partly by the same circumstances that gave rise to Indian fetishism, we cannot help admiring that colony of thinkers which long resisted the progress of despotism, and whose destruction was the revenge of intolerance and tyranny.

38. *Places for celebrating Mysteries.*—The mysteries, as in other countries, were celebrated in subterranean caverns, here excavated in the solid rock, and surpassing in grandeur of conception and finish of execution anything to be seen elsewhere.

The temples of Elephanta, Ellora, and Salsette, consisting of large halls and palaces, chapels, pagodas, cells for thousands of priests and pilgrims, adorned with pillars and columns, obelisks, bas-reliefs, gigantic statues of deities, elephants and other sacred animals, all carved out of the living rock, are especially noteworthy. In the sacellum, only accessible to the initiated, the supreme Deity was represented by the lingam, which was used more or less by all ancient nations to represent his creative power, though in India it was also typified by the petal and calyx of the lotus.

39. *Initiation.*—The periods of initiation were regulated by the increase and decrease of the moon, and the mysteries were divided into four degrees, and the candidate might be initiated into the first at the early age of eight years. He was then prepared by a Brahmin, who became his spiritual guide for the second degree, the probationary ceremonies of which consisted in incessant occupation in prayers, fastings, ablutions, and the study of astronomy. In the hot season he sat exposed to five fires, four blazing around him, with the sun above; in the rains he stood uncovered; in the cold season he wore wet clothing. To participate in the high privileges which the mysteries were believed to confer, he was sanctified by the sign of the cross, and subjected to the probation of the pastos, the tomb of the sun, the coffin of Hiram, darkness, hell, all sym-

bolical of the first three properties (11). His purification being completed, he was led at night to the cavern of initiation. This was brilliantly illuminated, and there sat the three chief hierophants, in the east, west and south, representing the gods Brahma, Vishnu, Siva, surrounded by attendant mystagogues, dressed in appropriate vestments. The initiation was begun by an apostrophe to the sun, addressed by the name of *Pooroosh,* here meaning the vital soul, or portion of the universal spirit of Brahm; and the candidate, after some further preliminary ceremonies, was made to circumambulate the cavern three times, and afterwards conducted through seven dark caverns, during which period the wailings of Mahadeva for the loss of Siva were represented by dismal howlings. The usual paraphernalia of flashes of light, of dismal sounds and horrid phantoms were produced to terrify and confuse the aspirant. Having arrived at the last cavern, the sacred conch was blown, the folding doors thrown open, and the candidate was admitted into an apartment filled with dazzling lights, ornamented with statues and emblematic figures richly decorated with gems, and scented with the most fragrant perfumes. This sacellum was intended to represent Paradise, and was actually so called in the temple of Ellora. With eyes riveted on the altar, the candidate was taught to expect the descent of the Deity in the bright pyramidal fire that blazed upon it; and in a moment of enthusiasm, thus artificially produced, the candidate might indeed persuade himself that he actually beheld Brahma seated on the lotus, with his four heads and arms, representing the four elements and the four quarters of the globe, and bearing in his hands the emblems of eternity and power, the circle and fire.

39a. *Brahm and Brahma.*—The reader will have noticed in one case I say Brahm and in the other Brahma; the latter is the body of the former, which is the Eternal Life. The terms corrrespond with those of Abyssal Deity and Virgin Sophia of Christian theosophy.

40. *The ineffable name Aum.*—The candidate was now supposed to be regenerated, and was invested with the white robe, tiara, and the sacred belt; a cross was marked on his forehead and a tau (49) upon his breast; the salagram or marginal black stone (18), to insure to him the perfection of Vishnu, and the serpent stone, an antidote against the bite of serpents, were delivered to him; and lastly, he was intrusted with the sacred name, which signified the solar fire, and united in its comprehensive meaning the great Trimurti, or combined principle on which the existence of all things is founded. This word was OM, or in a triliteral form AUM, to represent the creative, preserving, and destroying power of the Deity, personified in Brahma, Vishnu, and Siva, the symbol of which was

an equilateral triangle. To this name, as the Royal Arch Masons to that of Iabulon, they attributed the most wonderful powers; and it could only be the subject of silent but pleasing contemplation, for its pronunciation was said to make earth and heaven tremble, and even the angels of heaven to quake with fear. The emblems around and the aporreta of the mysteries were then explained, and the candidate instructed that by means of the knowledge of OM he was to become one with the Deity. With the Persians the syllable HOM meant the tree of life, a tree and a man at the same time, the dwelling-place of the soul of Zoroaster; and with them also, as with the Indians, it was forbidden on pain of death to reveal it. In this secret name, involving the rejection of polytheism, and comprising the knowledge of nature, we have the golden thread that unites ancient and modern secret societies.

41. *The Lingam.*—One of the emblems found in the sacellum, and which in fact is found everywhere on the walls of Indian temples, was the lingam, which represented the male principle, and which passed from India to Egypt, Greece and Scandinavia. The worship of this symbol could not but lead to great abuses, especially as regarded the gymnosophists.

42. *The Lotus.*—The lotus, the lily of the Nile, held sacred also in Egypt, was the great vegetable

amulet of eastern nations. The Indian gods were always represented as seated on it. It was an emblem of the soul's freedom when liberated from its earthly tabernacle, the body; for it takes root in the mud deposited at the bottom of a river, vegetates from the germ to a perfect plant, and afterwards rising proudly above the waves, it floats in air, as if independent of any extraneous aid. It is placed on a golden table, as the symbol of Siva, on the top of Mount Menu, the holy mountain of India, the centre of the earth, worshipped by Hindoos, Tartars, Montchurians and Mongols. It is supposed to be in Northern India, to have three peaks, composed of gold, silver and iron, on which reposes the trine deity Brahma, Vishnu, and Siva. Geographically this mountain is evidently the tableland of Tartary, whose southern boundary is formed by the Himalayas. This custom of accounting a three-peaked mountain holy was not confined to India alone, but prevailed also among the Jews. Thus Olivet, near Jerusalem, had three peaks, which were accounted the residence of the Deity—Chemosh, Milcom, Ashtoreth (2 Kings xxiii. 13). In Zechariah (xiv. 4) the feet of the Almighty are placed on the two outer peaks of this mountain during the threatened destruction of Jerusalem; while the mountain itself is made to split asunder at the centre peak from east to west, leaving a great valley between the divided parts.

IV.

EGYPTIAN MYSTERIES.

43.

NTIQUITY of Egyptian Civilization.—
All Egypt is an initiation. A long and
narrow strip of land, watered by immense floods and surrounded by immense
solitudes—such is Egypt. Very high and steep
rocks protected it from the incursions of the nomadic
tribes, and thus a valley, a river, and a race sufficed
to create, if not the most ancient, at least one of the
most ancient and illustrious cultures, a world of
marvels, at a time when Europeans went naked,
and dyed their skins, as Cæsar found the ancient
Britons, and when the Greeks, armed with bows
and arrows, led a nomadic existence. The Egyptians, many thousand years before the Trojan war,
had invented writing, as is proved, for instance, by
the hieratic papyrus of the time of Rameses II., full
of recipes and directions for the treatment of a great

variety of diseases, and now in the Berlin Museum. They also knew many comforts of life, which our pride calls modern; and the Greek writers, whom the Egyptian priests called *children*, are full of recollections of that mysterious land, recording the father Nile, Thebes with its hundred gates, the Pyramids, Lake Meroe, the Labyrinth, the Sphinx, and the statue of Memnon saluting the rising sun.

44. *Temples of Ancient Egypt.*—Egyptian chronology, the reproof and paragon of all others, is graven on imperishable monuments. But those obelisks, sacred to the sun, by their conical form like that of the flame; those labyrinths, those human-headed birds, typifying the intelligent soul; those scarabei, signifying creative power; those sphinxes, representing force, the lion or sun, and man; those serpents expressing life and eternity (57); those strange combinations of forms; those hieroglyphics —they long remained secrets for us, and perhaps always were a secret for the Egyptian people that in fear and silence erected the pyramids—all these symbols constituted the language of one of the vastest and most elaborate secret societies that ever existed. Penetrating into those gigantic temples which seem the work of an extinct race, different from ours, as fossil quadrupeds are different from those now living; traversing those cloisters, which after many windings lead to the innermost sanctuary, we are seized by a singular

thought—that of the silence and solitude which ever reigned within those edifices into which the people were not allowed to penetrate; only the few were admitted, and we moderns are the first profane that have set foot within the hallowed precincts. The temple of Luxor is the vastest on earth—six propylæa with long files of columns, and colossi and obelisks and sphinxes; six cloisters—every new generation of kings for seventy centuries added some new portion and inscribed on the walls the history of its deeds, and every new addition removed the faithful further from the seat of the god; the marvel and mystery increased. The sixth propylæum is not finished; it is a chapter of history broken off in the middle, and will never be completed. The walls and pillars of the temples were covered with religious and astronomical representations, and from the fact of many of these pictures showing human beings in various states of suffering and under torture, it has been assumed that the Egyptian ritual was cruel, like the Mexican (74, 77); but such is not the case; the pictures are only representations of the punishments said to be inflicted on the wicked in another life.

45. *Egyptian Priests and Kings.*—The priestly caste, possessing all the learning, ruled first and alone; but in its own defence it armed a portion of the population; the rest it kept down by superstition, or disarmed and weakened it by corruption.

To Plato, who saw it from a distance, this government seemed stupendous, and he idealized it; it was for him the "city of God," the pattern republic. Nevertheless, as was inevitable, might rebelled against doctrine, the soldiery broke the rein of the priesthood, and by the side of the pontiffs arose the kings, or to speak more correctly, the two series proceeded in parallels; that of the priests was not set aside, it had its palaces, the temples, strong like fortresses, along the Nile, which were at the same time splendid abodes, agricultural establishments, commercial dépôts, and caravan stations; its members appointed and ruled the kings themselves, regulating the most minute acts of their daily conduct; they were the depositaries of the highest offices, and as the learned savans, magistrates, and physicians, enjoyed the first honours. Their chief colleges were at Thebes, Memphis, Heliopolis, and Saïs; they possessed a great portion of the land, which they caused to be cultivated; paid no taxes, but collected tithes. They formed indeed the elect, privileged, and only free portion of the nation.

46. *Exoteric and Esoteric Doctrines.*—The priests were no followers of the idolatrous faith of the people; but to have undeceived the latter would have been dangerous for themselves. The true doctrine of the unity of God, therefore, which was their secret, was only imparted to those that after many trials

had been initiated into the mysteries. Their doctrines, like those of all other priesthoods, were therefore exoteric and esoteric; and the mysteries were of two kinds, the greater and the less, the former being the mysteries of Osiris and Serapis, the latter those of Isis. The mysteries of Osiris were celebrated at the autumnal equinox; those of Serapis at the summer solstice; and those of Isis at the vernal equinox.

47. *Egyptian Mythology.*—Though want of space does not allow me fully to enter upon the vast subject of Egyptian mythology, yet a few words thereon are necessary to render its bearing on the mysteries clear, and also to show its connection with many of the rites of modern freemasonry.

That all the symbols and ceremonies of all the ancient creeds originally had a deep and universal cosmic meaning has already been shown (9, 10), but at the time when the mysteries were most flourishing that meaning was to a great extent lost, and a merely astronomical one substituted for it, as will be seen from the following explanations:—

Osiris, represented in Egypt by a sceptre surmounted by an eye, to signify him that rules and sees, symbolizes the sun. He is killed by Typhon, a serpent engendered by the mud of the Nile. But Typhon is a transposition of Python, derived from the Greek word πύθω, "to putrefy," and means nothing else but the noxious vapours arising from steaming mud, and thus concealing the sun; wherefore in the Greek mythology Apollo—another name for the sun—is said to have slain Python with his arrows, that is to say, dispelled the vapours by his rays. Osiris having been killed by Python—to which, however, the wider meaning of the sun's imaginary disappearance, or death, during the winter season, was attached—Isis, his wife, or the moon, goes in search of him, and at last finds his body, cut into fourteen pieces, that is to say, into as many parts as there are days between the full moon and the new; she collects all the pieces, with one important exception, for which she made a substitution which gave rise to a worship resembling that of the lingam in India.

But although to the vulgar crowd Isis was only the moon, to the initiated she was the Universal Mother, the primordial harmony and beauty, called in Egyptian "Iophis," which the Greeks turned into "Sophia,"[1] whence the Virgin Sophia of theosophy. Hence also the many names by which Isis was known (54), indicating the multifarious aspects she necessarily assumed. Her image was worshipped at Saïs under the emblem of "Isis veiled," with

---

[1] By a transposition of consonants, common enough in the formation of new words; Typhon from Python is an instance already mentioned; *forma*, from μορφή, is another.

this inscription :—" I am all that has been, all that is, and all that will be, and no mortal has drawn aside my veil."

Apis, or the Bull, was an object of worship throughout all the ancient world, because formerly the zodiacal sign of the Bull opened the vernal equinox (69).

48. *The Phœnix.*—The Egyptians began the year with the rising of the dog-star or Sirius. But making no allowance for the quarter of a day which finishes the year, the civil year every four years began one day too soon, and so the beginning of the year went successively through every one of the days of the natural year in the space of four times 365, which makes 1,460 years. They fancied they blessed and made all the seasons to prosper by making them thus to enjoy one after another the feast of Isis, which was celebrated along with that of Sirius, though it was frequently very remote from that constellation; wherefore they introduced the image of dogs, or even the real and living animals, preceding the chariots of Isis. When in the 1461st year the feast again coincided with the rising of the star Sirius, they looked upon it as a season of plenty, and symbolized it by a bird of singular beauty, which they called Phœnix (*deliciis abundans*), saying that it came to die upon the altar of the sun, and that out of its ashes there arose a little

worm, that gave birth to a bird perfectly like the preceding.

49. *The Cross.*—Among the astronomical symbols we must not omit the Cross. This sign really signifies the fire, as we have seen (11. ix.), but in Egypt it was simply the Nilometer, consisting of an upright pole with a cross-bar, that was raised or lowered according to the swelling or decrease of the river. It was frequently surmounted by a circle, typifying the deity that governs this important operation. Now, the overflow of the Nile was considered the salvation of Egypt, and hence the sign came to be looked upon with great veneration and to have occult virtues attributed to it, such as the power of averting evil; wherefore the Egyptians hung small figures of the cross, or rather the letter T, with a ring attached to it, the *crux ansata,* round the necks of their children and of sick persons; they applied it to the string or fillets with which they wrapped up their mummies, where we still find it; it became in fact an amulet (*amolitio malorum*). Other nations adopted the custom, and hence the cross or the letter T, whereby it was symbolized throughout the ancient world, was supposed to be a sign or letter of more than ordinary significance. In the mysteries, the *crux ansata* was the symbol of eternal life. But the cross was worshipped as an astronomical sign in other countries. We have seen that in India the

neophyte was sanctified by the sign of the cross (39), which in most ancient nations was a symbol of the universe, pointing as it does to the four quarters of the compass; and the erection of temples on the cruciform principle is as old as architecture itself. The two great pagodas of Benares and Mathura are erected in the form of vast crosses, of which each wing is equal in extent, as is also the pyramidal temple of New Grange in Ireland. But the older and deeper meaning of the cross is shown in (11); it refers to the fire, and the double quality everywhere observable in nature. The triple tau is the Royal Arch Mason's badge.

50. *Places of Initiation.*—In Egypt and other countries (India, Media, Persia, Mexico) the place of initiation was a pyramid erected over subterranean caverns. The pyramids, in fact, may be looked upon, considering their size, shape, and solidity, as artificial mountains, covering buried cities. Their form not only symbolically represented the ascending flame, but also had a deeper origin in the conical form, which is the primitive figure of all natural products. And the Great Pyramid, the tomb of Osiris, was erected in such a position and to such a height, that at the spring and autumnal equinoxes the sun would appear exactly at midday upon the summit of the pyramid, seeming to rest upon this immense pedestal, when his worshippers, extended at the base, would contemplate the great Osiris as

well when he descended into the tomb as when he arose from it triumphant.

51. *Process of Initiation.*—The candidate, conducted by a guide, was led to a deep, dark well or shaft in the pyramid, and, provided with a torch, he descended into it by means of a ladder affixed to the side. Arrived at the bottom, he saw two doors—one of them barred, the other yielding to the touch of his hand. Passing through it, he beheld a winding gallery, whilst the door behind him shut with a clang that reverberated through the vaults. Inscriptions like the following met his eye: " Whoso shall pass along this road alone, and without looking back, shall be purified by fire, water, and air; and overcoming the fear of death, shall issue from the bowels of the earth to the light of day, preparing his soul to receive the mysteries of Isis." Proceeding onward, the candidate arrived at another iron gate, guarded by three armed men, whose shining helmets were surmounted by emblematic animals, the Cerberus of Orpheus. Here the candidate had offered to him the last chance of returning, if so inclined. Electing to go forward, he underwent the trial by fire, by passing through a hall filled with inflammable substances in a state of combustion, and forming a bower of fire. The floor was covered with a grating of red-hot iron bars, leaving, however, narrow interstices where he might safely place his foot. Having surmounted this obstacle, he has to

encounter the trial by water. A wide and dark canal, fed by the waters of the Nile, arrests his progress. Placing the flickering lamp upon his head, he plunges into the canal, and swims to the opposite bank, where the greatest trial, that by air, awaits him. He lands upon a platform leading to an ivory door, bounded by two walls of brass, into each of which is inserted an immense wheel of the same metal. He in vain attempts to open the door, when, espying two large iron rings affixed to it, he takes hold of them; but suddenly the platform sinks from under him, a chilling blast of wind extinguishes his lamp, the two brazen wheels revolve with formidable rapidity and stunning noise, whilst he remains suspended by the two rings over the fathomless abyss. But ere he is exhausted the platform returns, the ivory door opens, and he sees before him a magnificent temple, brilliantly illuminated, and filled with the priests of Isis clothed in the mystic insignia of their offices, the hierophant at their head. But the ceremonies of initiation do not cease here. The candidate is subject to a series of fastings, which gradually increase for nine times nine days. During this period a rigorous silence is imposed upon him, which if he preserve inviolate, he is at length fully initiated into the esoteric doctrines of Isis. He is led before the triple statue of Isis, Osiris, and Horus,—another symbol of the sun,—where he swears never to publish the things revealed to him in the sanctuary, and first drinks the water of Lethe presented to him by the high priest, to forget all he ever heard in his unregenerate state, and afterwards the water of Mnemosyne, to remember all the lessons of wisdom imparted to him in the mysteries. He is next introduced into the most secret part of the sacred edifice, where a priest instructs him in the application of the symbols found therein. He is then publicly announced as a person who has been initiated into the mysteries of Isis—the first degree of the Egyptian rites.

52. *Mysteries of Serapis.*—These constituted the second degree. We know but little of them, and Apuleius only slightly touches upon them. When Theodosius destroyed the temple of Serapis there were discovered subterraneous passages and engines wherein and wherewith the priests tried the candidates. Porphyry, in referring to the greater mysteries, quotes a fragment of Cheremones, an Egyptian priest, which imparts an astronomical meaning to the whole legend of Osiris, thus confirming what has been said above. And Herodotus, in describing the temple of Minerva, where the rites of Osiris were celebrated, and speaking of a tomb placed in the most secret recess, as in Christian churches there are calvaries behind the altar, says: " It is the tomb of a god whose name I dare not mention."

Calvary is derived from the Latin word *calvus*, "bald," and figuratively "arid," "dried up;" pointing to the decay of nature in the winter season.

53. *Mysteries of Osiris.*—These formed the third degree, or summit of Egyptian initiation. In these the legend of the murder of Osiris by his brother Typhon was represented, and the god was personated by the candidate. (As we shall see hereafter, the Freemasons exactly copy this procedure in the master's degree, substituting for Osiris, Hiram Abiff, one of the three grand masters at the building of Solomon's temple.) The perfectly initiated candidate was called *Al-om-jak*, from the name of the Deity (40), and the dogma of the unity of God was the chief secret imparted to him. How great and how dangerous a secret it was may easily be seen when it is borne in mind that centuries after the institution of the mysteries, Socrates lost his life for promulgating the same doctrine.

54. *Isis.*—The many names assumed by Isis have already been alluded to. She was also represented with different emblems, all betokening her manifold characteristics. The lucid round, the snake, the ears of corn, and the sistrum represent the titular deities of the Hecatæan (Hecate, Goddess of Night), Bacchic, Eleusinian, and Ionic mysteries, that is, the mystic rites in general for whose sake the allegory was invented. The black palla in which she is

wrapped, embroidered with a silver moon and stars, denotes the time in which the mysteries were celebrated, namely, in the dead of night. Her names, to return to them, are given in the following words, put into her mouth by Apuleius in his "Golden Ass," which is a description of the mysteries under the guise of a fable:—" Behold, Lucius, I, moved by thy prayers, am present with thee; I who am nature, the parent of things, the queen of all the elements, the primordial progeny of the ages, the supreme of divinities, the sovereign of the spirits of the dead, the first of the celestials, the first and universal substance, the uniform and multiform aspect of the uncreated essence; I who rule by my nod the luminous summits of the heavens, the breezes of the sea, and the silence of the realms beneath, and whose one divinity the whole orb of the earth venerates under a manifold form, by different rites, and a variety of appellations. Hence the early Phrygians call me Pessinuntica, mother of the gods; the Attic aborigines, Cecropian Minerva; the floating Cyprians, Paphian Venus; the arrow-bearing Cretans, Diana Dictynna; the three-tongued Sicilians, Stygian Proserpine; and the Eleusinians, the ancient goddess Ceres. Some also call me Juno, others Bellona, others Hecate, and others Rhamnusia. The Ethiopians, the Arii, and the Egyptians, skilled in ancient learning, honour me with rites peculiarly appropriate, and call me by my true name, Queen Isis." From this it is quite clear that Isis was not simply the moon to the initiated. In the sanctuary the multifarious forms are reduced to unity; the many idols are reduced to the one divinity, *i. e.* primeval power and intelligence.

V.

METAMORPHOSES OF THE LEGEND OF ISIS.

55.

SPREAD *of Egyptian Mysteries.*—The irradiations of the mysteries of Egypt shine through and animate the secret doctrines of Phœnicia, Asia Minor, Greece, and Italy. Cadmus and Inachus brought them into Greece at large, Orpheus into Thrace, Melampus into Argos, Trophonius into Bœotia, Minos into Crete, Cinyras into Cyprus, and Erechtheus into Athens. And as in Egypt the mysteries were dedicated to Isis and Osiris, so in Samothrace they were sacred to the mother of the gods, in Bœotia to Bacchus, in Cyprus to Venus, in Crete to Jupiter, in Athens to Ceres and Proserpine, in Amphissa to Castor and Pollux, in Lemnos to Vulcan, and so to others in other places; but their end, as well as nature, was the same in all—to teach monotheism and a future state.

56. *Dionysiac or Bacchic Mysteries.*—These were divided into the greater and the less. The latter were celebrated every year at the autumnal equinox, and females were admitted to them, wearing the creative emblem suspended round their necks. They ended with the sacrifice of an unclean animal, which was eaten by the worshippers. Then aspirants and initiated proceeded with sacred dances towards the temple. The Canephoroi, carrying golden vases full of the choicest fruits, were followed by the bearers of the creative emblem, who were furnished with long poles, and were crowned with ivy, a herb sacred to Bacchus, or the sun personified. Now came other celebrants habited as women, but performing all the repulsive actions of drunken men. The next night the ceremonies of initiation were performed, in which the fable of Bacchus slain by the Titans was scenically represented, the aspirant acting the part of Bacchus.

The greater mysteries were celebrated every three years at the vernal equinox, in the neighbourhood of a marsh, like the festival of Saïs, in Egypt. On the night preceding the initiation. the spouse of the hierophant sacrificed a ram. She represented the spouse of Bacchus, and when seated as such on the throne, the priests and initiated of both sexes exclaimed: "Hail, spouse, hail, new light!" The aspirant was purified by fire, water, and air, passing through trials similar to those described elsewhere (*e. g.* 39), and finally, was introduced into the sanctuary crowned with myrtle and dressed in the skin of a fawn.

57. *Sabazian Mysteries.*— Sabazius was a name of Bacchus, probably derived from Siva or some cognate form, whose astronomical meaning is the planetary system of countless suns and stars. The mysteries were performed at night, and represented the amours of Jupiter, in the form of a serpent, and Proserpina. A golden—others say a living—serpent was introduced into the bosom of the candidate, who exclaimed, "Evoe! Sabai! Bacchi! Anes! Attes! Hues!" Evoe or Eve in most languages of antiquity meant both serpent and life; a recollection of the name of Adam's wife, and the origin of the serpent-worship of the ancient world. When Moses lifted up a brazen serpent in the Wilderness, the afflicted Hebrews knew that it was a sign of preservation. Sabai has already been explained; Hues and Attes were other names of Bacchus. These mysteries continued to be celebrated to the last days of paganism, and in the days of Domitian, 7,000 initiated were found in Rome alone.

58. *Mysteries of the Cabiri.*—The name of the Cabiri was derived originally from Phœnicia; the word signifies " powerful." There were four gods— Aschieros, Achiochersus, Achiochersa, and Camillus. The last was slain by his three brothers, who carried

away with them the reproductive organs; and this allegorical murder was celebrated in the secret rites. Camillus is the same as Osiris, Adonis, and others, all subject to the same mutilation, all symbolizing the sun's loss of generative power during winter. The chief places for the celebration of these mysteries were the islands of Samothrace and Lemnos. The priests were called Corybantes. There is much perplexity connected with this subject; since, besides what is mentioned above, the mysteries are also said to have been instituted in honour of Atys, the son of Cybele. Atys means the sun, and the mysteries were celebrated at the vernal equinox, and there cannot, therefore, be any doubt that, like all the other mysteries in their period of decay, they represented the enigmatical death of the sun in winter and his regeneration in the spring. The ceremonies lasted three days. The first day was one of sadness: a cruciform pine with the image of Atys attached to it was cut down, the mutilated body of Atys having been discovered at the foot of such a tree; the second day was a day of trumpets, which were blown to awaken the god from his deathlike sleep; and the third day, that of joy, was the day of initiation and celebration of his return to life.

59. *Eleusinian Mysteries.*—The Eleusinian mysteries were celebrated in honour of Ceres, the Isis of Greece; whilst Osiris appears as Proserpine—for the death of Osiris and the carrying off of Proserpine

to the infernal regions symbolize the same thing, viz. the sun's disappearance during the winter season. The mysteries were originally celebrated only at Eleusis, a town of Attica, but eventually extended to Italy and even to Britain. Like all other mysteries, they were divided into the greater and the less, and the latter, like the Bacchic and Cabiric rites, lasted nine days, and were merely preparatory, consisting of lustrations and sacrifices. The ceremonies of initiation into the greater mysteries were opened by the herald exclaiming: "Retire, O ye profane." The aspirant was presented naked, to signify his total helplessness and dependence on Providence. He was clothed with the skin of a calf. An oath of secrecy was then administered, and he was asked: "Have you eaten bread?" The reply was "No." Proserpine cannot return to the earth because she has eaten of the fruit of the infernal regions; Adam falls when he tastes of earthly fruit. "I have drunk the sacred mixture, I have been fed from the basket of Ceres; I have laboured; I have entered into the bed." That is to say, he had been placed in the pastos, in which the aspirant for initiation was immured during the period of his probation (39). He was then made to pass through a series of trials, similar in character to those adopted in other mysteries, after which he was introduced into the inner temple, where he beheld the statue of the goddess Ceres, surrounded by a dazzling light. The candidate, who had heretofore been called a *mystes*, or novice, was now termed *epoptes*, or eye-witness, and the secret doctrine was revealed. The assembly was then closed with the Sanscrit words, "*Konx om pax*," the meaning of which is uncertain. According to Captain Wilford, the words Candscha om Pacsha, of which the above is a Greek corruption, are still used at the religious meetings and ceremonies of the Brahmins—another proof, if it were needed, that the mysteries are of Eastern origin.

60. *Doors of Horn and Ivory.*—The sixth book of the "Æeneid," and the "Golden Ass" of Apuleius, contain descriptions of what passed in the celebration of the Eleusinian mysteries. In the former work, Æneas and his guide, having finished their progress through the infernal regions, are dismissed through the ivory gate of dreams. But there was another gate of horn through which the aspirant entered; for all caverns of initiation had two gates; one called the *descent* to hell, the other the *ascent* of the just. The ancient poets said that through the gate of horn issued true visions, and through the gate of ivory, false. Now from this, and the fact that Æneas and his guide issue through it, it has been inferred by some critics that Virgil meant to intimate, that all he had said concerning the infernal regions was to be considered a fable. But such could not be the poet's intention; what he really implied was

that a future state was a real state, whilst the representations thereof in the mysteries were only shadows. The ivory gate itself was no other than the sumptuous door of the temple through which the initiated came out when the ceremony was over.

61. *Suppression of Eleusinian Mysteries.*—These mysteries survived all others; they shone with great splendour when the secret worship of the Cabiri, and even of Egypt, had already disappeared, and were not suppressed until the year 396 of our era by the pitiless Theodosius the Great, who, in his zeal for the Christian religion, committed the greatest cruelties against unbelievers.

62. *The Thesmophoria.*—The term signifies a legislative festival, and refers specially to the symbolic rites forming part of the festival consecrated to Ceres, who was said to have given to the Greeks sound laws founded on agriculture and property, in memory of which, chosen women in the solemn processions of the Thesmophoria carried at Eleusis the tablets on which the laws were written; hence the name of the festival, which was one of legislation and semination. We have only fragmentary notices concerning these festivals, though we derive some information from Aristophanes' "Thesmophoriazusæ," which, however, is very slight, as it would have been dangerous for him, in alluding to these mysteries, to employ more than general and simple designations. We discover, however, that they

were celebrated in the month of October, and lasted three or four days. Females only took part in them, and it was death for a man to enter the temple. Every tribe of Athens chose two females born in wedlock and married, and distinguished for virtue. The men who possessed a capital of three talents were compelled to give their wives the money necessary to defray the cost of the festivals. For nine days also there was to be total forbearance between married couples; for the Thesmophoria not only had reference to agriculture, but also to the more intimate relations between man and wife. As Ceres or the Earth mourned for the absence of Proserpine, or the Sun, so the Athenian women mourned during the celebration for the absence of the light of love; and as Ceres is at length cheered up by the homely beverage offered by Baubo, so a personage called Iambe, with absurd jokes and gross gestures, restores the attendants to a more joyous mood.

63. *Aim of Grecian Mysteries more Moral than Religious.*—The object of the initiation into the mysteries of Greece was more moral than religious, differing in this from the Indian and Egyptian mysteries, that were religious, scientific, and political. For at the time of their introduction into Greece science had ceased to be the prerogative of the few; the political life of that country had stirred up the energy of the people and made it the architect of its own greatness. We therein behold already the dawn

of a new era; the decay of the ancient nature-worship, and a tendency to, and endeavour on the part of mankind after, inquiry and free striving, to overcome nature; which is diametrically opposed to the spirit of antiquity, which consisted in the total resignation and surrender of the individual to the influences of the All.

VI.

CHINESE AND JAPANESE MYSTERIES.

64.

CHINESE *Metaphysics.*—In Chinese cosmogony we discover traces of the once universally prevailing knowledge of the properties of eternal nature. Matter—the first material principle—is assumed to act upon itself, and thus to evolve the dual powers. This first material principle is called *Tai-Keik,* and described as the first link in the chain of causes; it is the utmost limit in the midst of illimitableness, though in the midst of nonentity there always existed an infinite *Le,* or "principle of order." The *Le* is called infinite, because it is impossible to represent it by any figure, since it is the "Eternal Nothing." This undoubted fragmentary tradition of the most ancient metaphysical system in the world has been ridiculed by many modern writers; but any reader will see that, however imperfectly expressed, it is the theosophic doctrine (11).

65. *Introduction of Chinese Mysteries.*—The Chinese practised Buddhism in its most simple form, and worshipped an invisible God, until a few centuries before the Christian era. From the teaching of Confucius, who lived five centuries before that era, it appears that in his time there were no mysteries; they only became necessary when the Chinese became an idolatrous nation. The chief end of initiation then was an absorption into the deity O-Mi-To Fo. *Omito* was derived from the Sanscrit *Armida*, "immeasurable," and *Fo* was only another name for Buddha. The letter Y represented the triune God, and was indeed the ineffable name of the Deity, the Tetractys of Pythagoras, and the Tetragrammaton of the Jews. The rainbow was a celebrated symbol in the mysteries, for it typified the re-appearance of the sun; and this not only in China, but even in Mexico (73).

66. *Parallel between Buddhism and Roman Catholicism.*—The general resemblance between Buddhism and Romanism is so marked that it is acknowledged by the Romanists themselves, who account for this fact by the supposition that Satan counterfeited the true religion. This correspondence holds in minute particulars. Both have a supreme and infallible head, the celibacy of the priesthood, monasteries and nunneries, prayers in an

unknown tongue, prayers to saints and intercessors, and especially, and principally too, a virgin with a child; also prayers for the dead, repetition of prayers with the use of a rosary, works of merit and supererogation; self-imposed austerities and bodily inflictions; a formal daily service consisting of chants, burning of candles, sprinkling of holy water, bowings, prostrations; fast days and feast days, religious processions, images and pictures and fabulous legends, the worship of relics, the sacrament of confession, purgatory, &c. In some respects their rites resemble those of the Jews; they propitiate the Supreme Deity with the blood of bulls and goats, and also offered holocausts. The resemblance is easily accounted for. Romanism and some other creeds are only modernized Buddhism; and many religions are but superstitious perversions of the knowledge of natural phenomena. The tradition about Prester John has its origin in this resemblance between Buddhism and a corrupted Christianity. In the twelfth century there was in China a great Mongol tribe professing Buddhism, which by travellers was mistaken for an Oriental Christian religion. The Nestorian Christians, dwelling among the Mongols, called its head *John the Priest*, and hence arose the tradition that in the heart of Asia there was a Christian Church, whose popes bore the title of *Prester John*.

67. *Lau-Tze*.—Confucius was the religious lawgiver of China, but Lau-Tze was its philosopher.

He excelled the former in depth and independence of thought. The word *Lau*, or *Le*, is difficult to render; the Chinese itself defines it as "a thing indefinite, impalpable, and yet therein are forms." Lau-Tze himself seems to make it equivalent to "intelligence." His philosophy is peaceful and loving, and in this respect presents various commendable points of resemblance to Christian doctrine.

68. *Modern Chinese Societies.*—The most noted is that of Thian-ti-wé, or the Union of Heaven and Earth, which has for its leading dogma the equality of mankind, and the duty of the rich to share their superfluity with the poor. The candidate, having successfully passed through the most severe trials, is conducted before the master, two members of the order cross their swords over his head, and draw blood from both, which they pour into the same cup,—a sacramental drink, to which both put their lips when the candidate has pronounced the oath. This association is spread through the southern provinces of China and the island of Java. In central and northern China there are two other societies, probably derived from the former, that of Pe-lian-kiao, or the Lotos, and that of Thian-li, or Celestial Reason. Henry Pottinger, in a despatch to Lord Aberdeen (1843), alludes to a fourth, saying: "The song being finished, Ke-Ying, the Chinese commissioner, having taken from his arm

a gold bracelet, gave it to me, informing me, at the same time, that he had received it in his tender youth from his father, and that it contained a mysterious legend, and that, by merely showing it, it would in all parts of China assure me a fraternal reception." Another society, formed at the beginning of this century, is that of the "Triad," whose object is to initiate the indolent and prejudiced Chinese into Western civilization. The society of the "White Waterlily," whose chief could not be discovered by the Chinese government, caused many and disastrous political disturbances.

69. *Japanese Mysteries.*—The Japanese held that the world was enclosed in an egg before the creation, which egg was broken by a bull—the ever-recurring astronomical allegory, alluding to the Bull of the zodiac, which in former times opened the seasons, the vernal equinox. It is the same bull Apis which Egypt adored (47), and which the Jews in the wilderness worshipped as the golden calf; also the bull which, sacrificed in the mysteries of Mithras, poured out its blood to fertilize the earth. The Japanese worshipped a deity who was styled the Son of the Unknown God, considered the creator of sun and moon, and called Tensio-Dai-Sin. The aspirants for initiation were conducted through artificial spheres, formed of movable circles, representing the revolutions of the planets. The mirror was a significant emblem of the all-seeing eye of their chief deity (11).

In the closing ceremony of preparation the candidate was enclosed in the pastos, the door of which was said to be guarded by a terrible divinity, armed with a drawn sword. During the course of his probation the aspirant sometimes acquired so high a degree of enthusiasm as to refuse to quit his confinement in the pastos, and to remain there until he literally perished of famine. To this voluntary martyrdom was attached a promise of never-ending happiness hereafter. Their creed indeed is Buddhism, slightly modified. "*Diabolo ecclesiam Christi imitante!*" exclaimed Xavier on seeing how the practices of the Japanese resembled those of the Romanists in Europe; and, as has been observed of Buddhism in China and Thibet, all the practices of the Japanese ritual are so tinged with the colour of Romanism, that they might well justify the exclamation of Xavier, who was neither a savant nor a philosopher (66).

70. *Japanese Doctrines.*—The god Tensio-Dai-Sin has twelve apostles, and the sun, the planetary hero, fights with monsters and the elements. The ministers of the Temple of the Sun wear tunics of the colour of fire, and annually celebrate four festivals, the third day of the third month, the fifth day of the fifth, the seventh day of the seventh, and the ninth day of the ninth month respectively; and at one of these festivals they represent a myth similar to that of Adonis, and nature is personified by a

priest dressed in many colours. The members of this society are called *Jammabos*, and the initiated are enjoined a long time to abstain from meat and to prepare themselves by many purifications.

71. *The Lama.*—The Grand Lama, the God of Thibet, becomes incarnate in man; thus much the priests reveal to the people. But the true religion, which consists of the doctrine of the supposed origin of the world, is only made known in the almost inaccessible mysteries. The man in whom the Grand Lama has for the time become incarnate, and who is the pontiff, is held in such veneration, that the people eat pastiles, accounted sacred, and made from the unclean remains of the food which had contributed to the sustenance of his body. This disgusting practice, however, with them is simply the result of their belief in the metempsychosis—parallel with the Indian doctrine of corruption and reproduction, symbolized by the use of cowdung in the purification of the aspirant; and its real meaning is to show that all the parts of the universe are incessantly absorbed, and pass into the substance of each other. It is upon the model of the serpent who devours his tail.

VII.

MEXICAN AND PERUVIAN MYSTERIES.

72.

MERICAN *Aborigines*. — Ethnologists can tell us as yet nothing as to the origin of the earliest inhabitants of the American continent; but if the reader will accept the theory propounded in the introduction to this work (6—9), he will be at no loss to answer the question. As nature in Asia brought forth the Caucasian races, so in the western hemisphere it gave birth to the various races peopling it. That one of them was a highly civilized race in prehistoric times is proved by the ruins of beautiful cities discovered in Central America; and all the antiquarian remains show that the religion of Mexico and Peru was substantially the same as that practised by the various nations of the East; and naturally so, for the moral and physical laws of the uni-

verse are everywhere the same, and, working in the same manner, produce the same results, only modified by climatic and local conditions.

73. *Mexican Deities.*—The religious system of the Mexicans bore a character of dark and gloomy austerity. They worshipped many deities, the chief of which were Teotl, the invisible and supreme being; Virococha, the creator; Vitzliputzli or Heritzilopochtli, the god of mercy, to whom the most sanguinary rites were offered (which proves that the Mexican priests were quite as inconsistent in this respect as the priestly bigots of Europe, who, in the name of the God of mercy, tortured, racked and burnt millions that differed from whatever creed had been set up as the orthodox and legalized one); Tescalipuca, the god of vengeance; Quetzalcoatl, the Mexican Mercury, whose name signifies the " serpent clothed with green feathers;" Mictlaneiheratl, the goddess of hell; Tlaloc-teatli, or Neptune; and Ixciana, or Venus. To Vitzliputzli was ascribed the renovation of the world, and his name referred to the sun. He was said to be the offspring of a virgin, who was impregnated by a plume of feathers, which descended from heaven into her bosom, invested with all the colours of the rainbow (65). He was represented in the figure of a man, with a dread-inspiring aspect. He was seated on a globe over a lofty altar, which was borne in procession during the celebration of the mysteries. His

right hand grasped a snake, the symbol of life, and representations of this reptile are found on all the temples of Mexico and Peru. Traces of the serpent-worship of the western world are also found in the states of Ohio and Iowa, where serpent mounds, formed of earth, 1,000 feet long or more, are still to be found. The office of Tescalipuca was to punish the sins of men by the infliction of plagues, famine, and pestilence. His anger could only be appeased by human sacrifices—thousands of men were frequently immolated to him in one single day.

74. *Cruelty of Mexican Worship.*—The temples of Mexico were full of horrible idols, which were all bathed and washed with human blood. The chapel of Vitzliputzli was decorated with the skulls of the wretches that had been slain in sacrifice; the walls and floor were inches thick with blood, and before the image of the god might often be seen the still palpitating hearts of the human victims offered up to him, whose skins served the priests for garments. This revolting custom, as a legend says, arose from the fact that Tozi, the "Grand Mother," was of human extraction. Vitzliputzli procured her divine honours by enjoining the Mexicans to demand her of her father for their queen; this being done, they also commanded him to put her to death, afterwards to flay her, and to cover a young man with her skin. It was in this manner she was stripped of her humanity, to be placed among the gods.

Another disgusting practice arising from this legend will be mentioned hereafter.

75. *Initiation into Mysteries.*—The candidate had to undergo all the terrors, sufferings, and penances practised in the Eastern world. He was scourged with knotted cords, his flesh was cut with knives, and reeds put into the wounds, that the blood might be seen to trickle more freely, or they were cauterized with red-hot cinders. Many perished under these trials. The lustrations were performed, not with water, but with blood, and the candidate's habit was not white, but black, and before initiation he was given a drink, which was said to dispel fear, which, indeed, it may have done in some degree by disturbing the brain. The candidate was then led into the dark caverns of initiation, excavated beneath the foundations of the mighty pyramidal temple of Vitzliputzli in Mexico, and passed through the mysteries which symbolically represented the wanderings of their gods, *i. e.* the course of the sun through the signs of the zodiac. The caverns were called "the path of the dead." Everything that could appal the imagination and test his courage was made to appear before him. Now he heard shrieks of despair and the groans of the dying; he was led past the dungeons where the human victims, being fattened for sacrifice, were confined, and through caverns slippery with half congealed blood; anon he met with the quivering frame of the dying man, whose heart had

just been torn from his body and offered up to their sanguinary god, and looking up he beheld in the roof the orifice through which the victims had been precipitated, for they were now immediately under the altar of Vitzliputzli. At length, however, he arrived at a narrow chasm or stone fissure, at the end of this extensive range of caverns, through which he was formally protruded, and received by a shouting multitude as a person regenerated or born again. The females, divesting themselves of their little clothing, danced in a state of nudity like the frantic Bacchantes, and, having repeated the dance three times, they gave themselves up to unbounded licentiousness.

76. *The Greater Mysteries.*—But as with Eastern nations, the Mexicans had, besides the general religious doctrines communicated to the initiated, an esoteric doctrine, only attainable by the priests, and not even by them until they had qualified themselves for it by the sacrifice of a human victim. The most ineffable degrees of knowledge were imparted to them at midnight and under severe obligations, whose disregard entailed death without remission. The real doctrine taught was astronomical, and, like the Eastern nations, they at their great festivals lamented the disappearance of the sun, and rejoiced at its re-appearance at the festival of the new fire, as it was called. All fire, even the sacred fire of the temple, having been extinguished, the population of

Mexico, with the priests at their head, marched to a hill near the city, where they waited till the Pleiades ascended the middle of the sky, when they sacrificed a human victim. The instrument made use of by the priests to kindle the fire was placed on the wound made in the breast of the prisoner destined to be sacrificed; and, when the fire was kindled, the body was placed on an enormous pile ready prepared, and this latter set on fire. The new fire, received with joyful shouts, was carried from village to village; where it was deposited in the temple, whence it was distributed to every private dwelling. When the sun appeared on the horizon the acclamations were renewed. The priests were further taught the doctrine of immortality, of a triune deity, of the original population, who—led by the god Vitzliputzli, holding in his hand a rod formed like a serpent, and seated in a square ark—finally settled upon a lake, abounding with the lotus, where they erected their tabernacle. This lake was the lake in the midst of which the city of Mexico originally stood.

77. *Human Sacrifices.*—No priest was to be fully initiated into the mysteries of the Mexican religion until he had sacrificed a human victim. This horrible rite, which the Spaniards, who conquered the country, often saw performed on their own captive countrymen, was thus performed:—The chief priest carried in his hand a large and sharp knife made of

flint; another priest carried a collar of wood; the other four priests who assisted arranged themselves adjoining the pyramidal stone, which had a convex top, so that the man to be sacrificed, being laid thereon on his back, was bent in such a manner that the stomach separated upon the slightest incision of the knife. Two priests seized hold of his feet and two more of his hands, whilst the fifth fastened round his neck the collar of wood. The high priest then opened his stomach with the knife, and tearing out his heart, held it up to the sun, and then threw it before the idol in one of the chapels on the top of the great pyramid where the rite was performed. The body was finally cast down the steps that wound all round the building. Forty or fifty victims were thus sacrificed in a few hours. Prisoners of rank or approved courage might escape this horrid death by fighting six Mexican warriors in succession. If they were successful their lives and liberty were granted to them; but if they fell under the strokes of their adversaries they were dragged, dead or living, to the sacrificial stone, and their hearts torn out.

78. *Clothing in Bloody Skins.*—We have already seen that the priests were clothed in the bloody skins of their victims. The same horrid custom was practised on other occasions. On certain festivals they dressed a man in the bloody skin just reeking from the body of a victim. Kings and

grandees did not think it derogatory to their dignity to disguise themselves in this manner, and to run up and down the streets, soliciting alms, which were applied to pious purposes. This horrible masquerade continued till the skin began to grow putrid. On another festival they would slay a woman and clothe a man with her skin, who thus equipped, danced for two days together with the rest of his fellow-citizens.

79. *Peruvian Mysteries.*—The Incas, or rulers of Peru, boasted of their descent from the sun and moon, which therefore were worshipped, as well as the great god Pacha-Camac, whose very name was so sacred that it was only communicated to the initiated. They also had an idol they termed Tanga-tango, meaning "One in three and three in one." Their secret mysteries, of which we know next to nothing, were celebrated on their great annual festival, held on the first day of the September moon, the people watching all night until the rising of the sun; and when he appeared the eastern doors of the great temple of Casco were thrown open, so that the sun's radiance could illuminate his image in gold placed opposite. The walls and ceiling of this temple were all covered over with gold plates, and the figure of the sun, representing a round face, surrounded with rays and flames, as modern painters usually draw the sun, was of such a size as almost to cover one side of the wall. It was,

moreover, double the thickness of the plates covering the walls. The Virgins of the Sun, who, like the Vestals of ancient Rome, had the keeping of the sacred fire entrusted to them, and were vowed to perpetual celibacy, then walked round the altar, whilst the priests expounded the mild and equitable laws of Peru; for, contrary to the practice of their near neighbours, the Mexicans, the Peruvians had no sanguinary rites whatever, though some Spanish writers, who, of course, could see no good in non-Catholics and pagans, charged them with sacrificing young children of from four to six years old "in prodigious numbers," and also with slaying virgins. The Spaniards, no doubt, alluded to some ill-understood symbolical rite.

VIII.

THE DRUIDS.

80.

THE *Druids, the Magi of the West.*—The secret doctrines of the Druids were much the same as those of the Gymnosophists and Brahmins of India, the Magi of Persia, the priests of Egypt, and of all other priests of antiquity. Like them, they had two sets of religious doctrines, exoteric and esoteric. Their rites were practised in Britain and Gaul, though they were brought to a much greater perfection in the former country, where the Isle of Anglesea was considered their chief seat. The word Druid is generally supposed to be derived from δρῦς, "an oak," which tree was particularly sacred among them, though its etymology may also be found in the Gaelic word *Druidh*, "a wise man" or "magician."

81. *Temples.*—Their temples, wherein the sacred

fire was preserved, were generally situate on eminences and in dense groves of oaks, and assumed various forms—circular, because a circle was an emblem of the universe; oval, in allusion to the mundane egg, from which, according to the traditions of many nations, the universe, or according to others, our first parents, issued; serpentine, because a serpent was the symbol of Hu, the Druidic Osiris; cruciform, because a cross is an emblem of regeneration (49); or winged, to represent the motion of the divine spirit. Their only canopy was the sky, and they were constructed of unhewn stones, their numbers having reference to astronomical calculations. In the centre was placed a stone of larger dimensions than the others, and worshipped as the representative of the Deity. The three principal temples of this description in Britain were undoubtedly those of Stonehenge and Abury in the south, and that of Shap in Cumberland. Where stone was scarce, rude banks of earth were substituted, and the temple was formed of a high vallum and ditch. The most Herculean labours were performed in their construction; Stukeley says that it would cost, at the present time, £20,000 to throw up such a mound as Silbury Hill.

82. *Places of Initiation.*—The adytum or ark of the mysteries was called a cromlech, and was used as the sacred pastos, or place of regeneration. It consisted of three upright stones, as supporters of

a broad, flat stone laid across them on the top, so as to form a small cell. Kit Cotey's House, in Kent, was such a pastos. Considerable space, however, was necessary for the machinery of initiation in its largest and most comprehensive scale. Therefore, the Coer Sidi, where the mysteries of Druidism were performed, consisted of a range of buildings, adjoining the temple, containing apartments of all sizes, cells, vaults, baths, and long and artfully-contrived passages, with all the apparatus of terror used on these occasions. Most frequently these places were subterranean; and many of the caverns in this country were the scenes of Druidical initiation. The stupendous grotto at Castleton, in Derbyshire, called by Stukeley the Stygian Cave, as well as the giants' caves at Luckington and Badminster, in Wilts, certainly were used for this purpose.

83. *Rites.*—The system of Druidism embraced every religious and philosophical pursuit then known in these islands. The rites bore an undoubted reference to astronomical facts. Their chief deities are reducible to two,—a male and a female, the great father and mother, Hu and Ceridwen, distinguished by the same characteristics as belonged to Osiris and Isis, Bacchus and Ceres, or any other supreme god and goddess representing the two principles of all being. The grand periods of initiation were quarterly, and determined by the course of the sun, and his arrival at the equinoctial and solstitial points.

But the time of annual celebration was May-eve, when fires were kindled on all the cairns and cromlechs throughout the island, which burned all night to introduce the sports of May-day, whence all the national sports formerly or still practised date their origin. Round these fires choral dances were performed in honour of the sun, who, at this season, was figuratively said to rise from his tomb. The festival was licentious, and continued till the luminary had attained his meridian height, when priests and attendants retired to the woods, where the most disgraceful orgies were perpetrated. But the solemn initiations were performed at midnight, and contained three degrees, the first or lowest being the Eubates, the second the Bards, and the third the Druids. The candidate was first placed in the pastos bed, or coffin, where his symbolical death represented the death of Hu, or the sun; and his restoration in the third degree symbolized the resurrection of the sun. He had to undergo trials and tests of courage similar to those practised in the mysteries of other countries (*e. g.* 26), and which therefore need not be detailed here.

The festival of the 25th of December was celebrated with great fires lighted on the tops of the hills, to announce the birth-day of the god Sol. This was the moment when, after the supposed winter solstice, he began to increase, and gradually to ascend. This festival indeed was kept not by the Druids only, but throughout the ancient world, from India to Ultima Thule. The fires, of course, were typical of the power and ardour of the sun, whilst the evergreens used on the occasion foreshadowed the results of the sun's renewed action on vegetation. The festival of the summer solstice was kept on the 24th of June. Both days are still kept as festivals in the Christian church, the former as Christmas, the latter as St. John's Day; because the early Christians judiciously adopted not only the festival days of the pagans, but also, so far as this could be done with propriety, their mode of keeping them; substituting, however, a theological meaning for astronomical allusions. The use of evergreens in churches at Christmas time is the Christian perpetuation of an ancient Druidic custom.

84. *Doctrines.*—The Druids taught the doctrine of one supreme being, a future state of rewards and punishments, the immortality of the soul and a metempsychosis. It was a maxim with them that water was the first principle of all things, and existed before the creation in unsullied purity (11), which seems a contradiction to their other doctrine that day was the offspring of night, because night or chaos was in existence before day was created. They taught that time was only an intercepted fragment of eternity, and that there was an endless succession of worlds. In fact, their doctrines were chiefly those of Pythagoras. They entertained

great veneration for the numbers three, seven, nineteen (the Metonic cycle), and one hundred and forty-seven, produced by multiplying the square of seven by three. They also practised vaticination, pretending to predict future events from the flights of birds, human sacrifices, by white horses, the agitation of water, and lots. They seem, however, to have possessed considerable scientific knowledge.

85. *Political and Judicial Power.*—Their authority in many cases exceeded that of the monarch. They were, of course, the sole interpreters of religion, and consequently superintended all sacrifices; for no private person was allowed to offer a sacrifice without their sanction. They possessed the power of excommunication, which was the most horrible punishment that could be inflicted next to that of death, and from the effects of which the highest magistrate was not exempt. The great council of the realm was not competent to declare war or conclude peace without their concurrence. They determined all disputes by a final and unalterable decision, and had the power of inflicting the punishment of death. And, indeed, their altars streamed with the blood of human victims. Holocausts of men, women, and children, inclosed in large towers of wicker-work, were sometimes sacrificed as a burnt-offering to their superstitions, which were, at the same time, intended to enhance the consideration of the priests, who were an ambitious race delighting in blood. The

Druids, it is said, preferred such as had been guilty of theft, robbery, or other crimes, as most acceptable to their gods; but when there was a scarcity of criminals, they made no scruple to supply their place with innocent persons. These dreadful sacrifices were offered by the Druids, for the public, on the eve of a dangerous war, or in the time of any national calamity; and also for particular persons of high rank, when they were afflicted with any dangerous disease.

86. *Priestesses.*—The priestesses, clothed in white, and wearing a metal girdle, foretold the future from the observation of natural phenomena, but more especially from human sacrifices. For them was reserved the frightful task of putting to death the prisoners taken in war, and individuals condemned by the Druids; and their auguries were drawn from the manner in which the blood issued from the many wounds inflicted, and also from the smoking entrails. Many of these priestesses maintained a perpetual virginity, others gave themselves up to the most luxurious excesses. They dwelt on lonely rocks, beaten by the waves of the ocean, which the mariners looked upon as temples surrounded with unspeakable prodigies. Thus the island of Sena or Liambis, The Saints, near Ushant, was the residence of certain of these priestesses, who delivered oracles to sailors; and there was no power that was not attributed to them. Others, living near the mouth of the Loire,

once a year destroyed their temple, scattered its materials, and, having collected others, built a new one—of course a symbolical ceremony; and if one of the priestesses dropped any of the sacred materials, the others fell upon her with fierce yells, tore her to pieces, and scattered her bleeding limbs.

87. *Abolition*.—As the Romans gained ground in these islands the power of the Druids gradually declined; and they were finally assailed by Suetonius Paulinus, governor of Britain under Nero, A.D. 61, in their stronghold, the Isle of Anglesey, and entirely defeated, the conqueror consuming many of them in the fires which they had kindled for burning the Roman prisoners they had expected to make—a very just retaliation upon these sanguinary priests. But though their dominion was thus destroyed, many of their religious practices continued much longer; and so late as the eleventh century, in the reign of Canute, it was necessary to forbid the people to worship the sun, moon, fires, etc. Certainly many of the practices of the Druids are still adhered to in Freemasonry; and some writers on this order endeavour to show that it was established soon after the edict of Canute, and that as thereby the Druidical worship was prohibited *in toto*, the strongest oaths were required to bind the initiated to secresy.

IX.

SCANDINAVIAN MYSTERIES.

88.

DROTTES.—The priests of Scandinavia were named Drottes, and instituted by Sigge, a Scythian prince, who is said afterwards to have assumed the name of Odin. Their number was twelve, who were alike priests and judges; and from this order proceeded the establishment of British juries. Their power was extended to its utmost limits, by being allowed a discretionary privilege of determining on the choice of human victims for sacrifice, from which even the monarch was not exempt—hence arose the necessity of cultivating the goodwill of these sovereign pontiffs; and as this order, like the Israelitish priesthood, was restricted to one family, they became possessed of unbounded wealth, and at last became so tyrannical as to be objects of terror to the whole community. Christianity, promising to relieve it from this yoke, was hailed with enthusiasm; and the inhabitants of Scandinavia, inspired with a thirst for vengeance on account of accumulated and long-continued suffering, retaliated with dreadful severity on their persecutors, overthrowing the palaces and temples, the statues of their gods, and all the paraphernalia of Gothic superstition. Of this nothing remains but a few cromlechs; some stupendous monuments of rough stone, which human fury could not destroy; certain ranges of caverns hewn out of the solid rock; and some natural grottos used for the purpose of initiation.

89. *Ritual.*—The whole ritual had an astronomical bearing. The places of initiation, as in other mysteries, were in caverns, natural or artificial, and the candidate had to undergo trials as frightful as the priests could render them. But instead of having to pass through seven caves or passages, as in the Mithraic and other mysteries, he descended through *nine*—the square of the mystic number three—subterranean passages, and he was instructed to search for the body of Balder, the Scandinavian Osiris, slain by Loke, the principle of darkness, and to use his utmost endeavours to raise him to life. To enter into particulars of the process of initiation would involve the repetition of what has been said before; it may therefore suffice to observe that the candidate on arriving at the

sacellum had a solemn oath administered to him on a naked sword, and ratified it by drinking mead out of a human skull. The sacred sign of the cross was impressed upon him, and a ring of magic virtues, the gift of Balder the Good, delivered to him.

90. *Astronomical Meaning Demonstrated.*—The first canto of the Edda, which apparently contains a description of the ceremonies performed on the initiation of an aspirant, says that he seeks to know the sciences possessed by the Æsas or gods. He discovers a palace, whose roof of boundless dimensions is covered with golden shields. He encounters a man engaged in launching upwards seven flowers. Here we easily discover the astronomical meaning: the palace is the world, the roof the sky; the golden shields are the stars, the seven flowers the seven planets. The candidate is asked what is his name, and replies Gangler, that is, the wanderer, he that performs a revolution, distributing necessaries to mankind; for the candidate personates the sun. The palace is that of the king, the epithet the ancient Mystagogues gave to the head of the planetary system. Then he discovers three seats; on the lowest is the king called Har, sublime; on the central one, Jafuhar, the equal of the Sublime; on the highest Tredie, the number three. These personages are those the neophyte beheld in the Eleusinian initiation (59), the hierophant, the

daduchus or torchbearer, and the epibomite or attendant on the altar; those he sees in Freemasonry, the master, and the senior and junior wardens, symbolical personifications of the sun, moon, and Demiurgus, or grand architect of the universe. But the Scandinavian triad is usually represented by Odin, the chief deity; Thor, his first-born, the reputed mediator between god and man, possessing unlimited power over the universe, wherefore his head was surrounded by a circle of twelve stars; and Freya, a hermaphrodite, adorned with a variety of symbols significant of dominion over love and marriage. In the instructions given to the neophyte, he is told that the greatest and most ancient of gods is called Alfader (the father of all), and has twelve epithets, which recall the twelve attributes of the sun, the twelve constellations, the twelve superior gods of Egypt, Greece, and Rome. Among the gods of the Scandinavian theogony there is Balder the Good, whose story, as already hinted above, formed the object of the initiatory ceremonies. Balder is Mithras, the sun's love. He foresees the danger that threatens him; he dreams of it at night. The other gods of Valhalla, the Scandinavian Olympus, to whom he reveals his sad forebodings, reassure him, and to guard against any harm befalling him, exact an oath from every thing in nature in his behalf, except from the mistletoe, which was omitted on account of its apparently inoffensive qualities. For an experiment, and in sport, the gods cast at Balder all kinds of missiles, without wounding him. Hoder the blind (that is, Fate), takes no part in the diversion; but Loke (the principle of evil, darkness, the season of winter) places a sprig in the hands of Hoder, and persuades him to cast it at the devoted victim, who falls pierced with mortal wounds. For this reason it was that this plant was gathered at the winter solstice by the Druids of Scandinavia, Gaul, and Britain, with a curved knife, whose form symbolized the segment of the zodiacal circle during which the murder of Balder took place. In the Edda of Snorro we have another legend of Odin and Freya, the Scandinavian Isis or Venus, giving an account of the wanderings of the latter in search of the former, which, of course, have the same astronomical meaning as the search of Isis for Osiris, of Ceres for Proserpine, etc. One of the chief festivals in the year, as with the Druids, was the winter solstice; and this being the longest night in the year, the Scandinavians assigned to it the formation of the world from primeval darkness, and called it "Mother Night." This festival was denominated "Yule," and was a season of universal festivity.

BOOK II.

EMANATIONISTS.

" A shameful strife,
A glowing life,
I weave on the whirring loom of Time,
The living garment of the Deity."
                        GOETHE, *Faust.*

AUTHORITIES.

Knorr. Cabala Denudata. 1677.
Freystadt. Cabalistische Philosophie. Königsberg, 1830.
Frank. La Cabala. Paris, 1843.
Münster. Versuch über die Alterthümer der Gnostiker. Anspach, 1790.
Schmidt. Ueber die Verwandtschaft der Gnostisch-theosophischen Lehren mit den Religions-systemen des Orients. Leipsic, 1828.
Matter. Histoire critique du Gnosticisme. Paris, 1847.

I.

THE CABALA.

91.

ITS Origin.—The Cabala is the summary of the labours of the sects of Judaism, and is occupied in the mystical interpretation of the Scriptures, and in metaphysical speculations concerning the Deity and the worlds visible and invisible. The Jews say that it was communicated to Moses by God Himself. Now, although it is not at all improbable that Moses did leave to his successors some secret doctrines, yet the fantastic doctrines of the Cabala concerning angels and demons are purely Chaldean; at Babylon the Jews ingrafted on Monotheism the doctrine of the Two Principles. Daniel, the pontiff of the Magi and prophet of the Jews, may be considered as the chief founder of the Cabala, which was conceived at Babylon, and received as the forbidden fruit of the strange woman.

92. *Its Progress.*—The ancient Jews, indeed, had some idea of angels, but did not ascribe to them any particular functions, though to each patriarch they assigned a special familiar spirit. The Alexandrian School made many additions to that foreign importation; Philo supplemented Daniel. The speculative portion of the Cabala, whose foundation consists in the doctrine of Emanation, was developed in that School; the philosophical systems of Pythagoras and Plato were combined with Oriental philosophy, and from these proceeded Gnosticism and Neo-platonism.

93. *Date of Cabala.*—The first documentary promulgation of the Cabala may roughly be stated to have taken place within the century before and half a century after our era. The greater culture of the Jewish people, the supreme tyranny of the letter of the law and rabbinical minuteness, furthered the spread of occult theology, whose chief text-books are the "Sepher-yetzirah," or Book of the Creation, probably by Akiba, and the "Zehar," the Book of Light, by Simon-ben-Joachai, the St. Thomas of the Cabala, whose work contains the sum of that obscure and strange system.

94. *The Book of the Creation.*—In this work Adam considers the mystery of the universe. In his monologue he declares the forces and powers of

reason, which attempts to discover the bond which unites in a common principle all the elements of things; and in this investigation he adopts a method different from the Mosaic. He does not descend from God to the creation, but, studying the universe, seeking the unity in variety and multiplicity, the law in the phenomenon, he ascends from the creation to God—a prolific method, but which leads the Cabalists to seek fantastic analogies between superior and inferior powers, between heaven and earth, between the things and the signs of thought. Hence arose all the arts of divination and conjuration, and the most absurd superstitions. According to cabalistic conception, the universe, which to Pythagoras is a symbol of the mysterious virtues of numbers, is only a marvellous page on which all existing things were written by the supreme artificer with the first ten numbers and the twenty-two letters of the Hebrew alphabet. The ten abstract numbers are the general forms of things, the "supreme categories of ideas." Thus, number one represents the spirit of the living God, the universal generative power; number two is the breath of the animating spirit; three is the aqueous, and four the igneous principle. The imprint of the letters on the universe is indestructible, and is the only character that can enable us to discover the Supreme Cause, to recompose the name of God, the Logos, written on the face of the world. Nor are all the letters of equal virtue; three, called the *mothers* have the precedence, and refer to the triads found in various physical and mental orders; seven others are called *double*, because from them arise the things constantly opposed to one another; the remaining twelve are called simple, and refer to twelve attributes of man.

95. *Different Kinds of Cabala.*—It is of two kinds, theoretical and practical. The latter is engaged in the construction of talismans and amulets, and is therefore totally unworthy of our notice. The theoretical is divided into the literal and dogmatic. The dogmatic is the summary of the metaphysical doctrines taught by the Cabalistic doctors. The literal is a mystical mode of explaining sacred things by a peculiar use of the letters of words. This literal Cabala is again subdivided into three branches, the first considering words according to the numerical value of the letters composing them. This branch is called Gematria, and for an example of it the reader is referred to Mithras (29,) the name of the sun, whose letters make up the number 365, the number of days during which the sun performs his course. The second branch is called Notaricon, and is a mode of constructing one word out of the initials or finals of many. Thus, of the sentence in Deut. xxx. 12, "Who shall go up for us to heaven?" in Hebrew מי יעלה לם השמימה, the initial letters of each word are taken to form the

word, מילה, "circumcision." The third mode is called Temura, or permutation of letters, such as is familiarly known as an anagram.

96. *Visions of Ezekiel.* — Cabalistic terms and inventions, not destitute of poetic ideas, lent themselves to the requirements of the mystics, sectaries, and alchymists. It suffices to consider that portion of the system whose object is the study of the visions of Ezekiel, to form an idea of the fantastic and mythological wealth of the Cabala.

In the visions of Ezekiel God is seated on a throne, surrounded with strange winged figures— the man, the bull, the lion, and the eagle, four zodiacal signs, like "the glory which he saw by the river of Chebar," that is, among the Chaldeans, famous for their astronomical knowledge. The rabbis call the visions the description of the celestial car, and discover therein profound mysteries. Maimonides reduced those visions to the astronomical ideas of his time; the Cabala surrounded them with its innumerable hosts of angels. Besides the angels that preside over the stars, elements, virtues, vices, passions, the lower world is peopled by genii of both sexes, holding a position between angels and men— the elemental spirits of the Rosicrucians. The good angels are under the command of Metatron, also called Sar Happanim, the angel of the Divine countenance. The evil angels are subject to Samuel, or Satan, the angel of death. Besides the Indian metempsychosis the Cabalists admit another, which they call "impregnation," consisting in a union of several souls in one body, which takes place when any soul needs the assistance of others to attain to the beatific vision.

97. *The Creation out of Nothing.*—The primitive Being is called the Ancient of Days, the ancient Ring of Light, incomprehensible, infinite, eternal, a closed eye. Before he manifested himself all things were in him, and he was called The Nothing, the Zero-world (9). Before the creation of the world the primitive light of God, Nothing, filled all, so that there was no void; but when the Supreme Being determined to manifest His perfections, He withdrew into Himself, and let go forth the first emanation, a ray of light, which is the cause and beginning of all that exists, and combines the generative and conceptive forces. He commenced by forming an imperceptible point, the point-world ; then with that thought He constructed a holy and mysterious form, and finally covered it with a rich vestment—the universe. From the generative and conceptive forces issued forth the first-born of God, the universal form, the creator, preserver, and animating principle of the world, Adam Kadmon, called the macrocosm ; whilst man, born out of and living in it, and comprising, in fact, what the typical or celestial man comprises potentially, is called the microcosm. But before the Eusoph or Infinite revealed Himself

in that form of the primitive man, other emanations, other worlds, had succeeded each other, which were called "sparks," which grew fainter the more distant they were from the centre of emanation. Around Adam Kadmon were formed the countless circles of posterior emanations, which are not beings having a life of their own, but attributes of God, vessels of omnipotence, types of creation. The ten emanations from Adam Kadmon are called Sephiroth, the "powers" of Philo, and the "æons" of the Gnostics.

98. *Diffusion of Cabalistic Ideas.*—Cabalistic ideas spread far and wide. In the middle ages we meet with them in a great number of strange practices and ceremonies. I will here merely allude to one, because it explains a sign still in use in many parts of the Continent. The double triangle (18) was regarded by the Jews as a cabalistic figure, to which they attributed the power of averting fire. Hence the German Jews in the middle ages placed it over the entrances of all their workshops and factories. Its use was afterwards restricted to breweries. Now it is the sign of beerhouses; whilst the pine branch, which is the ancient thyrsus, announces the sale of wine.

Without specifying how much the philosophic systems of Spinoza and Schelling are indebted to them, and without speaking of the Hebrew sects still existing—which may be considered as the sequels of the Cabalistic school, and which include that of the "New Saints," founded by Israel, called the Thaumaturgist, in Podolia, in 1740, and that of the "Zohariti," the Illuminated, founded by Jacob Franck, who attempted, by a kind of philosophical syncretism, to reconcile the ancient and the modern revelation,—we meet with Cabalistic ideas in the most lasting superstitions, in the Schools, Academies, and Masonic Lodges. The rituals of the Mystics, Freemasons, Illuminati, and Carbonari, abound with them, as I shall successively point out.

II.

THE GNOSTICS.

99.

CHARACTER *of Gnosticism.*—The leading ideas of Platonism are also found in the tenets of the Gnostics, and they continued, during the second and third centuries, the schools that raised a barrier between recondite philosophy and vulgar superstition. Under this aspect Gnosticism is the most universal heresy, the mother of many posterior heresies, even of Arianism, and reappears among the alchymists, mystics, and modern transcendentalists.

100. *Doctrines.*—The Gnostics assumed an infinite, invisible Being, an abyss of darkness, who, unable to remain inactive, diffused himself in emanations, decreasing in perfection the further they were removed from the centre that produced them. They had their grand triad, whose personifications,

Matter, the Demiurgus, and the Saviour, comprised and represented the history of mankind and of the world. The superior emanations, partakers of the attributes of the Divine essence, are the "æons," distributed in classes, according to symbolical numbers. Their union forms the "pleroma," or the fulness of intelligence. The last and most imperfect emanation of the pleroma, according to one of the two grand divisions of Gnosticism, is the Demiurgus, a balance of light and darkness, of strength and weakness, who, without the concurrence of the unknown Father, produces this world, there imprisoning the souls, for he is the primary evil, opposed to the primary good. He encumbers the souls with matter, from which they are redeemed by Christ, one of the sublime powers of the pleroma, the Divine thought, intelligence, the spirit. For humanity is destined to raise itself again from the material to the spiritual life; to free itself from nature, and to govern it, and to live again in immortal beauty.

According to the other party of the Gnostics, the Demiurgus was the representative and organ of the highest God, who was placed by the Divine will especially over the Jewish people, as their Jehovah. Men are divided into three classes: the terrestrial men, of the earth earthy, tied and bound by matter; the spiritual men, the Pneumatikoi, who attain to the Divine light; the Psychikoi, who only rise up to the Demiurgus. The Jews, subject to Jehovah, were Psychikoi; the Pagans were Terrestrial men; the true Christians or Gnostics, Pneumatikoi.

101. *Development of Gnosticism.*—Simon Magus; Menander, his successor; Cerinthus, the apostle of the Millennium, and some others who lived in the first century, are looked upon as the founders of Gnosticism, which soon divided into as many sects as there arose apostles. This may be called the obscure period of Gnosticism. But at the beginning of the second century the sect of Basilides of Alexandria arose, and with it various centres of Gnosticism in Egypt, Syria, Rome, Spain, &c. Basilides assumed 365 æons or cycles of creation, which were expressed by the word *abraxas*, whose letters, according to their numerical value in Greek, produce the number 365. By "abraxas" was meant, in its deeper sense, the Supreme God; but the reader will at once detect the astronomical bearing, and remember the words Mithras and Belenus, which also severally represent that number, and the Supreme God, viz. the sun. Valentinus also is a famous Gnostic, whose fundamental doctrine is that all men shall be restored to their primeval state of perfection; that matter, the refuge of evil, shall be consumed by fire, which is also the doctrine of Zoroaster, and that the spirits in perfect maturity shall ascend into the pleroma, there to enjoy all the delights of a perfect union with their companions. From the Valentinians sprang the

Ophites, calling themselves so after the serpent that by tempting Eve brought into the world the blessings of knowledge; and the Cainites, who maintained that Cain had been the first Gnostic in opposition to the blind, unreasoning faith of Abel, and therefore persecuted by the Demiurgus, Jehovah. The Antitacts (opponents to the law), like the Ishmaelites at a later period, taught their adepts hatred against all positive religions and laws. The Adamites looked upon marriage as the fruit of sin; they called their lascivious initiation "paradise;" held all indulgence in carnal delights lawful, and advocated the abolition of dress. The Pepuzians varied their initiations with the apparition of phantasms, among whom was a woman crowned with the sun and twelve stars, and having the moon under her feet—the Isis of Egypt and the Ceres of Greece. They found in the Apocalypse all their initiatory terminology. A Gnostic stone, represented in the work of Chifflet, shows seven stars of equal size with a larger one above; these probably mean the seven planets and the sun. There are, moreover, figured on it a pair of compasses, a square, and other geometrical emblems. Thus all religious initiations are ever reducible to astronomy and natural phenomena.

102. *Spirit of Gnosticism.*—The widely opposite ideas of polytheism, pantheism, monotheism, the philosophical systems of Plato, Pythagoras, Hera-

clitus, together with the mysticism and demonology that after the Jewish captivity created the Cabala—all these went towards forming Gnosticism. And the aristocracy of mind, powerful and numerous as none had ever been before, that arose in the first centuries of our era, even when adopting the new faith, could not but loathe the thought of sharing it completely with the crowd of freed and unfreed slaves around them—with the low and poor in spirit. The exclusiveness of Gnosticism was undoubtedly, next to the attractiveness of its dogmas, one of the chief reasons of its rapid propagation and its lasting influence on modern religious systems.

BOOK III.

RELIGION OF LOVE.

Les croisés, pendant leur séjour en Orient, ont étudié toutes les variantes qui caractérisèrent les sectes chrétiennes. Ils se sont attachés aux doctrines des gnosticiens et des manichéens, qui leur paraissaient moins altérées que celle des prêtres de Rome.—RAGON.

AUTHORITIES.

Wolf. Manichæismus ante Manichæos. Hamburg, 1707.
Baur. Sur le Manichéisme des Cathares. Tübingen, 1831.
Millot. Vie des Troubadours.
Fabre d'Olivet. Poésies occitaniques du XIIIe siècle. Paris, 1803.
Diez. Die Poesie der Troubadours. Zwickau, 1826.
Dinaux. Les Trouveurs de la Flandre et du Tournaisan. Paris, 1839.
Hauriel. Histoire de la Poésie provençale.
Galvani. Osservazioni sulla Poesia de' Trovatori. Modena, 1839.
Schmidt. Geschichte der Albigenser.
Büsching. Ritterzeit und Ritterwesen. Leipsic, 1823.
Mills. History of Chivalry. London, 1825.
Aroux. Les Mystères de la Chevalerie. Paris, 1858.

I.

SONS OF THE WIDOW.

103.

*RIGIN of Religion of Love.*—A Persian slave, whose powerful imagination brought forth a desolating doctrine, but extraordinary by originality of invention and variety of episodes, three centuries after the appearance of Christ, and when Orientalism was on the point of disappearing from the West, founded a theogony and instituted a sect which revived Eastern influence in Europe, and by means of the Crusades spread schism and revolt throughout the Catholic world. The action of this rebellious disciple of Zoroaster, of this restorer of the ancient faith of the Magi, mixed with Christian forms and Gnostic symbols, had an extension and duration which, though called in doubt by the past, modern criticism discovers in the intrinsic phi-

losophy of a great part of the sects formed in the bosom of Catholicism. At the head of this gigantic movement of intelligence and conscience, which devoted itself to the most singular superstitions in order to shake off the yoke of Rome, are Gnosticism and Manichæism, Oriental sects, the last and glorious advance of a theogony, which, seeing the rule of so large a portion of the earth pass away from itself, undertook to recover it with mysteries and the evocation of poetic phantoms.

104. *Manes.*—Manes, redeemed from slavery by a rich Persian widow, whence he was called the " son of the widow," and his disciples " sons of the widow," of prepossessing aspect, learned in the Alexandrian philosophy, initiated into the Mithraic mysteries, traversed the regions of India, touched on the confines of China, studied the evangelical doctrines, and so lived in the midst of many religious systems, deriving light from all, and satisfied by none. He was born at a propitious moment, and his temperament fitted him for arduous and fantastic undertakings and schemes. Possessing great penetration and an inflexible will, he comprehended the expansive force of Christianity, and resolved to profit thereby, masking Gnostic and Cabalistic ideas under Christian names and rites. In order to establish this Christian revelation, he called himself the Paraclete announced by Christ to His disciples, attributing to

himself, in the Gnostic manner, a great superiority over the Apostles, rejecting the Old Testament, and allowing to the sages of the pagans a philosophy superior to Judaism.

105. *Manichæism.*—The dismal conceptions of a dualism, pure and simple, the eternity and absolute evil of matter, the non-resurrection of the body, the perpetuity of the principle of evil,—these preside over the compound that took its name from him, and confound Mithras with Christ, the Gospel with the Zend-Avesta, Magism with Judaism. The Unknown Father, the Infinite Being, of Zoroaster, is entirely rejected by Manes, who divides the universe into two dominions, that of light, and that of darkness, irreconcilable, whereof one is superior to the other; but, great difference, the first, instead of conquering the latter into goodness, reduces it to impotence, conquers, but does not subdue or convince it. The God of light has innumerable legions of combatants (æons), at whose head are twelve superior angels, corresponding with the twelve signs of the zodiac. Satanic matter is surrounded by a similar host, which, having been captivated by the charms of the light, endeavours to conquer it; wherefore the head of the celestial kingdom, in order to obviate this danger, infuses life into a new power, and appoints it to watch the frontiers of heaven. That power is called the "Mother of Life," and is the soul of the world,

the "Divine," the primitive thought of the Supreme Ens, the heavenly "Sophia" of the Gnostics. As a direct emanation of the Eternal it is too pure to unite with matter, but a son is born unto it, the first man, who initiates the great struggle with the demons. When the strength of the man fails him, the "Living Spirit" comes to his assistance, and, having led him back to the kingdom of light, raises above the world that part of the celestial soul not contaminated by contact with the demons—a perfectly pure soul, the Redeemer, the Christ, who attracts to Himself and frees from matter the light and soul of the first man. In these abstruse doctrines lies concealed the Mithraic worship of the sun. The followers of Manes were divided into "Elect" and "Listeners;" the former had to renounce every corporeal enjoyment, everything that can darken the celestial light in us; the second were less vigorously treated. Both might attain immortality by means of purification in an ample lake placed in the moon (the baptism of celestial water), and sanctification in the solar fire (the baptism of celestial fire), where reside the Redeemer and the blessed spirits.

106. *Life of Manes.*—The career of Manes was chequered and stormy, a foreshadowing of the tempests that were to arise against his sect. After having enjoyed the unstable favour of the Court, and acquired the fame of a great physician, he found himself unable to save the life of one of the sons of

the prince. He was consequently exiled, and roved through Turkestan, Hindostan, and the Chinese empire. He dwelt for one year in a cave, living on herbs, during which time his followers, having received no news from him, said that he had ascended to heaven, and were believed, not only by the " Listeners," but by the people. The new prince recalled him to court, showered honours on him, erected a sumptuous palace for him, and consulted him on all state affairs. But the successor of this second prince made him pay dearly for this short happiness, for he put him to a cruel death.

107. *Progress of Manichœism.*—The government of the sect already existing with degrees, initiatory rites, signs and pass-words, was continued by astute chiefs, who more and more attracted to themselves the Christians by the use of orthodox language, making them believe that their object was to recall Christianity to its first purity. But the sect was odious to the Church of Rome, because it had issued from rival Persia; and so for two hundred years it was banished from the empire, and the Theodosian Codex is full of laws against it. Towards the end of the fourth century it spread in Africa and Spain. It had peace and flourished under the mother of the Emperor Anastasius (491-518); but Justin renewed the persecution. Changing its name, seat, and figurative language, it spread in Bulgaria, Lombardy (Patarini), France (Cathari, Albigenses, &c.),

united with the Saracens and openly made war upon the Emperor, and its followers perished by thousands in battle and at the stake; and from its secular trunk sprang the so-called heresies of the Hussites and Wyckliffites, which opened the way for Protestantism. In those gloomy middle ages, in fact, arose those countless legions of sectaries, bound by a common pact, whose existence only then becomes manifest when the sinister light of the burning pile flashes through the darkness in which they conceal themselves. The Freemasons undoubtedly, through the Templars, inherited no small portion of their ritual from them; they were very numerous in all the courts, and even in the dome of St. Peter, and baptized in blood with new denominations and ordinances.

108. *Doctrines.*—The sacred language of Manichæism was most glowing, and founded on that concert of voices and ideas, called in Pythagorean phraseology the "harmony of the spheres," which established a connection between the mystic degrees and the figured spheres by means of conventional terms and images; and it is known that the Albigenses and Patarini recognized each other by signs. A Provençal Patarino, who had fled to Italy in 1240, everywhere met with a friendly reception, revealing himself to the brethren by means of conventional phrases. He everywhere found the sect admirably organized, with churches, bishops, and

apostles of the most active propaganda, who overran France, Germany, and England. The Manichæan language, moreover, was ascetic, and loving, and Christian; but the neophyte, after having once entered the sect, was carried beyond, and gradually alienated from the Papal Church. The mysteries had two chief objects in view—that of leading the neophyte, by first insensibly changing his former opinions and dispositions, and then of gradually instructing him in the conventional language, which, being complicated and varied, required much study and much time. But not all were admitted to the highest degrees. Those that *turned back*, or could not renounce former ideas, remained always in the Church, and were not introduced into the sanctuary. These were simple Christians and sincere listeners, who, out of zeal for reform, often encountered death, as, for instance, the canons of Orleans, who were condemned to the stake by King Robert in 1022. But those who did not turn back were initiated into all those things which it was important should be known to the most faithful members of the sect. The destruction of Rome, and the establishment of the heavenly Jerusalem spoken of in the Apocalypse, were the chief objects aimed at.

109. *Spread of Religion of Love.*—The religion of love did not end with the massacre of the Albigenses, nor were its last echoes the songs of the troubadours; for we meet with it in a German sect

which in 1550 pretended to receive a supernatural light from the Holy Spirit. In Holland, also, a sect of Christians arose in 1580, called the "Family of Love," which spread to England, where it published many books, and flourished about the time of Cromwell, and seems to have had some connection with the Puritans.

II.

THE GAY SCIENCE.

110.

TRANSITION *from Ancient to Modern Initiations.* — An order of facts now claims our attention which in a certain manner signalizes the transition from ancient to modern initiations. An extraordinary phenomenon in social conditions becomes apparent, so strikingly different from what we meet with in antiquity as to present itself as a new starting point. Hitherto we have seen the secret organizing itself in the higher social classes, so as to deprive the multitude of truths whose revelation could not have taken place without injury and danger to the hierarchy. At the base we find polytheism, superstition; at the summit deism, rationalism, the most abstract philosophy. Truly those peoples were to be pitied, who, slaves of ignorance and corruption, erected with their own hands the prisons of truth and the temples of imposture, who adored idols and idolized form, superficiality, and appearance.

111. *Spirit of Ancient Secret Societies.*—The secret societies of antiquity were theological, and theology frequently inculcated superstition; but in the deepest recesses of the sanctuary there was a place where it would laugh at itself and the deluded people, and draw to itself the intelligences that rebelled against the servitude of fear, by initiating them into the only creed worthy of a free man. To that theology, therefore, otherwise very learned and not cruel, and that promoted art and science, much may be forgiven, attributing perhaps not to base calculation, but to sincere conviction and thoughtful prudence, the dissimulation with which it concealed the treasures of truth and knowledge, that formed its power, glory, and, in a certain manner, its privilege.

112. *Spirit of Modern Societies.*— In modern times the high religious and political spheres have no secrets, for they have no privilege of knowledge, nor initiations which confer on those higher in knowledge the right to sit on the seat of the mighty.

113. *Cause and Progress of Heresy.*—But the pyramid was overthrown; the lofty summit fell, and the ample massive base became visible, and no one, without being guilty of an anachronism and preparing for himself bitter disappointments, can seek

the truth where there is but a delusive show of truth. Whoever persists in making any mendacious height the object of his ambition, removes his eyes from the horizon which, lit up by the dawn, casts light around his feet, while his head is yet in darkness. Henceforth secret societies are popular and religious, not in the sense of the constituted and official church, but of a rebellious and sectarian church; and since at a period when the authority of the church is paramount, and religion circulates through all the veins of the state, no change can be effected without heresy, so this must necessarily be the first aspect of political and intellectual revolt. This heresy makes use of the denial and rejection of official dogmas in order to overthrow the hated clerocracy, and to open for itself a road to civil freedom.

114. *Efforts and Influence of Heretics.*— The Papacy was necessarily the first cradle of the new conspirators, and from the heresies arose the sects, of which none was more extensive and active than the Albigenses. This great fact of opposition and reaction has no parallel in antiquity, where the very schools of philosophy adopted the forms of the mysteries; and it is a fact which imparts an immense momentum to modern history, and surrounds with lustre popular movements and personalities. This great energy proceeded from heretical and sectarian schools, and struggled in the dark to

conquer in the light. The sect of the Albigenses, the offspring of Manichæism, fructified in its turn the germs of the Templars and Rosicrucians, and of all those associations that continued the struggle and fought against ecclesiastical and civil oppression.

115. *The Albigenses.*—It is to be noticed that the object of the Albigenses in so far differed from that of all posterior sects, that its blows were intended for Papal Rome alone; and wholly Papal was the revenge taken through the civil arm, and with priestly rage. The Albigenses were the Ghibellines of France, and combined with all who were opposed to Rome, especially with Frederick II. and the Arragonese, in maintaining the rights of kings against the pretensions of the Papal See. Their doctrines had a special influence on the University of Bologna, wholly imperial; Dante was imperialistic, tainted with that doctrine, and therefore hated by the Guelphs.

116. *Tenets of Albigenses.*—Toulouse was the Rome of that church which had its pastors, bishops, provincial and general councils, like the official church, and assembled under its banners the dissenters of a great portion of Europe, all meditating the ruin of Rome and the restoration of the kingdom of Jerusalem. The rising in Provence gathered strength from the circumstances in which it took place. The Crusaders had revived eastern Manichæism, placing Europe in immediate contact with sophisticated

Greece, and Mahomedan and Pantheistic Asia. The East, moreover, contributed Aristotle and his Arab commentators, to which must be added the subtleties of the cabala and the materialism of ideas. Philosophy, republicanism, and industry assailed the Holy See. Various isolated rebellions had revealed the general spirit, and wholesale slaughter had not repressed it; the rationalism of the Waldenses connected itself with the German mysticism of the Rhine and the Netherlands, where the operatives rose against the counts and the bishops. Every apostle that preached pure morality, the religion of the spirit, the restoration of the primitive church, found followers; the century of Saint Louis is the century of unbelief in the Church of Rome, and the *Impossibilia* of Sigero foreshadowed those of Strauss.

117. *Aims of Albigenses.*—The heresy of the Albigenses made such progress along the shores of the Mediterranean that several countries seemed to separate from Rome, whilst princes and emperors openly favoured it. Not satisfied with already considering impious Rome overthrown, the Albigenses suddenly turned towards the Crusaders, at first looked at with indifference, hoping to make Jerusalem the glorious and powerful rival of Rome, there to establish the seat of the Albigenses, to restore the religion of love in its first home, to found on earth the heavenly Jerusalem, of which

Godfrey of Bouillon was proclaimed king. This was the man who had carried fire and sword into Rome, slain the anti-Cæsar Rodolphe, "the king of the priests," and thrust the Pope out of the holy city, deserving thereby, and by the hopes entertained of him, the infinite praises for his piety, purity, and chastity, bestowed on him by the troubadours, who originally appeared in the first quarter of the twelfth century, in the allegorical compositions known by the name of the "Knight of the Swan." It was a project which assigned an important part to the Templars, who perhaps were aware of and sharers in it.

118. *Religion of the Troubadours.*—Troubadours and Albigenses drew closer together in persecution; their friendship increased in the school of sorrow. They sang and fought for one another, and their songs expired on the blazing piles; wherefore it appears reasonable to consider the troubadours as the organizers of that vast conspiracy directed against the Church of Rome, the champions of a revolt which had not for its guide and object material interests and vulgar ambition, but a religion and a polity of love. Here love is considered, not as an affection which all more or less experience and understand, but as an art, a science, acquired by means of the study and practice of sectarian rites and laws; and the artists under various names appear scattered throughout many parts of Europe. It is difficult, indeed, to determine the boundaries

within which the Gay Science was diffused. The singers of love are met with as the troubadours of the Langue d'Oc and the Langue d'Oïl, the minnesängers and minstrels.

119. *Difficulty to understand the Troubadours.*—The singers of Provence—whose language was by the Popes called the language of heresy—are nearly unintelligible to us, and we know not how to justify the praises bestowed upon their poetry by such men as Dante, Petrarch, Chaucer; nor dare we, since we do not understand their verses, call their inspiration madness, nor deny them the success they undoubtedly achieved. It appears more easy and natural to think that those free champions of a heresy who were not permitted clearly to express their ideas, preferred the obscure turns of poetry and light forms that concealed their thoughts, as the sumptuous and festive courts of love perhaps concealed the " Lodges " of the Albigenses from the eyes of the Papal Inquisition. The same was done for political purposes at various periods. Thus we have Gringore's *La Chasse du Cerf des Cerfs* (a pun designating Pope Julius II., by allusion to the *servus servorum*), in which that Pope is held up to ridicule.

120. *Poetry of Troubadours.*—Arnaldo Daniello was obscure even for his contemporaries; according to the Monk of Montaudon, " no one understands his songs," and yet Dante and Petrarch praise him above every other Provencal poet, calling him the

"great Master of Love," perhaps a title of sectarian dignity, and extolling his style, which they would not have done had they not been able to decipher his meaning. The effusions of the Troubadours were always addressed to some lady, though they dared not reveal her name; what Hugo de Brunet says applies to all: "If I be asked to whom my songs are addressed, I keep it a secret. I pretend to such a one, but it is nothing of the kind." The mistress invoked, there can be no doubt, like Dante's Beatrice, was the purified religion of love, personified as the Virgin Sophia.

121. *Degrees among Troubadours.*—There were four degrees, but the "Romance of the Rose" divides them into four and three, producing again the mystic number seven. This poem describes a castle, surrounded with a sevenfold wall, which is covered with emblematical figures, and no one was admitted into the castle that could not explain their mysterious meaning. The troubadours also had their secret signs of recognition, and the "minstrels" are supposed to have been so called because they were the "ministers" of a secret worship.

122. *Courts of Love.*—I have already alluded to these; they probably gave rise to the Lodges of Adoption, the Knights and Nymphs of the Rose &c. (*which see*). The decrees pronounced therein with pedantic proceedings, literally interpreted, are frivolous or immoral; and therefore incompatible

with the morals and manners of the Albigenses, which were on the whole pure and austere. The Courts of Love may therefore have concealed far sterner objects than the decision of questions of mere gallantry; and it is noticeable that these courts, as well as the race of troubadours, become extinct with the extinction of the Albigenses by the sword of De Montfort and the fagots of the Inquisition.

III.

THE CONSOLATION.

123.

ISTORICAL *Notices.*—Italy, though watched by Rome, nay, because watched, supported the new doctrines. Milan was one of the most active *foci* of the Cathari; in 1166 that city was more heretical than catholic. In 1150 there were Cathari at Florence, and the women especially were most energetic in the dissemination of the dogmas of the sect which became so powerful as to effect in the city a revolution in favour of the Ghibellines. At Orvieto Catharism prevailed in 1125, and was persecuted in 1163; the persecution was most fierce at Verona, Ferrara, Modena, &c. In 1224 a great number of these sectaries met in Calabria and Naples, and even Rome was full of them. But Lombardy and Tuscany were always the chief seats of this revolt.

124. *Doctrines and Tenets.*—But we have only

scanty notices of this sect, because, unlike other heretical associations, it sought to conceal its operations. It bore great resemblance to Manichæism and the dogmas of the Albigenses, like which latter, it concealed its doctrines not only from the world at large, but even from its proselytes of inferior degrees. They believed in the metempsychosis, assuming that to attain to the light, seven such transmigrations were required; but, as in other cases, this was probably an emblematic manner of speaking of the degrees of initiation. They had communistic tendencies, and were averse to marriage; philanthropists, above all they led industrious lives, combined saving habits with charity, founded schools and hospitals, crossed lands and seas to make proselytes, denied to magistrates the right of taking away life, did not disapprove of suicide, and preceded the Templars in their contempt of the cross. They could not understand how Christians could adore the instrument of the death of the Saviour, and said that the cross was the figure of the beast mentioned in the Apocalypse and an abomination in a holy place. They performed their ceremonies in woods, caverns, remote valleys; wherefore those belonging to this heresy and others deriving from it could well answer the question: Where did our ancient brethren meet before there were any lodges? In every place. They were accused of strangling or starving the dying, and of burning children;

charges also brought against the Mithraics, Christians, Gnostics, Jews, and quite recently against the Irish Roman Catholics. The accusation, as in the other cases, probably arose from some symbolical sacrifice, literally interpreted by their opponents. They had four sacraments, and the *consolation* consisted in the imposition of hands, or baptism of the Holy Spirit; which, bestowed only on adults, remitted sins, imparted the consoling spirit, and secured eternal salvation. During persecutions the ceremonies were shortened and were held at night and secretly; the lighted tapers symbolized the baptism of fire. At the ceremony of initiation the priest read the first eighteen verses of the gospel of St. John, a custom still practised in some masonic degrees. In remembrance of his initiation the novice received a garment made of fine linen and wool, which he wore under his shirt; the women a girdle, which they also wore next to the skin just under the bosom.

IV.

CHIVALRY.

125.

ORIGINAL *Aim.*—An idea of conservation and propagandism produced the association of the San Greäl, whose members professed to be in search of the vase of truth, which once contained the blood of the Redeemer; or, to leave metaphorical language, to bring back the Christian Church to apostolic times, to the true observance of the precepts of the gospel. At the Round Table, a perfect figure, which admitted neither of first nor of last, sat the Knights, who did not attain to that rank and distinction but after many severe trials. Their degrees at first were three, which were afterwards raised to seven, and finally, at the epoch of their presumed fusion with the Albigenses, Templars and Ghibellines, to thirty-three. The chief grades, however, may be said to have been—1, Page; 2, Squire; 3, Knight.

126. *Knights the Military Apostles of the Religion of Love.*—This association was above all a proud family of apostles and missionaries of the Religion of Love, military troubadours, who, under the standards of justice and right, fought against the monstrous abuses of the Theocratic *régime*, consoled the "widow"—perhaps the Gnostic Church—protected the "sons of the widow"—the followers of Manes —and overthrew giants and dragons, inquisitors and churchmen. The powerful voice of the furious Roland, which made breaches in the granite rocks of the mountains, is the voice of that so-called heresy which found its way into Spain, thus anticipating the saying of Louis XIV., "There are no longer any Pyrenees." This may seem a startling assertion, but it is nevertheless true. Of course I do not now speak of the chivalry of feudal times, but of that which existed even before the eleventh century, that issued from the womb of Manichæism and Catharism, and was altogether hostile to Rome. But even at that period the Papal church acted on the principle afterwards so fully carried out by the Jesuits, of directing what they could not suppress; and having nothing more to fear than spiritualism, whether mystical, Platonic, or chivalric, Rome, instead of opposing its current, cunningly turned it into channels where, instead of being destructive to the Papacy, it became of infinite advantage to it.

127. *Tenets and Doctrines.*—Those who com-

posed the romances of the Round Table and the San Greäl were well acquainted with the Gallic triads, the mysteries of the theological doctrines of the Bards and Celtic myths. These romances have their origin in the phenomena of the natural world, and the San Greäl is only a diminutive Noah's Ark. From Chaucer's "Testament of Love," which seems founded on the "Consolation of Philosophy," by Boëthius, it has been supposed that the love of chivalry was the love of woman, in its highest, noblest, and most spiritualized aspect. But the lady-love of the knight in the early period of chivalry was the Virgin Sophia, or philosophy personified. The phraseology employed in the rites of initiation, the religious vows taken on that occasion, the tonsure to which the knights submitted, with many other circumstances, sufficiently indicate that the love so constantly spoken of has no reference to earthly love. This applies especially to the knights who may be called Voluntary Knights, and whose charter is the curious book called "Las Siete Partidas," by Alfonso, King of Castile and Leon. Their statutes greatly resembled those of the Templars and Hospitallers; they were more than any other a religious order, bound to very strict lives; their clothes were of three colours, and—strange coincidence—analogous with those with which Dante beheld Beatrice clothed, and the three circles he describes towards the end of "Paradise." They had two meals a day, and drank only water, a regimen scarcely fit for a militia whose duties were not always spiritual; for, besides their special duties, they were also subject to all the rules of chivalry, and bound to protect the weak against the strong, to restore peace where it had been disturbed, to serve their body (the Lodge), and protect the (evangelical) religion. They are said to have branded their right arms in sign of their fraternity; but this is perhaps only a figure of the baptism of fire and the Spirit, one of the most essential rites of the Religion of Love.

BOOK IV.

ISHMAELITES.

And he will be a wild man; his hand will be against every man, and every man's hand against him.
Gen. xvi. 12.

AUTHORITIES.

Makrizi. Description of Egypt and Cairo.
Sacy. Chrestomathie Arabe.
Pococke. Spec. Hist. Arab. Edit. Whitc.
Hammer. Origin, Power, and Fall of the Assassins.
Malcolm. History of Persia.
Rousseau. Mémoires sur les Ismaélites.
Silv. de Sacy. Exposé de la Religion des Druses. Paris 1838.
Wolff. Drusen und ihre Vorläufer. London, 1856.

I.

THE LODGE OF WISDOM.

128.

ARIOUS Sects sprung from Manichœism.—Manichæism was not the only secret association that sprang from the initiations of the Magi. In the seventh century of our era we meet with similar societies, possessing an influence not limited to the regions in which they arose, variations of one single thought, which aimed at combining the venerable doctrines of Zoroaster with Christian belief. Of these societies or sects the following may be mentioned: the followers of Keyoumerz; the worshippers of Servan, infinite time, the creator and mover of all things; disciples of Zoroaster properly so called; Dualists; Gnostics, admitting two principles, the Father and the Son, at war and reconciled by a third celestial power; and lastly the followers of Mastek, the most formidable and disastrous of all, preaching universal equality and liberty, the irresponsibility of man, and the community of property and women.

129. *Secret Doctrines of Islamism.*—The Arabs having rendered themselves masters of Persia, the sects of that country set to work to spread themselves among Islamism, in order to undermine its base. In Islamism even we find indications of an exoteric and an esoteric doctrine. The punctuated initials which Mahomet put at the head of each chapter, according to Mahomedan teachers, contain a profound secret, which it is a great crime to reveal. The name mufti, which is equivalent to *key,* intimates that the priests of Islamism are the living keys of a secret doctrine. But the conquered revenged themselves on the conquerors. The Persian sects examined the Koran, pointed out its contradictions, and denied its divine origin. And so there arose in Islamism that movement, which attacks dogmas, destroys faith, and substitutes for blind belief free inquiry. False systems are fruitful in schisms. A great and enduring harmony is impossible in error; truth alone is one, but error has many forms.

130. *The Candidati.*—From among the many sects which arose I will mention only one, that of the *Sefidd-Schamegan,* the *Candidati,* or those *clothed in white,* whose habitat was the Caucasus, and at whose head was the Veiled Prophet. Hakem-ben-Haschem wore a golden mask, and taught that God put on a human form from the day He commanded

the angels to adore the first man, and that from the same day the divine nature was transmitted from prophet to prophet down to him; that after death evil men would pass into beasts, whilst the good should be received into God; and he, who considered himself very good, in order that no trace should be found of his body, and the people should think that, like Romulus, he had ascended to heaven—threw himself into a pit filled with corrosive matter, which consumed him.

131. *Cruelty of Babeck the Gay.*—The fury with which the sects of Islam contested the government of conscience and political power has scarcely a parallel in the history of religion. Extermination had no bounds. A revolutionary heresiarch, who preached communism, Babeck *the Gay,* for twenty years filled the caliphate of Bagdad with death and ruin—a dismal gaiety! A million of men are said to have perished through him, and one of the ten executioners he had in his pay boasted of having slaughtered twenty thousand; and he himself died laughing by the hand of one of his colleagues. But these murders were not all due to hostile religious views; political ambition had as great a share in them. The caliphate, whose power was growing from day to day, raised open and secret opponents, and a violent reaction set in.

132. *The Ishmaelites.*—Egypt especially seems as if predestined to be the birthplace of secret societies,

of priests, warriors, and fanatics. It is the region of mysteries. The spreading light seems not to affect it. Cairo has succeeded the ancient Memphis, the doctrine of the Lodge of Wisdom that of the Academy of Heliopolis. Abdallah determined secretly to overthrow the caliphate and to uphold the rights of Mahomet the son of Ishmael, the descendant of the prophet by Fatima. The new sect succeeded in delivering from prison Obeidallah, the pretended descendant of Ishmael, and in placing him on the throne of Mahdia, and subsequently one of his successors on that of Cairo, thus subjecting Egypt to the sway of the descendants of Fatima. The caliphs of Egypt, more grateful than princes usually are, favoured the doctrine that had gained them the throne.

133. *Teaching of the Lodge of Cairo.*—The *Doial-Doat*, or supreme missionary or judge, shared the power with the prince. Meetings were held in the Lodge of Cairo, which contained many books and scientific instruments; science was the professed object, but the real aim was very different. The course of instruction was divided into nine degrees. The first sought to inspire the pupil with doubts, and with confidence in his teacher who was to solve them. For this purpose captious questions were to show him the absurdity of the literal sense of the Koran, and obscure hints gave him to understand that under that shell was hidden a sweet and nutritious kernel;

but the instruction went no further unless the pupil bound himself by dreadful oaths to blind faith in, and absolute obedience to, his instructor. The second inculcated the recognition of the imaums, or directors, appointed by God as the fountains of every kind of knowledge. The third informed him of the number of those blessed or holy imaums, and that number was the mystical seven. The fourth informed him that God had sent into the world seven legislators, each of whom had seven coadjutors, and who were called *mutes*, whilst the legislators were called *speakers*. The fifth informed him that each of these coadjutors had twelve apostles. The sixth placed before the eyes of the adept, advanced so far, the precepts of the Koran, and he was taught that all the dogmas of religion ought to be subordinate to the rule of philosophy; he was also instructed in the systems of Plato and Aristotle. The seventh degree embraced mystical pantheism. The eighth again brought before him the dogmatic precepts of the Mahomedan law, estimating it at its just value. The ninth degree, finally, as the necessary result of all the former, taught that nothing was to be believed, and that everything was lawful.

134. *Progress of Doctrines.*—These were the ends aimed at—human responsibility and dignity were to be annihilated; the throne of the descendants of Fatima was to be surrounded with an army of assassins, a formidable body-guard; a mysterious

militia was to be raised, that should spread far and wide the fame and terror of the caliphate of Cairo, and inflict fatal blows on the abhorred rule of Bagdad. The missionaries spread widely, and in Arabia and Syria partisans were won, to whom the designs of the order were unknown, but who had with fearful solemnity sworn blind obedience. The nocturnal labours of the Lodge of Cairo lasted a century; and its doctrines, which ended with denying all truth, morality, and justice, necessarily produced something very extraordinary. So terrible a shock to the human conscience led to one of those phenomena that leave a sanguinary and indelible trace on the page of history.

II.

THE ASSASSINS.

135.

FOUNDATION *of Order.*—Only Arabia and Syria could have been the theatre of the dismal deeds of the "Old Man," or rather "Lord of the Mountain." Hassan Sabbah was one of the *days* or missionaries of the School of Cairo, a man of adventurous spirit, who, having greatly distinguished himself, acquired much influence at Cairo. This influence, however, excited the envy of others, who succeeded in having him exiled. He had been put on board a ship to take him out of the country, but a storm arising, all considered themselves lost. But Hassan, assuming an authoritative air, exclaimed, "The Lord has promised me that no evil shall befal me." Suddenly the storm abated, and the sailors cried, "A miracle!" and became his followers. Hassan traversed Persia, preaching and making proselytes, and having seized the fortress of Alamut, on the borders of Irak and Dilem, which he called the " House of Fortune," he there established his rule.

136. *Influence of Hassan.*—What kind of rule? The history of his time is full of his name. Kings in the very centre of Europe trembled at it; his powerful arm reached everywhere. Philip Augustus of France was so afraid of him that he dared not stir without his guard around him; and perhaps the otherwise implacable Lord of the Mountain forgave him because of his fear. At first he showed no other intention but to increase the sway of the caliphate of Cairo, but was not long before throwing off the mask, because his fierce character submitted with difficulty to cunning and hypocrisy. He reduced the nine degrees into which the adherents of the Lodge of Cairo were divided to seven, placing himself at the head, with the title of *Seydna* or *Sidna*, whence the Spanish *Cid*, and the Italian *Signore*. The term Assassins is a corruption of *Hashishim*, derived from *hashish* (the hemp plant), with which the chief intoxicated his followers when they entered on some desperate enterprise.

137. *Catechism of the Order.*—To regulate the seven degrees he composed the Catechism of the Order. The first degree recommended to the missionary attentively to watch the disposition of the candidate, before admitting him to the order. The

second impressed it upon him to gain the confidence of the candidate, by flattering his inclinations and passions; the third, to involve him in doubts and difficulties by showing him the absurdity of the Koran; the fourth, to exact from him a solemn oath of fidelity and obedience, with a promise to lay his doubts before his instructor; and the fifth, to show him that the most famous men of Church and State belonged to the secret order. The sixth, called " Confirmation," enjoined on the instructor to examine the proselyte concerning the whole preceding course, and firmly to establish him in it. The seventh finally, called the " Exposition of the Allegory," gave the keys of the sect.

138. *Devotion of Followers.*—The followers were divided into two great hosts, " self-sacrificers " and " aspirants." The first, despising fatigues, dangers, and tortures, joyfully gave their lives whenever it pleased the great master, who required them either to protect himself or to carry out his mandates of death. The victim having been pointed out, the faithful, clothed in a white tunic with a red sash, the colours of innocence and blood, went on their mission, without being deterred by distance or danger. Having found the person they sought, they awaited the favourable moment for slaying him; and their daggers seldom missed their aim. Conrad of Montferrat, having either quarrelled with the Lord of the Mountain, or excited the

jealousy of some Christian princes who wished for his removal, was one of the first victims of the sect. Two Assassins allowed themselves to be baptized, and placing themselves beside him, seemed only intent on praying; but the favourable opportunity presenting itself, they slew him, and one of them took refuge in a church. But hearing that the prince had been carried off still alive, he again forced his way into Montferrat's presence, and stabbed him a second time; and then expired, without a complaint, amidst refined tortures.

139. *The Imaginary Paradise.*—How was such devotion secured? The story goes that whenever the chief had need of a man to carry out any particularly dangerous enterprise, he had recourse to the following stratagem:—In a province of Persia, now named Sigistan, was the famous valley Mulebat, containing the palace of Alladin, another name of the Lord of the Mountain. This valley was a most delightful spot, and so protected by high mountains terminating in perpendicular cliffs, that from them no one could enter the valley, and all the ordinary approaches were guarded by strong fortresses. The valley was cultivated as the most luxurious gardens, with pavilions splendidly furnished, their sole occupants being the most lovely and charming women. The man selected by the lord to perform the dangerous exploit was first made drunk, and in this state carried into the valley,

where he was left to roam whithersoever he pleased. On coming to his senses sufficiently to appreciate the beautiful scenery, and to enjoy the charms of the sylph-like creatures, that kept him engaged all the time in amorous dalliance, he was made to believe that this was Elysium ; but ere he wearied or became satiated with love and wine, he was once more made drunk, and in this state carried back to his own home. When his services were required, he was again sent for by the lord, who told him that he had once permitted him to enjoy paradise, and if he would do his bidding he could luxuriate in the same delights for the rest of his life. The dupe, believing that his master had the power to do all this, was ready to commit whatever crime was required of him.

140. *Sanguinary Character of Hassan.*—In that inaccessible nest the vulture-soul of its master was alone with his own ambition; and the very solitude, which constituted his power, must at times have weighed heavy upon him. And so it is said that he composed theological works, and gave himself up to frequent religious exercises. And this need not surprise us; theological studies are no bar to ferocity, and mystical gentleness is often found united with sanguinary fury. But he killed with calculation, to gain fame and power, to inspire fear and secure success. A Persian caliph thought of attacking and dispersing the sect, and found on his pillow a dagger and a

letter from Hassan, saying, "What has been placed beside thy head may be planted in thy heart." In spite of years he remained sanguinary to the last. With his own hand he killed his two sons: the one for having slain a *day*, and the other for having tasted wine. He did not design to found a dynasty, or regular government, but an order, sect, or secret society; and perhaps his sons perished in consequence of badly disguising their desire to succeed him.

141. *Further Instances of Devotion in Followers.*—The obedience of the faithful did not cease with Hassan's death, as the following will show. Henry, Count of Champagne, had to pass close by the territory of the Assassins; one of the successors of Hassan invited him to visit the fortress, which invitation the count accepted. On making the round of the towers, two of the "faithful," at a sign from the "Lord," stabbed themselves to the heart, and fell at the feet of the terrified count; whilst the master coolly said, "Say but the word, and at a sign from me you shall see them all thus on the ground." The Sultan having sent an ambassador to summon the rebellious Assassins to submission, the lord, in the presence of the ambassador, said to one of the faithful, "Kill thyself!" and he did it; and to another, "Throw thyself from this tower!" and he hurled himself down. Then turning to the ambassador, he said, "Seventy thousand followers obey

me in the same manner. This is my reply to your master." The only exaggeration in this is probably in the number, which by some writers is never estimated above forty thousand, many of whom moreover were not "faithful ones," but only aspirants.

142. *Christian Princes in league with Assassins.*—Several Christian princes were suspected of conniving at the deeds of the Assassins. Richard of England is one of them; and it has been the loyal task of English writers to free him from the charge of having instigated the murder of that Conrad of Montferrat spoken of above. There also existed for a long time a rumour that Richard had attempted the life of the King of France through Hassan and his Assassins. The nephew of Barbarossa, Frederick II., was excommunicated by Innocent II. for having caused the Duke of Bavaria to be slain by the Assassins; and Frederick II., in a letter to the King of Bohemia, accuses the Duke of Austria of having by similar agents attempted his life. Historians also mention an Arab who, in 1158, was discovered in the imperial camp at the siege of Milan, and on the point of stabbing the emperor. Who had armed that Assassin? It is not known. Mutual distrust existed amongst the rulers of Europe, and the power of Hassan and his successors increased in accordance with it.

143. *Extinction of Sect.*—There was a period when

a prior or lord, less corrupt or cruel than his predecessors, attempted to restore the Ishmaelite faith and to purge Alamat from the abominations that polluted it; but it was either mere pretence, or he was unsuccessful. His successors became only more ferocious. And it was only just that death should visit those that sent forth decrees of death; that suspicion and treachery should pursue those who spread them among men; that crime should destroy what crime had built up. The rock which was the chief residence of the Lords of the Mountain became the seat of hatred and plotting. The fathers looked upon their sons with jealous fear, and these impatiently awaited the death of their parents. They avoided one another, and, when obliged to meet, one would wear under his clothes a coat of mail, and the other redouble his guards. Parricide was punished with parricide; and this implacable Nemesis filled with horror and remorse the descendants of Hassan. The cup of poison avenged the dagger. But the measure was full; the Mongolians, led by Prince Hulagu in 1256, attacked and overthrew the Assassins, and the world was delivered from the reproach which the existence of such a sect had brought upon it.

III.

THE DRUSES.

144.

ORIGIN *of Sect of Druses.*—The Ishmaelites of Egypt and Syria may be found even to this day in some of the sects of Islam. Their primitive physiognomy reveals itself but faintly; but their profile is seen in the lineaments of some of the heretical families wandering in the wilderness or on Mount Lebanon; objects of inquietude to the Turkish government, of wonder to travellers, and of study to science. Of these the Druses, living in northern Syria, and possessing about forty towns and villages, are perhaps the most remarkable. Their sect may be said to date its rise from the supposed incarnation of God in Hakem Biamr Allah, publicly announced at Cairo in 1029. This Hakem was the sixth caliph of Egypt; and Darazi, his confessor, took an active part in promoting the imposture, which, however, was at first so badly received that he was compelled to take refuge in the deserts of Lebanon. Hamze, a Persian mystic and vizier of Hakem, was more successful, and is considered the real founder of the sect.

145. *Doctrines.*—The Druses believe in the transmigration of souls; but probably it is merely a figure, as it was to the Pythagoreans. Hakem is their prophet; and they have seven commandments, religious and moral. The first of these is veracity, by which is understood faith in the unitarian religion they profess, and the abhorrence of that lie which is called polytheism, incredulity, error. To a brother perfect truth and confidence are due; but it is allowable, nay, a duty, to be false towards men of another creed. The sect is divided into three degrees, Profanes, Aspirants, and Wise. A Druse who has entered the second, may return to the first degree, but incurs death if he reveals what he has learned. In their secret meetings they are supposed to worship a calf's head; but as their religious books are full of denunciations against idolatry, and as they also compare Judaism, Christianity, and Mahomedanism to a calf, it is more probable that this effigy represents the principle of falsehood and evil, Iblis, the rival and enemy of Hakem. The Druses have also been accused of licentious orgies; but, according to the evidence of resident Christians, a young Druse, as soon as he is initiated, gives up all dissolute habits, and becomes, at least in appearance, quite another man, meriting, as in other initiations, the title of

" new born." They have a peculiar phraseology, and recognize each other by enigmatic sentences. They claim, in fact, some connection with the Freemasons, who have degrees called the " United Druses," and " Commanders of Lebanon."

146. *Recent Events.*—Besides the forty towns and villages occupied by the Druses exclusively, they also divide possession of about four hundred towns and villages more with the Maronites, who in 1860 provoked hostilities with the Druses, which ended in much bloodshed. Since then the latter have been placed under the protection of a governor appointed by the Porte.

BOOK V.

KNIGHTS TEMPLARS.

The Templars were one of the most celebrated knightly orders during the Crusades; their whole institution, acts, and tragical fate, are attractive to the feelings and the fancy.—DE QUINCEY.

AUTHORITIES.

Du Puy.   Documents relating to the Trial of the Templars. 1650.
Nicolai.   The Templars.   1780.
Moldenhauer.   Procès-Verbal.   1791.
Du Puy.   Condemnation of Templars.   Brussels, 1713.
Recherches Historiques sur les Templiers.   Paris, 1835.
Michelet.   History of France.   Vol. IV.
James.   Dark Scenes of History.   London, 1850.

THE TEMPLARS.

147.

OUNDATION of Order.—The Order of the Knights of the Temple arose out of the Crusades. In 1118 nine valiant and pious knights formed themselves into an association which united the characters of the monk and the knight. They selected for their patroness "*La douce mère de Dieu,*" and bound themselves to live according to the rules of St. Augustine, swearing to consecrate their swords, arms, strength, and lives, to the defence of the mysteries of the Christian faith; to pay absolute obedience to the Grand Master; to encounter the dangers of the seas and of war, whenever commanded, and for the love of Christ; and even when opposed singly to three infidel foes not to retreat. They also took upon themselves the vows of chastity and poverty, promised not to go over to any other Order, nor to surrender any wall or foot of land. King Baldwin II. assigned them a portion of his palace, and, as it stood near the Church of the Temple, the abbot gave them a street leading from it to the palace, and hence they styled themselves " Soldiery of the Temple" (*militia templi*).

148. *Progress of the Order.*—The first nine years which elapsed after the institution of the Order, the Templars lived in great poverty; Hugh des Payens and Godfrey of St. Omer, the founders, had but one war-horse between them, a fact commemorated on the seal of the Order, which represents two knights seated on one charger. Soon after, Pope Honorius confirmed the Order, and appointed a white mantle —to which Eugenius III. affixed a red cross on the breast—to be the distinguishing dress of the Templars. The Order also assumed a banner formed of cloth, striped white and black, called *Beauséant* (in old French a piebald horse), which word became the battle-cry of the knights. The banner bore a cross and the inscription, " *Non nobis, Domine, sed nomini tuo da gloriam.*" Thenceforth many knights joined the Order, and numerous powerful princes bestowed considerable possessions upon it. Alfonso, king of Arragon and Navarre, even appointed the Templars his heirs, though the country refused to ratify the bequest. Thus they became the richest proprietors in Europe, until they possessed about nine thousand commanderies, situated in various countries of Europe and in Palestine, with an annual rental of one hundred and twelve million francs.

149. *Account of Commanderies.*—Their commanderies were situate in their eastern and western provinces, the former embracing Jerusalem, Tripoli, Antioch, Cyprus; the latter, Portugal, Castile and Leon, Arragon, France, including Flanders and the Netherlands, England, Ireland, Germany, Italy, and Sicily. Whilst Jerusalem was in the hands of the Christians, the chief seat of the Templars was in that city; afterwards it was transferred to Paris, where they erected the large building until lately known as the Temple. It was in this building that Philip the Fair took refuge on the occasion of a riot which took place in 1306, where the Templars protected him until the fury of the people had calmed down. The Knights, it is said, incautiously displayed to the royal cupidity their immense treasures. On a subsequent, but far more momentous rising, the pile which served an ungrateful King for an asylum, became the prison of an unfortunate successor; recently this memento of royal perfidy, and of an avenging fate that struck the innocent, has been levelled to the ground.

150. *Imputations against the Order.*—Towards the end of the twelfth century the Order counted about thirty thousand members, mostly French, and the Grand Master was generally chosen from among the French. Through the great number of their affiliated members they could raise a large army in any part of the Eastern world; and their fleet monopolized

the commerce of the Levant. Hence they departed from their original humility and piety. Palestine was lost, and they made no effort to recover it; but frequently drew the sword—which was only to be used in the service of God, as they understood the phrase—in the feuds and warfares of the countries they inhabited. They became proud and arrogant. When dying, Richard Cœur de Lion said, "I leave avarice to the Cistercian monks, luxuriousness to the begging friars, pride to the Templars;" and yet perhaps they only felt their own power. The English Templars had dared to say to Henry III., "You shall be king as long as you are just;" portentous words which supplied matter for meditation to that Philip of France who, like many other princes, wished to be unjust with impunity. In Castile, the Templars, Hospitallers, and Knights of St. John, combined against the King himself. Perhaps they aimed at universal dominion, or at the establishment of a Western sovereignty, like the Teutonic Knights of Prussia, the Hospitallers in Malta, or the Jesuits in Paraguay? But there is scarcely any ground for these imputations, especially the first, considering that the members of the Order were scattered all over the earth, and might at the utmost have attempted to seize the government of some individual state, as that of Arragon for instance; but not to carry out a scheme for which even the forces of Charlemagne had been inadequate.

Accusations better founded were, that they had disturbed the kingdom of Palestine by their rivalry with the Hospitallers; had concluded leagues with the infidels; had made war upon Cyprus and Antiochia; had dethroned the King of Jerusalem, Henry II.; had devastated Greece and Thrace; had refused to contribute to the ransom of Saint Louis; had declared for Arragon against Anjou—an unpardonable crime in the eyes of France—with many other accusations. But their greatest crime was that of being exceedingly wealthy; their downfall was therefore determined upon.

151. *Plots against the Order.*—Philip the Fair had spent his last sou. The victory of Mons, worse than a defeat, had ruined him. He was bound to restore Guyenne, and was on the point of losing Flanders. Normandy had risen against a tax which he had been obliged to withdraw. The people of the capital were so opposed to the government, that it had been found necessary to prohibit meetings of more than five persons. How was money to be obtained under these circumstances? The Jews could give no more, because all they had had been extorted from them by fines, imprisonment, and torture. It was necessary to have recourse to some grand confiscation, without disgusting the classes on whom the royal power relied, and leading them to believe, not that booty was aimed at, but the punishment of evil doers, to the

greater glory of religion and the triumph of the law. At the instigation of Philip the Fair libels were published against the Order of the Knights Templars, in which the most absurd charges were made against the members, accusing them of heresy, impiety, and worse crimes. Great weight was attached to the statements made against the Templars by two renegades of the Order, the Florentine Roffi Dei, and the prior of Montfaucon, which latter, having been condemned by the Grand Master to imprisonment for life for his many crimes, made his escape, and became the accuser of his former brethren.

152. *Attentions paid to Grand Master.*—Bertrand de Got, who by the influence of the French King had become Pope under the title of Clement V., was now urged by the former to fulfil the last of the five conditions on which the King had enabled him to ascend the chair of St. Peter. The first four conditions had been named, but Philip had reserved the naming of the fifth till the fit moment should arrive ; and from his subsequent conduct there can be no doubt that the destruction of the Order of the Temple was the condition that was in the King's mind when he thus alluded to it. The first step was to get the Grand Master, James de Molay, into his power. At the request of the Pope that he would come to France to concert measures for the recovery of the Holy Land, he left Cyprus and

came to Paris in 1307, accompanied by sixty knights, and bringing with him 150,000 florins of gold, and so much silver that it formed the lading of twelve horses, which he deposited in the Temple in that city. To lull him into false security, the King, whose plan was not yet quite ripe for execution, treated the Grand Master with the greatest consideration, made him the godfather of one of his sons, and chose him with some of the most distinguished persons to carry the pall at the funeral of his sister-in-law. The following day he was arrested with all his suite, and letters having in the meantime been sent to the King's officers in the provinces on the 13th of October, 1307, to seize upon all the Templars, their houses and property throughout the kingdom, many thousand members of the Order, knights and serving brothers, were thus made prisoners.

153. *Charges against the Templars.* — The Templars were accused of denying Christ, the Virgin, and the Saints, and of spitting and trampling on the cross; of worshipping in a dark cave an idol in the figure of a man covered with an old human skin, and having two bright and lustrous carbuncles for eyes; of anointing it with the fat of young children roasted, of looking upon it as their sovereign God; of worshipping the devil in the form of a cat; of burning the bodies of dead Templars and giving the ashes to the younger

brethren to eat and drink mingled with their food. They were charged with various unnatural crimes, frightful debaucheries, and superstitious abominations, such as only madmen could have been guilty of. To make them confess these crimes they were put to the torture, not only in France, but also in England, for Edward II. leagued with Philip to destroy the Order. Many knights in the agonies of the torture confessed to the crimes they were charged with, hundreds expired under it without making any confession, many starved or killed themselves in other ways in prison. The trial was protracted for years; the persecution extended to other countries; in Germany and Spain and Cyprus the Order was acquitted of all guilt; in Italy, England, and France, however, their doom was sealed, though for a moment there seemed a chance of their escaping, for the Pope seeing that Philip and Edward had seized all the money and estates of the Templars, and seemed inclined to deprive him of his share of the spoil, began to side with the Order. But on some concessions being made to him by the two Kings, he again supported them; though in the end we find him complaining of the small share of the booty that came into his hands.

154. *Burning of Knights.*—The tedious progress of the sham trial was occasionally enlivened by the public execution of knights who refused to acknowledge crimes of which they were not guilty. Fifty-

nine gallant knights were led forth in one day to the fields at the back of the nunnery of St. Antoine, where stakes had been driven into the ground, and fagots and charcoal collected. The knights were offered pardon if they would confess; but they all refused and were burned by slow fires. At Senlis nine were burned, and many more in other places. On all these occasions, as well as in the awful scenes of the torture-chamber, the Dominican friars were the mocking witnesses.

155. *James de Molay.*—The Grand Master remained in prison five years and a half; and there is no doubt that he was repeatedly put to the torture. The confession he was said to have made was probably a forgery. Finally, on the 18th March, 1313, he and Guy, the Grand Preceptor of the Order, were burnt by a slow fire on a small island in the Seine, between the royal gardens and the church of the Hermit Brethren, where afterwards the statue of Henry IV. was erected, both to the last moment asserting the innocence of the Order.

156. *Mysteries of the Knights Templars.*—Without laying too much stress on confessions extorted by violence, or denunciations proceeding from revenge, cupidity, and servility, it is manifest that the Templars, in their ordinances, creed, and rites, had something which was peculiar and secret, and totally different from the statutes, opinions, and ceremonies of other religio-military associations. Their

long sojourn in the East, in that dangerous Palestine which overflowed with schismatic Greeks and heretics, who, driven from Constantinople, took refuge with the Arabs; their rivalry with the Hospitallers; their contact with the Saracen element; finally, the loss of the Holy Land, which injured them in the opinion of the world, and rendered their lives idle— all these and many other circumstances would act on this institution in an unforeseen manner, differing from the tendencies of the original constitution, and mix up therewith ideas and practices little in accordance with, nay, in total antagonism to, the orthodox thought that had originated, animated, and strengthened this military brotherhood.

157. *The Temple and the Church.*—The very name may in a certain manner point to a rebellious ambition. Temple is a more august, a vaster and more comprehensive denomination than that of Church. The Temple is above the Church; this latter has a date of its foundation, a local habitation; the former has always existed. Churches fall; the Temple remains as a symbol of the parentage of religions, and the perpetuity of their spirit. The Templars might thus consider themselves as the priests of that religion, not transitory, but permanent; and the aspirants could believe that the Order constituting them the defenders of the Temple, intended to initiate them into a second and better Christianity, into a purer religion. Whilst

the Temple meant for the Christian the Holy Sepulchre, it recalled to the Mussulman the Temple of Solomon; and the legend which referred to this latter served as a bond to the rituals of the Freemasons and other secret societies.

158. *The Temple the Symbol of the Holy Spirit.*—In another sense, the Church may be called the house of Christ; but the Temple is the house of the Holy Spirit. It is that religion of the Spirit which the Templars inherited from the Manichæans, from the Albigenses, from the sectarian chivalry that had preceded them. Defenders of the Sepulchre of Christ, they remained faithful to their trust, but considered that He had come on earth only to preach in the name of the Eternal Spirit, to whom their principal worship was addressed; and, like the Gnostics and Manichæans, they celebrated Pentecost rather than Easter, because in the former the Divine Spirit itself had descended and spread itself over the face of the earth. This, in a certain sense, was an amplification, and in another a denial, of the Catholic dogma. The Holy Spirit is the universal conscience.

159. *Doctrines of Templars.*—The initiatory practices, the monuments, even the trial, show this prevalence of the religion of the Spirit in the secret doctrines of the Temple. The Templars drew a great portion of their sectarian and heterodox tendencies from the last epic cycle of the middle ages—from that

period in which chivalry, purified and organized, became a pilgrimage in search of the San Greäl, the mystic cup that received the blood of the Saviour; from that epoch in which the East, in invasions, armed and unarmed, with the science of the Arabs, with poetry and heresies, had turned upon the West.

160. *Initiation.*—Much has been said about the mode of initiation—that it took place at night in the chapel, in the presence of the chapter, all strangers being strictly excluded; that licentious rites attended it, and that the candidate was compelled to deny, curse, and spit upon the cross—that cross for which they had shed so much of their own blood, sacrificed so many of their own lives. We have seen that this was one of the chief accusations brought against the Order. Was there any truth in it? It seems most probable there was; but the practice may be explained as in the following paragraph.

161. *Cursing and Spitting on the Cross Explained.*—Such a practice need not surprise us in an age in which churches were turned into theatres, in which sacred things were profaned by grotesque representations, in which the ancient mysteries were reproduced to do honour, in their way, to Christ and the saints. The reader may also bear in mind the extraordinary scenes afterwards represented in the Miracle Plays. Now the aspirant to the Templar degree was at first introduced as a

sinner, a bad Christian, a renegado. He denied, in fact, after the manner of St. Peter; and the renunciation was frequently expressed by the odious act of spitting on the cross. The fraternity undertook to restore this renegado, to raise him all the higher the greater his fall had been. Thus at the Festival of the Idiots, the candidate presented himself as it were in a state of imbecility and of degradation, to be regenerated by the Church. These comedies, rightly understood at first, were in course of time falsely interpreted, scandalizing the faithful, who had lost the key of the enigma. The Templars had adopted similar ceremonies. They were scions of the Cathari (123) and Manichæans. Now the Cathari despised the cross (124), and considered it meritorious to tread it under foot. But with the Templars this ceremony was symbolical, as was abundantly proved during their trial; and had indeed reference to Peter's thrice-repeated denial of Christ.

162. *The Templars the Opponents of the Pope.*— But there may have been another and special reason for introducing this ceremony, and ever keeping the treachery of Peter before the mind of the members of the Order. We have seen that the Templars, during and in consequence of their sojourn in the East, attached themselves to the doctrines of the Gnostics and Manichæans,—as is sufficiently attested, were other proofs wanting, by the Gnostic and caba-

listic symbols discovered in and on the tombs of Knights Templars,—which appeared to them less perverted than those of the priests of Rome. They also knew the bad success the proclamation of Christ's death on the cross had had at Athens, in consequence of Æschylus' tragedy, "Prometheus Vinctus," wherein Oceanus denied his friend, when God made him the sacrifice for the sins of mankind, just as Peter, who lived by the ocean, did with regard to Christ. The Templars, therefore, came to the conclusion that all these gods, descended from the same origin, were only religious and poetic figures of the sun; and, seeing the bad use made of the doctrines connected therewith by the clergy, they renounced St. Peter, and became Johannites, or followers of St. John. There was thus a secret schism, and according to some writers, it was this, together with the opposition to Roman Catholicism which it implied, as well as their great wealth, which was among the causes of their condemnation by the court of Rome.

163. *Baphomet.* — The above explanation may also afford a clue to the meaning and name of the idol the Templars were accused of worshipping. This idol represented a man with a long white beard, and the name given to it was *Baphomet,* a name which has exercised the ingenuity of many critics, but the only conclusions arrived at by any of them as to its origin and meaning, and deserving

consideration, are those of Nicolai, who assumes that it was derived from βαφὴ μήτιος, the "baptism of wisdom," and that the image, which sometimes had three heads, represented God, the universal Father; and that of De Quincey, to which latter I myself incline, that the figure, sometimes represented with two heads only, meant the two chiefs against whom the Templars directed their hostility, viz. the Pope and Mahomet, and in the name Baphomet they intertwisted the names of both, by cutting off the first two letters of Mahomet, and substituting Bap or Pap, the first syllable of Papa. Thus by this figure the Templars expressed their independence of the Church and the Church creed; and an initiated member was called a "friend of God, who could speak with God, if he chose;" that is, without the intermediation of the Pope and the Church. Hence it becomes sufficiently plain why the secret was looked upon as inviolable, and was so well kept that we can only conjecture its import.

164. *Effects of the Downfal of the Knights of the Temple.* — With the Templars perished a world; chivalry, the crusades, ended with them. Even the Papacy received a tremendous shock. Symbolism was deeply affected by it. A greedy and arid trading spirit rose up. Mysticism, that had sent such a glow through past generations, found the souls of men cold, incredulous. The reaction was violent, and the Templars were the first to fall

under the rude blows of the West, that longed to rebel against the East, by which it had hitherto been in so many ways permeated, ruled, and oppressed.

165. *Connexion with Freemasonry.*—The Freemasons assert a connexion with the Templars; and there is a society calling themselves Templars whose chief seat is at Paris, and whose branches extend into England and other countries. They say that James de Moulay before his death appointed a successor, and that since then there has been an unbroken line of Grand Masters down to the present time, a list of which is given by the Order of the Temple at Paris. But true Freemasonry, of which Freemasons, as a rule, know nothing, existed before the Templars, as I shall show when speaking of the Masonic Orders. A simple allusion to the alleged connexion therefore is all that is needed here.

BOOK VI.
FREE JUDGES.

AUTHORITIES.

Berck. Geschichte der westphälischen Vehmgerichte. Bremen, 1814.
Kohlrausch. Deutsche Geschichte.
Wigant. Das Vehmgericht. Ham. 1825.
Koop. Verfassung der heimlichen Gerichte. Göttingen, 1794.
Hütter. Das Vehmgericht. Leipzig, 1798.
Troos. Sammlung merkwürdiger Urkunden für die Geschichte des Vehmgerichts. 1826.
Usener. Die freien und heimlichen Gerichte Westphalens. Frankfort, 1832.
De Bock. Histoire du Tribunal Secret. Metz, 1801.
Memoirs of the Secret Societies of Italy. London, 1821.

I.

THE HOLY VEHM.

166.

ORIGIN and object of Institution.—In this book we are introduced to an order of secret societies altogether different from preceding ones. Hitherto they were religious or military in their leading features; but those we are now about to give an account of were judicial in their operations, and arose during the period of violence and anarchy that distracted the German empire after the outlawry of Henry the Lion, somewhere about the middle of the thirteenth century. The most important of these were the secret tribunals of Westphalia, known by the name of *Vehm-Gerichte,* or the *Holy Vehm.* The supreme authority of the emperor had lost all influence in the country; the imperial assizes were no longer held; might and violence took the place of right and justice; the feudal lords tyrannized over the people; whosoever dared, could. To seize the guilty, whoever they might be, to punish them before they were aware of the blow with which they were threatened, and thus to secure the chastisement of crime—such was the object of the Westphalian judges, and thus the existence of this secret society, the instrument of public vengeance, is amply justified, and the popular respect it enjoyed, and on which alone rested its authority, explained.

167. *Officers and Organization.*—The Westphalia of that period comprehended the country between the Rhine and the Weser; its southern boundary was formed by the mountains of Hesse, its northern, by Friesland. *Vehm* or *Fehm* is according to Leibnitz derived from *fama,* as the law founded on common fame. But *fem* is an old German word, signifying condemnation, which may be the proper radix of Vehm. These courts were also called *Fehmding, Freistühle,* " free courts," *heimliche Gerichte, heimliche Achten, heimliche beschlossene Achten,* "secret courts," "free bann," and *verbotene Gerichte,* "prohibited courts." No rank of life excluded a person from the right of being initiated, and in a Vehmic code discovered at Dortmund, and whose reading was forbidden to the profane under pain of death, three degrees are mentioned; the affiliated of the first were called *Stuhlherren,* "lords justices;" those of the second, *Schöppen (scabini, échevins)*; those of the third, *Frohnboten,* "messengers." Two courts were held, an *offenbares Ding,* "open court," and the *heimliche*

Acht, "secret court." The members were called *Wissende,* "the knowing ones," or the *initiated.* The clergy, women and children, Jews and heathens, and as it would appear the higher nobility, were exempt from its jurisdiction. The courts took cognizance of all offences against the Christian faith, the Gospel, and the Ten Commandments.

168. *Language and Rules of Initiated.*—The initiated had a secret language; at least we may infer so from the initials S. S. S. G. G., found in Vehmic writings preserved in the archives of Herfort, in Westphalia, that have puzzled the learned, and by some are explained as meaning, *Stock, Stein, Strick, Gras, Grein,* stick, stone, cord, grass, woe. At meals the members are said to have recognized each other by turning the points of their knives towards the edge, and the points of their forks towards the centre, of the table. A horrible death was prepared for a false brother, and the oaths to be taken were as fearful as some prescribed in the higher degrees of Freemasonry. The affiliated promised, among other things, to serve the secret Vehm before anything that is illumined by the sun or bathed by rain, or to be found between heaven and earth; not to inform any one of the sentence passed against him; and to denounce, if necessary, his parents and relations, calling down upon himself, in case of perjury, the malediction of all, and the punishment of being hanged seven feet higher

than all others. One form of oath, contained in the archives of Dortmund, and which the candidate had to pronounce kneeling, his head uncovered, and holding the forefinger and the middle finger of his right hand upon the sword of the president, runs thus: " I swear perpetual devotion to the secret tribunal; to defend it against myself, against water, sun, moon and stars, the leaves of the trees, all living beings; to uphold its judgments and promote their execution. I promise moreover that neither pain, nor money, nor parents, nor anything created by God, shall render me perjured."

169. *Procedure.*—The first act of the procedure of the Vehm was the accusation, made by a *Freischöppe*. The person was then cited to appear; if not initiated, before the open court, and woe to the disobedient! The accused that belonged to the order was at once condemned; and the case of the unaffiliated was transferred to the secret tribunal. A summons was to be written on parchment and sealed with at least seven seals; six weeks and three days were allowed for the first, six weeks for the second, and six weeks and three days for the third. When the residence of the accused was not known, the summons was exhibited at a cross-road of his supposed county, or placed at the foot of the statue of some saint or affixed to the poor-box, not far from some crucifix or humble wayside chapel. If the accused was a knight, dwelling in his fortified

castle, the *Schöppen* were to introduce themselves at night, under any pretence, into the most secret chamber of the building and do their errand. But sometimes it was considered sufficient to affix the summons, and the coin that always accompanied it, to the gate, to inform the sentinel of the fact that the citation had been left, and to cut three chips from the gate, to be taken to the *Freigraf*, as proofs. If the accused appeared to none of the summonses, he was sentenced *in contumacia*, according to the laws laid down in the " Mirror of Saxony ; " the accuser had to bring forward seven witnesses, not to the fact charged against the absent person, but to testify to the well-known veracity of the accuser, whereupon the charge was considered as proved, and the Imperial ban was pronounced against the accused, which was followed by speedy execution. The sentence was one of outlawry, degradation, and death; the neck of the convict was condemned to the halter, and his body to the birds and wild beasts; his goods and estates were declared forfeited, his wife a widow, and his children orphans. He was declared *fehmbar*, *i. e.* punishable by the Vehm, and any three initiated that met with him were at liberty, nay, enjoined, to hang him on the nearest tree. If the accused appeared before the court, which was presided over by a count, who had on the table before him a naked sword and a withy halter, he, as well as his accuser, could each bring thirty friends as witnesses, and be represented by their attorneys, and also had the right of appeal to the general chapter of the secret closed tribunal of the Imperial chamber, generally held at Dortmund. When sentence was once definitively spoken for death, the culprit was hanged immediately.

170. *Execution of Sentences.*—Those condemned in their absence, and who were pursued by at least a hundred thousand persons, were generally unaware of the fact. Every information thereof conveyed to him was high treason, punishable by death; the emperor alone was excepted from the law of secresy; merely to hint that "good bread might be eaten elsewhere," rendered the speaker liable to death for betraying the secret. After the condemnation of the accused a document bearing the seal of the count was given to the accuser, to be used by him when claiming the assistance of other members to carry out the sentence; and all the initiated were bound to grant him theirs, were it even against their own parents. A knife was stuck in the tree on which the person had been hanged, to indicate that he had suffered death at the hands of the Holy Vehm. If the victim resisted, he was slain with daggers; but the slayer left his weapon in the wound to convey the same information.

171. *Decay of the Institution.*—These secret tribunals inspired such terror that the citation by a Westphalian free count was even more dreaded

than that of the emperor. In 1470 three free counts summoned the emperor himself to appear before them, threatening him with the usual course in case of contumacy; the emperor did not appear, but pocketed the affront. By the admission of improper persons, and the abuse of the right of citation, the institution—which in its time had been a corrective of public injustice—gradually degenerated. The tribunals were, indeed, reformed by Rupert; and the Arensberg reformation and Osnaburgh regulations modified some of the greatest abuses, and restricted the power of the Vehm. Still it continued to exist, and was never formally abolished. But the excellent civil institutions of Maximilian and of Charles V., the consequent decrease of the turbulent and anarchic spirit, the introduction of the Roman law, the spread of the Protestant religion, conspired to give men an aversion for what appeared now to be a barbarous jurisdiction. Some of the courts were abolished, exemptions and privileges against them multiplied, and they were prohibited all summary proceedings. But a shadow of them remained, and it was not till French legislation, in 1811, abolished the last free court in the county of Münster, that they may be said to have ceased to exist. But it is not many years since that certain citizens in that locality assembled secretly every year, boasting of their descent from the ancient free judges.

172. *Kissing the Virgin.*—There is a tradition

that one of the methods of putting to death persons condemned to that fate by the secret tribunals was the following:—The victim was told to go and kiss the statue of the Virgin which stood in a subterranean vault. The statue was of bronze and of gigantic size. On approaching it, so as to touch it, its front opened with folding doors and displayed its interior set full with sharp and long spikes and pointed blades. The doors were similarly armed, and on each, about the height of a man's head, was a spike longer than the rest, the two spikes being intended when the doors were shut to enter the eyes and destroy them. The doors having thus opened, the victim by a secret mechanism was drawn or pushed into the dreadful statue, and the doors closed upon him. There he was cut and hacked by the knives and spikes, and in about half a minute the floor on which he stood—which was in reality a trap-door—opened, and allowed him to fall through. But more horrible torture awaited him; for underneath the trap-door were six large wooden cylinders, disposed in pairs one below the other. There were thus three pairs. The cylinders were furnished all round with sharp blades; the distance between the uppermost pair of parallel cylinders was such that a human body could just lie between them; the middle pair was closer together, and the lowest very close. Beneath this horrible apparatus was an opening in which could be heard the rushing of water. The mechanism that opened the doors of the statue also set in motion the cylinders, which turned towards the inside. Hence when the victim, already fearfully mangled and blinded, fell through the trap-door he fell between the upper pair of cylinders and was thus drawn in between them, his body being cut on all sides by the knives set round the cylinders. In this mutilated condition, the quivering mass fell between the second and more closely approaching pair of cylinders, and was now actually hacked through and through and thrown on the lowest and closest pair, where it was reduced to small pieces which fell into the brook below, and were carried away; thus leaving no trace of the awful deed that had been accomplished.

II.

THE BEATI PAOLI.

173.

CHARACTER *of the Society.*—The notices of this sect, which existed for many years in Sicily, are so scanty, that we may form a high idea of the mystery in which it shrouded itself. It had spread not only over the island, where it created traditional terror, but also over Calabria, where it was first discovered, and cruelly repressed and punished by the feudatories, who saw their power assailed by it. A popular institution, in opposition to the daily arrogance of baronial or kingly power, it knew not how to restrain itself within the prescribed limits, and made itself guilty of reprehensible acts, so that it was spoken of in various ways by its contemporaries.

174. *Tendencies and Tenets.*—We have already seen that it had connections with the Holy Vehm, and its statutes were somewhat similar to this tribunal; but it is to be observed that it proceeded

from that spiritual movement which produced the reaction of the Albigenses, the propaganda of the Franciscans, and the reformatory asceticism of the many heretics who roamed through Italy and the rest of Europe, preaching opposition to Rome, and organizing a crusade against the fastuous and corrupt clerocracy. Among these heretics we must remember the abbot Gioachimo, whose prophecies and strange sayings reappear in the *Evangelium Æternum* of John of Parma, a book which was one of the text-books of the Sicilian judges. The *Evangelium Æternum*, a tissue of cabalistic and Gnostic eccentricities, was, by the Beati Paoli, preferred to the Old and New Testaments; they renounced belief in dualism, and made God the creator of evil and death—of evil, because he placed the mystical apple in the mystical garden; of death, because he ordained the deluge, and destroyed Sodom and Gomorrah.

175. *Account of a Sicilian Writer.*—Amidst the general silence of historians, the account of a Sicilian writer, which was published only in 1840, and is still generally unknown, may be considered the only document concerning this family of Avengers, who at the extreme end of Italy reproduced the struggles and terrors of the Westphalian tribunals. This writer says:—" In the year 1185, at the nuptials of the Princess Constance, daughter of the first King Roger of Sicily, with Henry, afterwards

Henry VI., Emperor of Germany, there was discovered the existence of a new and impious sect, who called themselves the Avengers, and in their nocturnal assemblies declared every crime lawful committed on pretence of promoting the public good. Of this we find an account in an ancient writer, who does not enter into further details. The King ordered strict inquiry to be made, and their chief, Arinulfo di Ponte Corvo, having been arrested, he was sentenced to be hanged with some of his most guilty accomplices; the less guilty were branded with a red-hot iron. The belief exists among the vulgar that this secret society of Avengers still exists in Sicily and elsewhere, and is known by the name of the Beati Paoli. Some worthless persons even go so far as to commend the impious institution. Its members abounded especially at Palermo, and Joseph Amatore, who was hanged on Dec. 17, 1704, was one of them. Girolamo Ammirata, comptroller of accounts, also belonged to this society, and suffered death on 27th April, 1725. Most came to a bad end, if not by the hands of justice, by the daggers of their associates. The famous *vetturino*, Vito Vituzzo of Palermo, was the last of the wretches forming the society of the Beati Paoli. He escaped the gallows, because he turned in time from his evil courses; and thenceforward he passed all day in St. Matthew's Church, whence he came to be known by the surname of the church mouse. The preceptors and masters of these vile men were heretics and apostates from the Minor Brethren of St. Francis, who pretended that the power of the pontiff and the priesthood had been bestowed on them by an angelic revelation. The house where they held their meetings is still in existence in the street *de' Canceddi*, and I paid it a visit. Through a gateway you pass into a courtyard, under which is the vault where the members met, and which receives its light through a grating in the stone pavement. At the bottom of the stairs is a stone altar, and at the side a small dark chamber, with a stone table, on which were written the acts and sentences of these murderous judges. The principal cave is pretty large, surrounded with stone seats, and furnished with niches and recesses where the arms were kept. The meetings were held at night by candle light. The derivation of the name, the Beati Paoli (Blessed Pauls), is unknown; but I surmise that it was adopted by the sect, because either the founder's name was Paul, or that he assumed it as that of a saint who, before his conversion, was a man of the sword, and, imitating him, was, during the day, a Blessed Paul, and at night at the head of a band of assassins, like Paul persecuting the Christians." Such is the author's account, which I have greatly abbreviated, omitting nearly all his invectives against the sect, of which very little is known, and whose existence evidently, in its day, was to some extent beneficial; for Sicilians, on suffering any injury or loss, for which they cannot apply to justice, are often heard to exclaim:—" Ah, if the Beati Paoli were still in being!"

BOOK VII.

ALCHYMISTS.

In our day men are only too much disposed to regard the views of the disciples and followers of the Arabian school, and of the late Alchymists, respecting transmutation of metals, as a mere hallucination of the human mind, and, strangely enough, to lament it. But the idea of the variable and changeable corresponds with universal experience, and always precedes that of the unchangeable.

LIEBIG.

> The alchymist he had his gorgeous vision
>   Of boundless wealth and everlasting youth;
> He strove untiringly, with firm decision,
>   To turn his fancies into glorious truth,
> Undaunted by the rabble's loud derision,
>   Condemning without reason, without ruth,
> And though he never found the pearl he sought,
> Yet many a secret gem to light he brought.

AUTHORITIES.

Ledoux. Dictionnaire hermétique. Paris, 1695.
Clef du Grand Œuvre. Paris, 1776.
Goldenfalck. Anecdotes alchimiques. Lyons, 1783.
Schmieder. Geschichte der Alchemie. Halle, 1832.
Kopp. Geschichte der Chemie. Leipsic, 1844.
Figuier. L'Alchimie et les Alchimistes. Paris, 1855.
Lévi. La Clef des Grands Mystères. Paris, 1861.
Lenglet du Fresnoy. Histoire de la Philosophie hermétique. Paris, 1742.
Suggestive Inquiry into the Hermetic Mystery. London, 1850.
Böhme. Works *passim.*
Fludd. Tractatus Theologo-Philosophicus. Oppenheim, 1617.
Neuhnsius. De Fratribus Rosæ-Crucis.
Semler. The Rosicrucians.
Mackey. Lexicon of Freemasonry.
De Quincey. Works. Supplemental vol. London, 1871.

I.

THE ALCHYMISTS.

176.

ASTROLOGY perhaps Secret Heresy.—The mystic astronomy of ancient nations produced judicial astrology, which, considered from this point of view, will appear less absurd. It was the principal study of the middle ages; and Rome was so violently opposed to it because, perhaps, it was not only heresy, but a wide-spread reaction against the Church of Rome. It was chiefly cultivated by the Jews, and protected by princes opposed to the papal supremacy. The Church was not satisfied with burning the books, but burned the writers; and the poor astrologers, who spent their lives in the contemplation of the heavens, mostly perished at the stake.

177. *Process by which Astrology degenerated.*— As it often happens that the latest disciples attach

themselves to the letter, understanding literally what in the first instance was only a fiction, taking the mask for a real face, so we may suppose astrology to have degenerated and become false and puerile. Hermes, the legislator of Egypt, who was revealed in the Samothracian mysteries, and often represented with a ram by his side—a constellation initiating the new course of the equinoctial sun, the conqueror of darkness—was revived in astrological practice; and a great number of astrological works, the writings of Christian Gnostics and Neo-Platonists, were attributed to him, and he was considered the father of the art from him called *hermetic*, and embracing astrology and alchymy, the rudimentary efforts of two sciences, which at first overawed ignorance by imposture, but, after labouring for centuries in the dark, conquered for themselves glorious thrones in human knowledge.

178. *Scientific Value of Alchymy.*—Though alchymy is no longer believed in as a true science, in spite of the prophecy of Dr. Girtanner, of Göttingen, that in the nineteenth century the transmutation of metals will be generally known and practised, it will never lose its power of awakening curiosity and seducing the imagination. The aspect of the marvellous which its doctrines assume, the strange renown attaching to the memory of the adepts, and the mixture of reality and illusion, of truths and chimeras which it presents, will always exercise a

powerful fascination upon many minds. And we ought also to remember that every delusion that has had a wide and enduring influence must have been founded, not on falsehood, but on misapprehended truth. This aphorism is especially applicable to Alchymy, which, in its origin, and even in its name, is identical with chemistry, the syllable *al* being merely the definite article of the Arabs. The researches of the Alchymists for the discovery of the means by which transmutation might be effected were naturally suggested by the simplest experiments in metallurgy and the amalgamation of metals; it is very probable that the first man who made brass thought that he had produced imperfect gold.

179. *The Tincture.*—The transmutation of the base metal was to be effected by means of the transmuting tincture, which, however, was never found. But it exists for all that; it is the power that turns a green stalk into a golden ear of corn, that fills the sour unripe apple with sweetness and aroma, that has turned the lump of charcoal into a diamond. All these are natural processes, which, being allowed to go on, produce the above results. Now, all base metals may be said to be imperfect metals, whose progress towards perfection has been arrested, the active power of the tincture being shut up in them in the first property of nature (11). If a man could take hold of the tincture universally diffused in

nature, and by its help assist the imprisoned tincture in the metal to stir and become active, then the transmutation into gold, or rather the manifestation (11) of the hidden life, could be effected. But this power or tincture is so subtle that it cannot possibly be apprehended; yet the Alchymists did not seek the non-existing, but only the unattainable.

180. *Aims of Alchymy.*—The three great ends pursued by Alchymy were the transmutation of base metals into gold by means of the philosopher's stone; the discovery of the panacea, or universal medicine, the elixir of life; and the universal solvent, which, being applied to any seed, should increase its fecundity. All these three objects are attainable by means of the tincture—a vital force, whose body is electricity, by which the two latter aims have to some extent been reached, for electricity will both cure disease and promote the growth of plants. Alchymy was then in the beginning the search after means to raise matter up to its first state, whence it was supposed to have fallen. Gold was considered, as to matter, what the ether of the eighth heaven was as to souls; and the seven metals, each called by the name of one of the seven planets, the knowledge of the seven properties really implied being lost—the Sun, gold; Moon, silver; Saturn, lead; Venus, tin; Mercury, iron; Mars, mixed

metal; Jupiter, copper,[1]—formed the ascending scale of purification, corresponding with the trials of the seven caverns or steps. Alchymy was thus either a bodily initiation, or an initiation into the mysteries, a spiritual Alchymy; the one formed a veil of the other, wherefore it often happened that in workshops where the vulgar thought the adepts occupied with handicraft operations, and nothing sought but the metals of the golden age, in reality, no other philosopher's stone was searched for than the cubical stone of the temple of philosophy; in fine, nothing was purified but the passions, men, and not metals, being passed through the crucible. Böhme, the greatest of mystics, has written largely on the perfect analogy between the philosophical work and spiritual regeneration.

181. *History of Alchymy.*—Alchymy flourished in Egypt at a very early age, and Solomon was said to have practised it. Its golden age began with the conquests of the Arabs in Asia and Africa, about the time of the destruction of the Alexandrian Library. The Saracens, credulous, and intimate with the fables of talismans and celestial influences, eagerly admitted the wonders of Alchymy. In the splendid courts of Almansor and Haroun al Raschid,

---

[1] New arrangement: Venus, copper; Mercury, mixed metal; Mars, iron; Jupiter, tin.

the professors of the hermetic art found patronage, disciples, and emolument. Nevertheless, from the above period until the eleventh century the only alchymist of note is the Arabian Geber, whose proper name was Abu Mussah Djafar al Sofi. His attempts to transmute the base metals into gold led him to several discoveries in chymistry and medicine. He was also a famous astronomer, but—*sic transit gloria mundi!*—he has descended to our times as the founder of that jargon known by the name of gibberish! The Crusaders brought the art to Europe, and about the thirteenth century Albertus Magnus, Roger Bacon, and Raymond Lully appeared as its revivers. Henry VI. of England engaged lords, nobles, doctors, professors, and priests to pursue the search after the philosopher's stone; especially the priests, who, says the king—(ironically?)—having the power to convert bread and wine into the body and blood of Christ, may well convert an impure into a perfect metal. The next man of note that pretended to the possession of the *lapis philosophorum* was Paracelsus, whose proper name was Philip Aureolus Theophrastus Paracelsus Bombastus, of Hohenheim, and whom his followers called " Prince of Physicians, Philosopher of Fire, the Trismegistus of Switzerland, Reformer of Alchymistical Philosophy, Nature's faithful Secretary, Master of the Elixir of Life and Philosopher's Stone, Great Monarch of Chymical Secrets." He introduced the term *alcahest* (probably a corruption of the German words "*all geist*," "all spirit"), to express the universal solvent. The Rosicrucians (184), of whom Dr. Dee was the herald, next laid claim to alchymistical secrets, and were, in fact, the descendants of the Alchymists; and it is for this reason chiefly that these latter have been introduced into this work, though they cannot strictly be said to have formed a secret society. The last of the English Alchymists seems to have been a gentleman of the name of Kellerman, who as lately as 1828 was living at Lilley, a village between Luton and Hitchin. There are, no doubt, at the present moment men engaged in the search after the philosopher's stone; we patiently wait for their discoveries.

182. *Specimen of Alchymistic Language.*—After Paracelsus the Alchymists divided into two classes: those that pursued useful studies, and those that took up the visionary fantastical side of Alchymy, writing books of mystical trash which they fathered on Hermes, Aristotle, Albertus Magnus, and others. Their language is now unintelligible. One brief specimen may suffice. The power of transmutation, called the Green Lion, was to be obtained in the following manner:—"In the Green Lion's bed the sun and moon are born, they are married and beget a king; the king feeds on the lion's blood, which is the king's father and mother, who are at the same time his brother and sister. I fear I betray the

secret, which I promised my master to conceal in dark speech from every one who does not know how to rule the philosopher's fire." Our ancestors must have had a great talent for finding out enigmas if they were able to elicit a meaning from these mysterious directions; still the language was understood by the adepts, and was only intended for them. Many statements of mathematical formulæ must always appear pure gibberish to the uninitiated into the higher science of numbers; still, these statements enunciate truths well understood by the mathematician. Thus, to give but one instance, when Hermes Trismegistus, in one of the treatises attributed to him, directs the adept to catch the flying bird and to drown it, so that it fly no more, the fixation of quicksilver by a combination with gold is meant.

183. *Personal Fate of the Alchymists.*—The Alchymists, though chemistry is greatly indebted to them, and in their researches they stumbled on many a valuable discovery, as a rule led but sad and chequered lives, and most of them died in the utmost poverty, if no worse fate befell them. Thus one of the most famous Alchymists, Bragadino, who lived in the last quarter of the sixteenth century, who obtained large sums of money for his pretended secret from the Emperor of Germany, the Doge of Venice, and other potentates, who boasted that Satan was his slave—two ferocious black dogs that always ac-

companied him being demons—was at last hanged at Munich, the cheat with which he performed the pretended transmutation having been discovered. The two dogs were shot under the gallows. But even the honest Alchymists were doomed—

> To lose good days that might be better spent,
> To waste long nights in pensive discontent;
> To speed to-day, to be put back to-morrow,
> To feed on hope, to pine with fear and sorrow;
> To fret their souls with crosses and with cares,
> To eat their hearts through comfortless despairs.
> Unhappy wights, born to disastrous end,
> That do their lives in tedious tendance spend!

II.

ROSICRUCIANS.

184.

*ERITS of the Rosicrucians.*—A halo of poetic splendour surrounds the Order of the Rosicrucians; the magic lights of fancy play around their graceful daydreams, while the mystery in which they shrouded themselves lends an additional charm to their history. But their brilliancy was that of a meteor. It just flashed across the realms of imagination and intellect, and vanished for ever; not, however, without leaving behind some permanent and lovely traces of its hasty passage, just as the momentary ray of the sun, caught on the artist's lens, leaves a lasting image on the sensitive paper. Poetry and romance are deeply indebted to the Rosicrucians for many a fascinating creation. The literature of every European country contains hundreds of pleasing fictions, whose machinery has been borrowed from their system of philosophy, though that itself

has passed away; and it must be admitted that many of their ideas are highly ingenious, and attain to such heights of intellectual speculation as we find to have been reached by the sophists of India. Before their time, alchymy had sunk down, as a rule, to a grovelling delusion, seeking but temporal advantages and occupying itself with earthly dross only; the Rosicrucians spiritualized and refined it by giving the chimerical search after the philosopher's stone a nobler aim than the attainment of wealth, namely, the opening of the spiritual eyes, whereby man should be able to see the supernal world, and be filled with an inward light to illumine his mind with true knowledge.

185. *Origin of Society doubtful.*—The society is of very uncertain origin. It is affirmed by some writers that from the fourteenth century there existed a society of physicists and alchymists who laboured in the search after the philosopher's stone; and a certain Nicolo Barnaud undertook journeys through Germany and France for the purpose of establishing a hermetic society. From the preface of the work, "Echo of the Society of the Rosy Cross," it moreover follows that in 1597 meetings were held to institute a secret society for the promotion of alchymy. Another indication of the actual existence of such a society is found in 1610, when the notary Haselmeyer pretended to have read in a MS. the *Fama Fraternitatis*, comprising all the

laws of the Order. Four years afterwards appeared a small work, entitled "General Reformation of the World," which in fact contains the *Fama Fraternitatis*, where it is related that a German, Christian Rosenkreuz, founded such a society in the fourteenth century, after having learnt the sublime science in the East. Of him it is related, that when, in 1378, he was travelling in Arabia, he was called by name and greeted by some philosophers, who had never before seen him; from them he learned many secrets, among others that of prolonging life. On his return he made many disciples, and died at the age of 150 years, not because his strength failed him, but because he was tired of life. In 1604 one of his disciples had his tomb opened, and there found strange inscriptions and a MS. in letters of gold. The grotto in which this tomb was found, by the description given of it, strongly reminds us of the Mithraic Cave. Another work, the "Confessio Fraternitatis Rosæ Crucis," contains an account of the object and spirit of the Order. It is a mixture of absurdity and fanaticism, and the most plausible solution is that the work is a satire on the philosophical follies of the time. It was written by Valentine Andrea of Herrenberg. But as the armorial bearings of the Andrea family were a *St. Andrew's cross and four roses*, he may also have meant to intimate that the Order of the Rosy Cross was an Order founded by himself.

186. *Origin of Name.*—The name is generally derived from the supposed founder of the Order, Rosenkreuz, Rose Cross; but according to others it is the compound of *ros*, dew, and *crux*, the cross. *Crux* is supposed mystically to represent LUX, or light, because the figure X exhibits the three letters LVX; and light, in the opinion of the Rosicrucians, is that which produces gold, whilst dew (*ros*) with the alchymists was the most powerful solvent of gold. Others say that the Order took its name from the rose, and the epopt was called *Rosa*, whilst their ritual affirmed that the rose is the emblem of the Son of God, who by the Evangelist is compared to that flower. But we have already seen in the account of the Eleusinian Mysteries what importance was attached to the rose, and that Apuleius makes Lucius to be restored to his primitive form by eating roses; and the "Romance of the Rose" was considered by the Rosicrucians as one of the most perfect specimens of Provençal literature, and as the allegorical *chef d'œuvre* of their sect. It is undeniable that this was coeval with chivalry, and had from thenceforth a literature rich in works, in whose titles the word *Rosa* is incorporated; as the *Rosa Philosophorum*, of which no less than ten occur in the *Artis Auriferæ quam Chemiam vocant* (Basilea, 1610). The connection of the Rosicrucians with chivalry, the Troubadours, and the Albigenses, cannot be denied. Like these, they swore the

same hatred to Rome, like these they called Catholicism the religion of hate. They solemnly declared that the Pope was Antichrist, and rejected pontifical and Mahomedan dogmas, styling them the beasts of the East and West.

187. *Statements concerning themselves.* — They pretended to feel neither hunger nor thirst, nor to be subject to age or disease; to possess the power of commanding spirits and attracting pearls and precious stones, and of rendering themselves invisible. They stated the aim of their society to be the restoration of all the sciences and especially of medicine; and by occult artifices to procure treasures and riches sufficient to supply the rulers and kings with the necessary means for promoting the great reforms of society then needed. They were bound to conform to five fundamental laws: 1. Gratuitously to heal the sick. 2. To dress in the costume of the country in which they lived. 3. To attend every year the meeting of the Order. 4. When dying to choose a successor. 5. To preserve the secret one hundred years.

188. *Poetical Fictions of Rosicrucians.*—These are best known from the work of Joseph Francis Borri, a native of Milan. Having preached against the abuses of the Papacy, and promulgated opinions which were deemed heretical, he was seized by order of the Inquisition and condemned to perpetual imprisonment. He died in the Castle of St.

Angelo in 1695. The work referred to is entitled "The Key of the Cabinet of Signor Borri," and is in substance nothing but the cabalistic romance entitled "The Count de Gabalis," published in 1670 by the Abbé de Villars. What we gather from this work is, that the Rosicrucians discarded for ever all the old tales of sorcery and witchcraft and communion with the devil. They denied the existence of incubi and succubi, and of all the grotesque imps monkish brains had hatched and superstitious nations believed in. Man, they said, was surrounded by myriads of beautiful and beneficent beings, all anxious to do him service. These beings were the elemental spirits; the air was peopled with sylphs, the water with undines or naiads, the earth with gnomes, and the fire with salamanders. These the Rosicrucian could bind to his service and imprison in a ring, a mirror, or a stone, and compel to appear when called, and render answers to such questions as he chose to put. All these beings possessed great powers, and were unrestrained by the barriers of space or matter. But man was in one respect their superior: he had an immortal soul, they had not. They could, however, become sharers in man's immortality, if they could inspire one of that race with the passion of love towards them. On this notion is founded the charming story of "Undine;" Shakespeare's Ariel is a sylph; the "Rape of the Lock," the Masque of "Comus," the poem of "Salamandrine," all owe their machinery to the poetic fancies of the Rosicrucians. Among other things they taught concerning the elemental spirits, they asserted that they were composed of the purest particles of the element they inhabited, and that in consequence of having within them no antagonistic qualities, being made of but one element (11) they could live for thousands of years. The Rosicrucians further held the doctrine of the *signatura rerum*, by which they meant that everything in this visible world has outwardly impressed on it its inward spiritual character. Moreover they said that by the practice of virtue man could even on earth obtain a glimpse of the spiritual world, and above all things discover the philosopher's stone, which however could not be found except by the regenerate, for " it is in close communion with the heavenly essence." According to them the letters INRI, the sacred word of the Order of Rose Croix, signified *Igne Natura Regenerando Integrat*.

189. *Progress and Extinction of Rosicrucians.*— After having excited much attention throughout Germany, the Rosicrucians endeavoured to spread their doctrines in France, but with little success. In order to attract attention they secretly posted certain notices in the streets of Paris, to this effect: " We, the deputies of the College of the Rosy Cross, visibly and invisibly dwell in the city. We teach

without books or signs every language that can draw men from mortal error," &c. &c. A work by Gabriel Ra̅nde gave them the final blow. Peter Mormio, not having succeeded in reviving the society in Holland, where it existed in 1622, published at Leyden, in 1630, a work entitled *Arcana Naturæ Secretissima*, wherein he reduced the secrets of the brethren to three, viz. perpetual motion, the transmutation of metals, and the universal medicine. The German Rosicrucians always called themselves the depositories and preservers of the Masonic dogma, which they asserted to have been confided to them by the English in the time of King Arthur. Faithful to the Johannite tradition they called their grand masters John I., John II., and so on. At first they had only three degrees besides the three symbolic degrees of freemasonry. The sect was also known in Sweden and Scotland, where it had its own traditions, claiming to be descended from the Alexandrian priesthood of Ormuzd, that embraced Christianity in consequence of the preaching of St. Mark, founding the society of Ormuzd, or of the "Sages of Light." This tradition is founded on the Manichæism preserved among the Coptic priests, and explains the seal impressed on the ancient parchments of the Order, representing a lion placing his paw on a paper, on which is written the famous sentence, "*Pax tibi, Marce Evangelista meus :*" from which we might infer that Venice had some connection with the spreading of that tradition. In fact, Nicolai tells us that at Venice and Mantua there were Rosicrucians, connected with those of Erfurt, Leipsic, and Amsterdam. And we also know that at Venice congresses of alchymists were held; and the connection between these latter and the Rosicrucians has already been pointed out. Nevertheless the Scotch and Swedish Rosicrucians called themselves the most ancient, and asserted Edward, the son of Henry III., to have been initiated into the Order in 1196, by Raymond Lully, the alchymist. The Fraternity of the Rosy Cross is still flourishing in England, the members being selected from the Masonic body; it has a governing Senate in London, with a Metropolitan College, while Provincial Colleges are established at Bristol, Manchester, Cambridge, Oxford, Edinburgh and Glasgow.

190. *Transition to Freemasons.*—From the Templars and Rosicrucians the transition to the Freemasons is easy. With these latter alchymy receives a wholly symbolical explanation; the philosopher's stone is a figure of human perfectibility. In the Masonic degree called the "Key of Masonry," or "Knight of the Sun," and the work "The Blazing Star," by Tschudi, we discover the parallel aims of the two societies. From the "Blazing Star" I extract the following portion of the ritual: "When the hermetic philosophers speak of gold and

silver, do they mean common gold and silver?"— "No, because common gold and silver are dead, whilst the gold and silver of the philosophers are full of life."—"What is the object of Masonic inquiries?"—"The art of knowing how to render perfect what nature has left imperfect in man."— "What is the object of philosophic inquiry?"— "The art of knowing how to render perfect what nature has left imperfect in minerals, and to increase the power of the philosopher's stone."—"Is it the same stone whose symbol distinguishes our first degrees?"—"Yes, it is the same stone which the Freemasons seek to polish." So also the Phœnix is common to hermetic and Masonic initiation, and the emblem of the new birth of the neophyte. Now we have already seen the meaning of this figure, and its connection with the sun. We might multiply comparisons to strengthen the parallelism between hidden arts and secret societies, and trace back the hermetic art to the mysteries of Mithras, where man is said to ascend to heaven through seven steps or gates of lead, brass, copper, iron, bronze, silver, and gold.

BOOK VIII.

FREEMASONS.

What mote it be?
      King Henry VI. of England.

AUTHORITIES.

Saint-Albin. Les Francs-Maçons. Paris, 1862.
Preston. Illustrations of Masonry.
Gadicke. Freimaurer Lexicon.
Mackey. Lexicon of Freemasonry.
Reghellini. Esprit du Dogme de la Franc-Maçonnerie.
Barruel. Histoire du Jacobinisme.
Robison. Proofs of a Conspiracy. London, 1799.
Lawrie. History of Freemasonry.
Heldmann. Les trois plus anciens Monuments de la Confraternité maçonnique allemande.
Lenning. Encyclopædie der Freimaurerei.
Ragon. Cours philosophique des Initiations anciennes et modernes. Paris, 1841.
Dermott. The Ahiman Rezon.
Oliver. Theocratic Philosophy of Freemasonry. London, 1840.
Pocket Companion of History of Freemasonry. London, 1764.
Oliver. History of Initiations. London, 1829.
Hutchinson. Spirit of Freemasonry.
Carlile. Manual of Freemasonry. London.
Fellows. Mysteries of Freemasonry. London, 1860.
Lenoir. La Franc-Maçonnerie rendue à sa véritable Origine.
Clavel. Histoire pittoresque de la Franc-Maçonnerie. Paris, 1844.
Ragon. Le Tuilier Général. Paris, 1861.
Rédarés. Etudes sur les Trois Grades de la Maçonnerie. Paris, 1859.
Eckert. Die Freimaurerei in ihrer wahren Bedeutung. Liège, 1854.

Kauffmann et Cherpin. Histoire philosophique de la Franc-Maçonnerie. Lyons, 1850.

De la Tierce. Histoire des Franc-Maçons. 1745.

De Widekind. Geschichte der Freimaurerei in Deutschland.

Lindner. Mac-Benach. Leipsic, 1819.

Bode. Einfluss der Freimaurer. Leipsic, 1788.

Règle maçonnique à l'Usage des Loges réunies et rectifiées de Convent-Général de Wilhelmsbad. Paris, 1829.

La Vérité sur les Sociétés secrètes en Allemagne. Paris, 1819.

Forgame. De l'Influence de l'Esprit philosophique et de celle des Sociétés secrètes. Paris, 1858.

Mounier. De l'Influence attribuée aux Philosophes, aux Francs-Maçons et aux Illuminés sur la Révolution de France. Paris, 1801.

Vie de Joseph Balsamo. Paris, 1791.

Mémoires authentiques pour servir à l'Histoire de Cagliostro. Strasburg, 1786.

Saint-Félix. Aventures de Cagliostro. Paris, 1854.

L'Adoption de la Maçonnerie des Femmes. 1775.

Saint-Victor. La Vraie Maçonnerie d'Adoption. London, 1779.

Ragon. Manuel Complet de la Maçonnerie des Dames. Paris, 1860.

Procédures de l'Inquisition de Portugal contre les Francs-Maçons. 1740.

Eybert. Les Martyrs de la Franc-Maçonnerie en Espagne. Paris, 1854.

Levesque. Aperçu général des principales Sectes maçonniques. Paris, 1821.

Dubreuil. Histoire des Francs-Maçons. Brussels, 1838.

Bedarride. De l'Ordre maçonnique de Misraim. Paris, 1845.

Vernhes. Défense de l'Ordre de Misraim.
Barginet. Discours sur l'Histoire de l'Ordre du Temple. 1833.
Vassal. Cours complet de Maçonnerie. Paris, 1832.
Abraham. Miroir de la Vérité.
Accary. La Maçonnerie du Grand Orient de France. Paris, 1857.
Bazot. Tableau historique, philosophique, et moral de la Maçonnerie en France.
La Madre loggia Dante Alighieri. Turin, 1863.
Programma Massonico adottato dalla Massoneria Italiana Ricostituta. 1863.
Organisation du Travail par l'Initiation maçonnique. Paris, 1844.
Marconis. Table de la Loi des Francs-Maçons. Paris, 1862.
Freemasons' Quarterly Review. London.
Moreau. L'Univers maçonnique. Paris, 1837.
Duplais. La Vraie Lumière; Journal des Francs-Maçons. Versailles, 1851-2.
Cherpin. Revue maçonnique. Lyons.
Peigne. Revue maçonnique. Paris.
Juge. Le Globe; Archives générales des Sociétés secrètes, non politiques. Paris.
The Secrets of Freemasonry Revealed. London, 1759.
A Master-Key to Freemasonry. London, 1760.
L'Ordre des Francs-Maçons trahi. Amsterdam, 1771.
Les plus secrèts Mystères de la Franc-Maçonnerie. Jerusalem (Paris), 1774.
Fatti ed Argomenti intorno alla Massoneria. Genova, 1862.
Masonry the same all over the World. Boston, 1830.

I.

THE LEGEND OF THE TEMPLE.

191.

ANCESTRY *of Hiram Abiff.*—Solomon, having determined on the erection of the Temple, collected artificers, divided them into companies, and put them under the command of Adoniram or Hiram Abiff, the architect sent to him by his friend and ally Hiram, King of Tyre. According to mythical tradition, the ancestry of the builders of the mystical temple was as follows: One of the Elohim, or primitive genii, married Eve and had a son called Cain; whilst Jehovah or Adonai, another of the Elohim, created Adam and united him with Eve to bring forth the family of Abel, to whom were subjected the sons of Cain, as a punishment for the transgression of Eve. Cain, though industriously cultivating the soil, yet derived little produce from it, whilst Abel leisurely tended his flocks. Adonai rejected the gifts and sacrifices of Cain, and stirred up strife between the sons of the Elohim, generated out of fire, and the sons formed out of the earth only. Cain killed Abel, and Adonai pursuing his sons, subjected to the sons of Abel the noble family that invented the arts and diffused science. Enoch, a son of Cain, taught men to hew stones, construct edifices, and form civil societies. Irad and Mehujael, his son and grandson, set boundaries to the waters and fashioned cedars into beams. Methusael, another of his descendants, invented the sacred characters, the books of Tau and the symbolic T, by which the workers descended from the genii of fire recognized each other. Lamech, whose prophecies are inexplicable to the profane, was the father of Jabal, who first taught men how to dress camels' skins; of Jubal, who discovered the harp; of Naamah, who discovered the arts of spinning and weaving; of Tubal-Cain, who first constructed a furnace, worked in metals, and dug subterranean caves in the mountains to save his race during the deluge; but it perished nevertheless, and only Tubal-Cain and his son, the sole survivors of the glorious and gigantic family, came out alive. The wife of Ham, second son of Noah, thought the son of Tubal-Cain handsomer than the sons of men, and he became progenitor of Nimrod, who taught his brethren the art of hunting, and founded Babylon. Adoniram, the descendant of Tubal-Cain, seemed called by God to lead the militia of the free men, connecting the sons of fire with the sons of thought, progress, and truth.

192. *Hiram, Solomon, and the Queen of Sheba.*—By Hiram was erected a marvellous building, the Temple of Solomon. He raised the golden throne of Solomon, most beautifully wrought, and built many other glorious edifices. But, melancholy amidst all his greatness, he lived alone, understood and loved by few, hated by many, and among others by Solomon, envious of his genius and glory. Now the fame of the wisdom of Solomon spread to the remotest ends of the earth; and Balkis, the Queen of Sheba, came to Jerusalem, to greet the great king and behold the marvels of his reign. She found Solomon seated on a throne of gilt cedar wood, arrayed in cloth of gold, so that at first she seemed to behold a statue of gold with hands of ivory. Solomon received her with every kind of festive preparation, and led her to behold his palace and then the grand works of the temple; and the queen was lost in admiration. The king was captivated by her beauty, and in a short time offered her his hand, which the queen, pleased at having conquered this proud heart, accepted. But on again visiting the temple, she repeatedly desired to see the architect who had wrought such wondrous things. Solomon delayed as long as possible presenting Hiram Abiff to the queen, but at last he was obliged to do so. The mysterious artificer was brought before

her, and cast on the queen a look that penetrated her very heart. Having recovered her composure, she questioned and defended him against the illwill and rising jealousy of the king. When she wished to see the countless host of workmen that wrought at the temple, Solomon protested the impossibility of assembling them all at once; but Hiram, leaping on a stone to be better seen, with his right hand described in the air the symbolical Tau, and immediately the men hastened from all parts of the works into the presence of their master; at this the queen wondered greatly, and secretly repented of the promise she had given the king, for she felt herself in love with the mighty architect. Solomon set himself to destroy this affection, and to prepare his rival's humiliation and ruin. For this purpose, he employed three fellow-crafts, envious of Hiram, because he had refused to raise them to the degree of masters, on account of their want of knowledge and their idleness. They were Fanor, a Syrian and a mason; Amru, a Phœnician and a carpenter; and Metusael, a Hebrew and a miner. The black envy of these three projected that the casting of the brazen sea, which was to raise the glory of Hiram to its utmost height, should turn out a failure. A young workman, Benoni, discovered the plot and revealed it to Solomon, thinking that sufficient. The day for the casting arrived, and Balkis was present. The doors that restrained the molten metal were opened, and torrents of liquid fire poured into the vast mould wherein the brazen sea was to assume its form. But the burning mass ran over the edges of the mould, and flowed like lava over the adjacent places. The terrified crowd fled from the advancing stream of fire. Hiram, calm, like a god, endeavoured to arrest its advance with ponderous columns of water, but without success. The water and the fire mixed, and the struggle was terrible; the water rose in dense steam and fell down in the shape of fiery rain, spreading terror and death. The dishonoured artificer needed the sympathy of a faithful heart; he sought Benoni, but in vain; the proud youth perished in endeavouring to prevent the horrible catastrophe when he found that Solomon had done nothing to hinder it.

Hiram could not withdraw himself from the scene of his discomfiture. Oppressed with grief, he heeded not the danger, he remembered not that this ocean of fire might speedily engulph him; he thought of the Queen of Sheba, who came to admire and congratulate him on a great triumph, and who saw nothing but a terrible disaster. Suddenly he heard a strange voice coming from above, and crying, "Hiram, Hiram, Hiram!" He raised his eyes and beheld a gigantic human figure. The apparition continued: "Come, my son, be without fear, I have rendered thee incombustible; cast thyself into the flames." Hiram threw himself into the furnace, and where others would have found death, he tasted ineffable delights; nor could he, drawn by an irresistible force, leave it, and asked him that drew him into the abyss: "Whither do you take me?" "Into the centre of the earth, into the soul of the world, into the kingdom of great Cain, where liberty reigns with him. There the tyrannous envy of Adonai ceases; there can we, despising his anger, taste the fruit of the tree of knowledge; there is the home of thy fathers." "Who then am I, and who art thou?" "I am the father of thy fathers, I am the son of Lamech, I am Tubal-Cain."

Tubal-Cain introduced Hiram into the sanctuary of fire, where he expounded to him the weakness of Adonai and the base passions of that god, the enemy of his own creature whom he condemned to the inexorable law of death, to avenge the benefits the genii of fire had bestowed on him. Hiram was led into the presence of the author of his race, Cain. The angel of light that begat Cain was reflected in the beauty of this son of love, whose noble and generous mind roused the envy of Adonai. Cain related to Hiram his experiences, sufferings, and misfortunes, brought upon him by the implacable Adonai. Presently he heard the voice of him who was the offspring of Tubal-Cain and his sister Naamah: "A son shall be born unto thee whom thou shalt indeed not see, but whose numerous descendants shall perpetuate thy race, which, superior to that of Adam, shall acquire the empire of the world; for many centuries they shall consecrate their courage and genius to the service of the ever ungrateful race of Adam, but at last the best shall become the strongest, and restore on the earth the worship of fire. Thy sons, invincible in thy name, shall destroy the power of kings, the ministers of the Adonai's tyranny. Go, my son, the genii of fire are with thee!" Hiram was restored to the earth. Tubal-Cain before quitting him gave him the hammer with which he himself had wrought great things, and said to him: " Thanks to this hammer and the help of the genii of fire, thou shalt speedily accomplish the work left unfinished through man's stupidity and malignity." Hiram did not hesitate to test the wonderful efficacy of the precious instrument, and the dawn saw the great mass of bronze cast. The artist felt the most lively joy, the queen exulted. The people came running up, astounded at this secret power which in one night had repaired everything.

One day the queen, accompanied by her maids, went beyond Jerusalem, and there encountered Hiram, alone and thoughtful. The encounter was decisive, they mutually confessed their love. Had-Had, the bird who filled with the queen the office of messenger of the genii of fire, seeing Hiram in the air make the sign of the mystic T, flew around his head and settled on his wrist. At this Sarahil, the nurse of the queen, exclaimed : " The oracle is fulfilled. Had-Had recognizes the husband which the genii of fire destined for Balkis, whose love alone she dare accept!" They hesitated no longer, but mutually pledged their vows, and deliberated how Balkis could retract the promise given to the king. Hiram was to be the first to quit Jerusalem; the queen, impatient to rejoin him in Arabia, was to elude the vigilance of the king, which she accomplished by withdrawing from his finger, while he was overcome with wine, the ring wherewith she had plighted her troth to him. Solomon hinted to the fellow-crafts that the removal of his rival, who refused to give them the master's word, would be acceptable unto himself; so when the architect came into the temple he was assailed and slain by them. Before his death, however, he had time to throw the golden triangle which he wore round his neck, and on which was engraven the master's word, into a deep well. They wrapped up his body, carried it to a solitary hill and buried it, planting over the grave a sprig of acacia.

Hiram not having made his appearance for seven days, Solomon, against his inclination, but to satisfy the clamour of the people, was forced to have him searched for. The body was found by three masters, and they, suspecting that he had been slain by the three fellow-crafts for refusing them the master's word, determined nevertheless for greater security to change the word, and that the first word accidentally uttered on raising the body should thenceforth be the word. In the act of raising it, the skin came off the body, so that one of the masters exclaimed "*Macbenach!*" (the flesh is off the bones!) and this word became the sacred word of the master's degree. The three fellow-crafts were traced, but rather than fall into the hands of their pursuers, they committed suicide and their heads were brought to Solomon. The triangle not having been found on the body of Hiram it was sought for and at last discovered in the well into which the architect had cast it. The king caused it to be placed on a triangular altar erected in a secret vault, built under the most retired part of the temple. The triangle was further concealed by a cubical stone, on which had been inscribed the sacred law. The vault, the existence of which was only known to the twenty-seven elect, was then walled up.

II.

ORIGIN. TRADITIONS.

193.

THE *First Masons.*—All nations, all states, all corporations, to increase their power and deduce from above their *raison d'être*, attribute to themselves a very ancient origin. This wish must be all the stronger in a society altogether ideal and moral, living the life of principles, which needs rather to seem to be, not coeval with, but anterior and superior to all others. Hence the claim set up by Freemasonry of being, not contemporary with the creation of man, but with that of the world; because light was before man, and prepared for him a suitable habitation, and light is the scope and symbol of Freemasonry. Now in the Introduction (6, 7) I have stated that there was from the very first appearance of man on the earth a highly favoured and civilized race, possessing a full knowledge of the laws and properties of nature, and which knowledge was embodied in mystical figures and schemes, such as were deemed appropriate emblems for its preservation and propagation. These figures and schemes are preserved in Masonry, though their meaning is no longer understood by the fraternity. I shall endeavour in these pages as much as possible to teach masons the real truths hidden under the symbols and enigmatical forms, which without a key appear but as absurd and debasing rites and ceremonies. The aim of all the secret societies of which accounts have been as yet or will be given in this work, except of those which were purely political, was to preserve such knowledge as still survived, or to recover what had been lost. And since Freemasonry is, so to speak, the *resumé* of the teachings of all those societies, dogmas in accordance with one or more of those taught in the ancient mysteries and other associations are to be found in Masonry; hence also it is impossible to attribute its origin to one or other specific society preceding it. Freemasonry is—or rather ought to be—the compendium of all primitive and accumulated human knowledge.

194. *Periods of Freemasonry.*—Masonic writers generally divide the history of the Order into two periods, the first comprising the time from its assumed foundation to the beginning of the last century, during which the Order admitted only masons, *i.e. operative* masons and artificers in

some way connected with architecture. The second or present period, they denominate the period of *Speculative* Masonry, when the Order no longer chooses its members only amongst men engaged in the raising of material structures, but receives into its ranks all who are willing to assist in building a spiritual temple, the temple of universal harmony and knowledge. Yet persons not working masons had ere then been admitted, for the records of a Lodge at Warrington, as old as 1648, note the admission of Colonel Mainwaring and the great antiquary Ashmole. Charles I., Charles II., and James II. also were initiated. But from what has been said above, it follows that true Masonry always was *speculative*, and that to deduce its origin from the ancient Dionysiac or any other kindred college is sheer nonsense. The name "masonic" was adopted by the society on its reconstruction in the last century, because the brotherhood of builders who erected the magnificent cathedrals and other buildings that arose during the middle ages, had lodges, degrees, landmarks, secret signs, and passwords, such as the builders of the temple of Solomon are said to have made use of. The Freemasons have also frequently been said to be descended from the Knights Templars, and thus to have for their object to avenge the destruction of that Order, and so to be dangerous to Church and State; yet this assertion was repudiated as early as 1535 in the " Charter of Cologne," wherein the Masons call themselves the Brethren of St. John, because St. John the Baptist was the forerunner of the Light. According to the same document the name of Freemasons was first given to the Brethren chiefly in Flanders, because some of them had been instrumental in erecting in the province of Hainault hospitals for persons suffering from St. Vitus's dance. And though some etymologists pretend the name to be derived from *massa*, a club, with which the doorkeeper was armed to drive away uninitiated intruders, we can only grant this etymology on the principle enunciated by Voltaire, that in etymology vowels go for very little, and consonants for nothing at all.

195. *Freemasonry derived from many Sources.*— But considering that Freemasonry is a tree the roots of which spread through so many soils, it follows that traces thereof must be found in its fruit; that its language and ritual should retain much of the various sects and institutions it has passed through before arriving at their present state, and in Masonry we meet with Indian, Egyptian, Jewish, and Christian ideas, terms, and symbols.

III.

RITES AND CUSTOMS.

196.

LIST of Rites.—Anciently, that is, before the rise of modern Masonry at the beginning of the last century, there was but one rite, that of the " Ancient, Free and Accepted Masons," or blue or symbolic Masonry; but vanity, fancy or interest soon led to the introduction of many new rites or modifications of the three ancient degrees. The following are the names of the rites now practised in Europe and America :—

1. York Rite, or Craft Masonry, of which an account will be given (205).—In America it consists of seven degrees :—The first three as in this country; 4. Mark Master; 5. Past Master; 6. Most Excellent Master; 7. Holy Royal Arch. All these also obtain in this country; the Royal Arch, being the most important, will be treated of in full (211).

II. French or Modern Rite.—It consists of seven degrees:—The first three the same as in Craft Masonry; 4. Elect; 5. Scotch Master; 6. Knight of the East; 7. Rose Croix. They are all astronomical.

III. Ancient and Accepted Scotch Rite.—It was organized in its present form in France early in the last century, though it derives its title from the claim of its founders, that it was originally instituted in Scotland. It is, next to the York rite, the most widely diffused throughout the masonic world. The administrative power is vested in Supreme Grand Councils, and the rite consists of thirty-three degrees, of which the 30th, Grand Elect Knight of Kadosh, is the most interesting, and particulars of which will be given under a separate head (214).

IV. The Ancient and Primitive Rite of Masonry or Order of Memphis: Privileges, Principles, and Prerogatives.—The Ancient and Primitive Rite of Masonry works thirty-three degrees, divided into three sections, embracing modern, chivalric, and Egyptian Masonry, as the latter was worked on the continent last century. The first section teaches morality, symbols, and philosophical research; and contains the degrees to Rose Croix (11-18°). The second section teaches science, philosophy, and political myth, and developes the sympathetic senses; it contains the degrees of a senate of hermetic philosophers to grand inspector (18-33°). The third section contains the Egyptian degrees, and occupies itself with high philosophy and religious myth. The Order rewards merit by six decorations:—1st, The Grand Star of Sirius; 2nd, the Decoration of Alidee; 3rd, the Decoration of the Grand Commander of the third series; 4th, the Lybic Chain; 5th, the Decoration of Eleusis; 6th, the Star of Merit in bronze, for the reward of literary merit and presence of mind and bravery either in Masons or non-Masons. These orders of chivalry, and all other high degrees of Masonry, are specially authorized by the laws of the Grand Lodge of England in the "Articles of Union" of 1813. The Order recognizes the degrees of all other rites, when legitimately obtained, so that a brother who has the Rose Croix, Kadosh, or Grand Inspector, or any other degree analogous to this rite under any other authority, may visit and participate in the same degrees of ancient and primitive Masonry.

It admits brethren of every and all political and religious creeds, for by the American revision of 1865, the Hindoo, the Parsee, the Jew, the Trinitarian and Unitarian Christian, the Mahommedan, &c., may attend its sublime ceremonies and lectures without any sacrifice of principle or of private convction, the rite breathing only pure Masonry— charity, love, and mutual tolerance—whilst adoring the Sublime Architect of the Universe, inculcating the immortality of the soul, and endless happiness for the good brother.

It embraces a far more extensive ritual of workable degrees than any other rite, every one of its thirty-three degrees having its appropriate and elaborate ceremonial easily arranged for conferment, and its titles are purged of ridiculous pretensions.

Its government is strictly representative, as in our own political constitution. The 32° and 31° are the 1st, 2nd, 3rd, and 4th officers of the *Chapter, Senate,* and *Council,* and form the *Mystic Temple* and *Judicial Tribunal,* the presiding officer, or Grand Master of Light, having the thirty-third degree to enable him to represent the province in the Sov. Sanc. (33-95°) or ruling body.

The Order relies more fully upon masonic worth, ability, and learning, than social standing and mere monetary qualifications, and seeks to extend masonic knowledge, justice, and morality. It levies only a small capitation fee upon each member admitted, to be hereafter devoted to charity and good works.

It admits Master Masons only in good standing under some constitutional Grand Lodge, and prohibits all interference with Craft Masonry, upon which its own thirty ceremonies form, and are intended to constitute, the most valuable and learned system of lectures extant; cultivating charity, tolerance, and brotherly love in the Masonic Order, and entering into no entangling alliances which too often prove their destruction.

Its watchword—Defence, not Defiance—maintaining the individual right of any brother to join any outside organization of Masonry suited to his religious or political opinions, and protesting against all interference of sectarian organizations.

v. Philosophic Scotch rite.

vi. Primitive Scotch rite, practised in Belgium.

vii. Ancient Reformed rite.

viii. Fessler's rite.

ix. Rite of the Grand Lodge of the Three Globes at Berlin.

x. Rite of Perfection.

xi. Rite of Misraim (223).

xii. Rite of the Order of the Temple.

xiii. Swedish rite.

xiv. Reformed rite.

xv. Schroeder's rite.

xvi. Rite of Swedenborg (*see* Book ix.).

xvii. Rite of Zinnendorf. Count Zinnendorf, physician of the emperor Charles VI., invented this rite, which was a modification of the Illuminism of Avignon, adding to it the mysteries of Swedenborg. His system consisted of seven degrees, divided into three sections: 1. Blue Masonry; 2. Red Masonry; 3. Capitular Masonry. The rite was never introduced into this country.

197. *Masonic Customs.*—Some masonic peculiarities may conveniently be mentioned here. Free-

masons frequently attend in great state at the laying of the foundation stones of public buildings; they follow a master to the grave, clothed with all the paraphernalia of their respective degrees; they date from the year of light. The Knights of the Sun, the 28th degree of the Scotch rite, acknowledge no era, but always write their date with seven noughts, 0,000,000. No one can be admitted into the masonic order before the age of 21, but an exception is made in this country and in France in favour of the sons of Masons, who may be initiated at the age of eighteen. Such a person is called a *Lewis* in England, and a *Louveteau* in France. This latter word signifies a young wolf; and the reader will remember that in the mysteries of Isis the candidate was made to wear the mask of a wolf's head. Hence a wolf and a candidate in these mysteries were synonymous. Macrobius, in his " Saturnalia," says that the ancients perceived a relationship between the sun, the great symbol of those mysteries, and a wolf; for as the flocks of sheep and cattle disperse at the sight of the wolf, so the flocks of stars disappear at the approach of the sun's light. And in Greek λύκος means both the sun and a wolf. There is a family of fellow-crafts that still derive their name from this idea. The adoption of the *louveteau* into the lodge takes place with a ceremony resembling that of baptism. The temple is covered with flowers, incense is burnt, and the godfather is enjoined not only to provide for the bodily wants of the new-born member, but also to bring him up in the school of truth and justice. The child receives a new name, generally that of a virtue, such as Veracity, Devotion, Beneficence; the godfather pronounces for him the oath of apprentice, in which degree he is received into the Order, which, in case he should become an orphan, supports and establishes him in life.

198. *Masonic Alphabet.*—The masonic alphabet preserves the angular character of primitive alphabets. Thirteen characters (9 + 4) compose the masonic system of writing. Hence all the sounds can only be represented by means of points, in the following manner:—

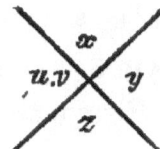

a.b	c.d	e.f
g.h	i.l	m.n
o.p	q.r	s.t

The letter *a* is written ⌐ ; the same sign with a dot in it, ⌐. , means *b*. The sign > means *u*, and with a dot >. , *v*. Masonic $_u^r$ abbreviations are always indicated by three dots, placed triangularly; thus, brother is abbreviated B ∴ . Lodge is written L ∴ or ▣∴ ; in the plural LL ∴ or ⌸∴ . Our common alphabet has an equally simple

Rites and Customs. 259

origin, as well as the Arabic numerals; they are all contained in the figure—

A, ᏏorᏴ, Ꮯ, dorᏞ, E, F, Ꮐ, H, I,
Ꮖ, K, L, M, N, Ꮜ, P, Ꮍ, R, Ꮞ, T,
U, V, X, Y, Z, Ꮜ, I, Ꮓ, Ꮤ, Ꮥ,
Ꮷ, ⁊, Ꮞ, Ꮍ.

IV.

THE LODGE.

199.

INTERIOR *Arrangement of Lodge.*—The arrangement of the lodge varies and will vary according to periods and degrees, but certain general rules are always followed in its construction. In an ancient French catechism the lodge is thus described: The lodge must have a vaulted ceiling, painted blue and covered with golden stars, to represent the heavens. The floor is called a mosaic floor; the term "mosaic" being derived from Moses; *i.e.* "drawn from the water," because by its variegated colours it represents the earth as covered with flowers again after the withdrawal of the waters of the Nile. There are three windows,—one east, one west, and a third south. There must also be two or three antechambers, so that the profane may catch no glimpse of what is going on in the lodge; and if some stranger should nevertheless intrude, the master exclaims, "It rains!" and the lodge is *ipso facto* dissolved. The lodge should be always hung with black; the brethren take their places according to their rank; the grand master in the east, the master in the south, and the novices at the north. When an apprentice is made, the lodge is brightly illuminated. The grand master, seated in his place, wears on his neck, appended to a large ribbon, a small square and compasses; before him stands a table on which lie the Gospel of St. John and a small hammer. At his side are the two stewards, the first of whom wears a level and the second a plumb of gold or silver. The masters and fellow-crafts stand around with the apprentices, all wearing white aprons of lamb's skin, and each carrying a naked sword. On the floor are designed figures, representing the steps that led to Solomon's temple, and the two pillars Jachin and Boaz, but which in reality symbolize the summer and winter solstices, the pillars of Hercules, the two pillars of Seth. Above are seen the sun, moon, and a large star. In the midst of the floor is a coffin, in which lies a man apparently dead, with his face turned upward and covered with his white apron smeared with blood, one hand resting on his breast, and the other extended towards the knee. In the corners of the room are substances easily combustible, such as sulphur, to kindle a fire instantaneously. This apparatus is somewhat altered when a fellow-craft or a master is to be made.

200. *Modern Lodge.*—The modern lodge is a large square hall, always, if possible, situated due east and west. Upon a dais ascended by three steps, opposite to the door of ingress, is seated the worshipful master; the altar is placed in the centre on four steps. A sky-blue canopy, dotted with stars, and having above it the shining triangle with the sacred name inscribed therein, covers the throne. To the left of the canopy is seen the sun, and to the right the moon. Another ornament is the blazing star, and the point within a circle, symbolizing the sun or the universe. A chest or ark also forms part of the masonic furniture. It represents the ark that was carried in the processions of ancient Egypt, and contained seeds of various plants, a winnowing fan, and *Osiridis pudendum*. To the west, at the sides of the door of ingress, stand two pillars of bronze, whose capitals represent pomegranates, and bearing on their fronts the initials J. and B. (Jachin and Boaz). The senior and junior wardens sit near the two columns, having before them a triangular table, covered with masonic emblems. Around the lodge there are ten other pillars connected by an architrave with the two pillars above mentioned. On the altar are placed a Bible, a square, a pair of compasses, and swords; three candelabra with long tapers are placed, one at the east at the foot of the steps, the second at the west, near the first warden, and the third at the south. The room is surrounded with benches for the members. In the lodges called Scotch, and in English and American lodges, the canopy that covers the master's throne is of crimson silk. In the United States, the worshipful master wears a cap adorned with black feathers and a large cockade of the same colour. The senior and junior wardens are seated in niches with fringed drapery, and wear, like heralds, staves of ebony sculptured like pillars.

201. *Officers.*—Besides the master and the wardens, who are figuratively called the *three lights*, the lodge has other officers—the orator, secretary, treasurer, master of the ceremonies, keeper of the seals, architect, steward, captain of the host, principal sojourner, inner and outer guard or tyler, and others. Every official occupies a place assigned to him, and has his proper jewels and badges, like the Egyptian, Hebrew, and Greek priests. Thus beside the jewels already mentioned, the treasurer wears cross keys; the secretary, cross pens; the senior deacon, a square and compass, with a sun in the centre; the junior deacon, a square and compass, with a moon in the centre; the steward, a cornucopia; the tyler, cross swords, &c. The names of most of the officers sufficiently indicate their duties; those that do not will be explained as they occur.

202. *Opening the Lodge.*—The meetings are generally held at night. The worshipful master, striking the altar with his mallet, " opens the

labours," and after having ascertained that the lodge is tyled, he turns to the junior warden and says: "Brother junior warden, your constant place in the lodge?" "In the south." "Why are you placed there?" "To mark the sun at its meridian, to call the brethren from labour to refreshment, and from refreshment to labour, that profit and pleasure may be the result." "Brother senior warden, your constant place in the lodge?" "In the west." "Why are you placed there?" "To mark the setting sun; to close the lodge by the command of the worshipful master, after seeing that every one has his just dues." "Why is the master placed in the east?" "As the sun rises in the east to open and enliven the day, so the worshipful master is placed in the east to open and enlighten his lodge, to employ and instruct the brethren." "At what hour are masons accustomed to begin their labours?" "At mid-day." "What hour is it, brother junior warden?" "It is mid-day." "Since this is the hour, and all is proved right and just, I declare the lodge open." The purely astronomical bearing of all this is self-evident, but will be more fully discussed hereafter.

V.

GENUINE AND SPURIOUS MASONRY.

203.

DISTINCTION *between Genuine and Spurious Masonry.*—Modern Freemasonry is divided into genuine and spurious. The former embraces the degrees of Entered Apprentice, Fellow-Craft, and Master Mason, which are known by the comprehensive name of Symbolic, and also of Blue Masonry, because the decorations are of that colour, which Blue Masonry is the only Masonry acknowledged by the Grand Lodge of England; the latter term is applied to all other degrees. Without the Royal Arch degree Blue Masonry is incomplete, for we have seen in the Legend of the Temple that, through the murder of Hiram, the master's word was lost; that word is not recovered in the master's degree, its substitute only being given; hence that lost word is recovered in the Royal Arch degree. Blue Masonry, in fact, answers to the lesser mysteries of the ancients, wherein in reality nothing but the exoteric doctrines were revealed; whilst spurious Masonry, or all subsequent degrees—for no one can be initiated into them who has not passed through the first three degrees—answers to the greater mysteries.

204. *Some Rites only deserve Special Mention.*—It would be an useless and unprofitable task to fully detail all the ceremonies practised in the lodges of Blue Masonry; and I shall, therefore, confine myself to giving such particulars of the three degrees as are most characteristic of the institution. As to spurious Masonry, its almost countless degrees form an incoherent medley of opposite principles, founded chiefly on Christian traditions and institutions, orders of knighthood, contested theological opinions, historical events; in fact, every important event or institution has afforded models for masonic mimicry. Of such as have been distinguished either by a philosophical spirit or influential action on the progress of mankind I shall speak at some length. The reader will, however, bear in mind that the ceremonies vary in different lodges and different countries, and that much that follows must be taken as typical, being modified according to local and other conditions and circumstances.

VI.

CEREMONIES OF INITIATION.

THE APPRENTICE, FELLOW-CRAFT, AND MASTER MASON.

205.

CEREMONIES *of Initiation. The Apprentice.*—The novice that is to be initiated into the first or apprentice degree is led into the lodge building by a stranger, and introduced into a remote chamber, where he is left alone for a few minutes. He is then deprived of all metal he has about him; his right knee, and sometimes his left side, are uncovered, and the heel of his left shoe is trodden down. His eyes are bandaged, and he is led into the closet of reflection, where he is told to stay without taking off the bandage, until he hears three knocks. At the signal, on uncovering his eyes he beholds on the walls hung with black inscriptions like the following:—" If idle curiosity draw thee hither, depart !" " If thou be afraid of being enlightened concerning thy errors, it profits thee not to stay here." " If thou value human distinctions, go hence ; here they are not known." After a deal of palaver between the brother who introduces the novice and the master, the candidate, having his eyes again bandaged and a cord passed round his neck, is introduced into the middle of the brethren, his guide pointing a naked sword to his breast. He is then questioned as to his object in coming hither, and on answering that he comes to be initiated into the secrets of Masonry, he is led out of the lodge and back again to confuse him. A large square frame covered with paper, such as circus-riders use, is then brought forward and held by two brethren. The guide then asks the master : " What shall we do with the profane ?" To which the master replies : " Shut him up in the cave." Two brethren seize the postulant and throw him through the paper-screen into the arms of two other brethren who stand ready to receive him. The folding doors, hitherto left open, are then shut with great noise, and by means of an iron ring and bar the closing with massive locks is imitated, so that the candidate fancies himself shut up in a dungeon. Some time then elapses in sepulchral silence. All at once the master strikes a smart blow, and orders the candidate to be placed beside the junior warden, and to be made to kneel. The master then addresses several questions to him, and instructs him on his duties towards the Order.

The candidate is then offered a beverage, with the intimation that if any treason lurks in his heart, the drink will turn to poison. The cup containing it has two compartments, the one holding sweet, the other bitter water; the candidate is then taught to say: "I bind myself to the strict and rigorous observance of the duties prescribed to Freemasons; and if ever I violate my oath"—(here his guide puts the sweet water to his lips, and having drunk some, the candidate continues)—"I consent that the sweetness of this drink be turned into bitterness, and that its salutary effect become for me that of a subtle poison." The candidate is then made to drink of the bitter water, whereupon the master exclaims: "What do I see? What means the sudden alteration of your features? Perhaps your conscience belies your words? Has the sweet drink already turned bitter? Away with the profane! This oath is only a test; the true one comes after." The candidate persisting nevertheless in his determination, he is led three times round the lodge; then he is dragged over broken chairs, stools, and blocks of wood; this trial over, he is told to mount the "endless stairs," and having, as he supposes, attained a great height, to cast himself down, when he only falls a few feet. This trial is accompanied by great noise, the brethren striking on the attributes of the order they carry in their hands, and uttering all kinds of dismal shouts. As a further trial, he is then passed through fire, rendered harmless by well-known conjuring tricks; his arm is slightly pricked, and a gurgling noise being produced by one of the brethren, the candidate fancies that he is losing much blood. Finally, he takes the oath, the brethren standing around him with drawn swords. The candidate is then led between the two pillars, and the brethren place their swords against his breast. The master of the ceremonies loosens the bandage without taking it off. Another brother holds before him a lamp that sheds a brilliant light. The master resumes: "Brother senior warden, deem you the candidate worthy of forming part of our society?" "Yes." "What do you ask for him?" "Light." "Then let there be light!" The master gives three blows with the mallet, and at the third the bandage is taken off, and the candidate beholds the light, which is to symbolize that which is to fill his understanding. The brethren drop their swords, and the candidate is led to the altar, where he kneels, whilst the master says: "In the name of the Grand Architect of the universe, and by virtue of the powers vested in me, I create and constitute thee masonic apprentice and member of this lodge." Then striking three blows with his mallet on the blade of the sword, he raises the new brother, girds him with the apron of white lamb's skin, gives him a pair of white gloves to be worn in the lodge, and another to be given to the lady he esteems best. He is then again led between the two pillars, and received by the brethren as one of them.

206. *Ceremonies of Initiation. The Fellow-Craft.*—The second degree of symbolic Freemasonry is that of fellow-craft. The apprentice, who asks for an increase of salary, is not conducted to the lodge like the profane by an unknown brother, nor are his eyes bandaged, because the light was made for him, but moves towards the lodge holding in his hand a rule, one of whose ends he rests on the left shoulder. Having reached the door, he gives the apprentice's knock, and having been admitted and declared the purpose for which he comes, he five times perambulates the lodge, whereupon he is told by the master to perform his last apprentice's work. He then pretends to square the rough ashlar. After a deal of instruction, very useless and pointless, he takes the oath, in which he swears to keep the secrets entrusted to him. Then there follows some more lecturing on the part of the master, chiefly on geometry, for which Masons profess a great regard, and to which the letter G seen in the lodge within an irradiation or star is said to refer.

207. *Ceremony of Initiation and Story of Hiram's Murder. The Master Mason.*—At the reception of a master, the lodge or "middle chamber" is draped with black, with death's heads, skele-

tons, and cross bones painted on the walls. A taper of yellow wax, placed in the east, and a dark lantern, formed of a skull having a light within, which shines forth through the eye-holes, placed on the altar of the most worshipful master, give just sufficient light to reveal a coffin, wherein the corpse is represented either by a lay-figure, a serving brother, or the brother last made a master. On the coffin is placed a sprig of acacia, at its head is a square, and at its foot, towards the east, an open compass. The masters are clothed in black, and wear large azure sashes, on which are represented masonic emblems, the sun, moon, and seven stars. The object of the meeting is said to be the finding of the word of the master that was slain. The postulant for admission is introduced after some preliminary ceremonies, having his two arms, breasts, and knees bare, and both heels slipshod. He is told that the brethren assembled are mourning the death of their grand master, and asked whether perhaps he was one of the murderers; at the same time he is shown the body or figure in the coffin. Having declared his innocence of any share in that crime, he is informed that he will on this occasion have to enact the part of Hiram (192), who was slain at the building of Solomon's temple, and whose history he is about to be told. The brother or figure in the coffin has in the meantime been removed, so that when the aspirant looks at it again, he finds it empty. The story of the murder of Hiram is then related. But the deed is not, as in the Legend of the Temple (192), attributed to Solomon's jealousy, but simply to Hiram's refusal to communicate the master's word to three fellow-crafts. The various incidents of the story are scenically enacted on the postulant. "Hiram," the master continues, "having entered the temple at noon, the three assassins placed themselves at the east, west, and south doors, and Hiram refusing to reveal the word, he who stood at the east door cut Hiram across the throat with a twenty-four-inch gauge. Hiram flew to the south door, where he received similar treatment, and thence to the west door, where he was struck on the head with a gavel, which occasioned his death." The applicant, at this part of the recital, is informed that he too must undergo trials, and is not to sink under the influence of terror, though the hand of death be upon him. He is then struck on the forehead and thrown down, and shams a dead man. The master continues: "The ruffians carried the body out at the west door, and buried it at the side of a hill"—here the postulant is placed in the coffin—"in a grave, on which they stuck a sprig of acacia to mark the spot. Hiram not making his appearance as usual, Solomon caused search to be made for him by twelve trusty fellow-crafts that were sent out, three east, three west, three south, and three north. Of the three who went east, one being weary, sat down on the brow of a hill, to rest himself, and in rising caught hold of a twig"—here a twig of that plant is put into the hand of the aspirant lying in the coffin —" which coming up easily, showed that the ground had been recently disturbed, and on digging he and his companions found the body of Hiram. It was in a mangled condition, having lain fourteen days, whereupon one of those present exclaimed *Macbenach!* which means 'the flesh is off the bones,' or 'the brother is smitten,' and became the master's word, as the former one was lost through Hiram's death; for though the other two masters, Solomon, and Hiram king of Tyre, knew it, it could only be communicated by the three grand masters conjointly. The covering of the grave being green moss and turf, other bystanders exclaimed, *Muscus domus, Dei gratia!* which according to Masonry is, "Thanks be unto God, our master has got a mossy house!" The exclamation shows that the Hebrew builders of Solomon's temple possessed a familiar knowledge of the Latin tongue! The body of Hiram could not be raised by the apprentice's or fellow-craft's grip, but only by the master's, or the lion's grip, as it is called. All this is then imitated by the master raising the aspirant in the coffin, who is then told the word, signs, and grips, and takes the oath.

208. *The Legend explained.*—Taken literally, the

story of Hiram would offer nothing so extraordinary as to deserve to be commemorated after three thousand years throughout the world by solemn rites and ceremonies. The death of an architect is not so important a matter as to have more honour paid to it than is shown to the memory of so many philosophers and learned men who have lost their lives in the cause of human progress. But history knows nothing of him. His name is only mentioned in the Bible, and it is simply said of him that he was a man of understanding and cunning in working in brass. Tradition is equally silent concerning him. He is remembered nowhere except in Freemasonry; the legend, in fact, is purely allegorical, and may bear a twofold interpretation, cosmological and astronomical.

Cosmologically, we find represented therein the dualism of the two antagonistic powers, which is the leading feature of all Eastern initiations. The dramatic portion of the mysteries of antiquity is always sustained by a deity or man who perishes as the victim of an evil power, and rises again into a more glorious existence. In the ancient mysteries, we constantly meet with the record of a sad event, a crime which plunges nations into strife and grief, succeeded by joy and exultation.

Astronomically, again, the parallel is perfect, and is in fact only another version of the legend of Osiris. Hiram represents Osiris, *i. e.*, the sun. The assassins place themselves at the west, south, and east doors, that is, the regions illuminated by the sun; they bury the body and mark the spot with a sprig of acacia. Twelve persons play an important part in the tragedy, viz. the three murderers (fellow-crafts), and nine masters. This number is a plain allusion to the twelve signs of the zodiac, and the three murderers are the three inferior signs of winter, *Libra*, *Scorpio*, and *Sagittarius*. Hiram is slain at the west door, the sun descends in the west. The acacia of Freemasonry is the plant found in all the ancient solar allegories, and symbolizing the new vegetation to be anticipated by the sun's resurrection. The acacia being looked upon by the ancients as incorruptible, its twigs were preferred for covering the body of the god-man to the myrtle, laurel, and other plants mentioned in the ancient mysteries. Hiram's body is in a state of decay, having lain fourteen days; the body of Osiris was cut into fourteen pieces (47). But according to other statements, the body was found on the seventh day; this would allude to the resurrection of the sun, which actually takes place in the seventh month after his passage through the inferior signs, that passage which is called his descent into hell. Hiram can only be raised by the lion's grip. It is through the instrumentality of Leo that Osiris is raised; it is when the sun re-enters that sign that he regains his former strength, that his restoration to life takes place. Masons in this degree call themselves the "children of the widow," the sun on descending into his tomb leaving nature —of which Masons consider themselves the pupils —a widow; but the appellation may also have its origin in the Manichæan sect, whose followers were known as the "sons of the widow" (103).

209. *The Raising of Osiris.*—A painting found on an Egyptian mummy, now in Paris, represents the death and resurrection of Osiris, and the beginning, progress, and end of the inundation of the Nile. The sign of the Lion is transformed into a couch, upon which Osiris is laid out as dead; under the couch are four canopi or jars of various capacities, indicating the state of the Nile at different periods. The first is terminated by the head of Sirius, or the Dog-Star, which gives warning of the approach of the overflow of the river; the second by the head of the Hawk, the symbol of the Etesian wind, which tends to swell the waters; the third by the head of a Heron, the sign of the south wind, which contributes to propel the water into the Mediterranean; and the fourth by that of the Virgin, which indicates that when the sun had passed that sign the inundation would have nearly subsided. To the above is superadded a large Anubis, who with an emphatic gesture, turning towards Isis, who has an empty throne on her head, intimates that the sun, by the aid of the Lion, had

cleared the difficult pass of the tropic of Cancer, and was now in the sign of the latter; and, although in a state of exhaustion, would soon be in a condition to proceed on his way to the south. The empty throne is indicative of its being vacated by the supposed death of Osiris. The reason why the hawk represents the north wind is, because about the summer solstice, when the wind blows from north to south, the bird flies with the wind towards the south. (Job xxxix. 26.) The heron signifies the south wind, because this bird, living on the worms hatched in the mud of the Nile, follows the course of the river down to the sea, just as the south wind does. To know the state of the Nile, and therefore their own personal prospects, the Egyptians watched the birds; hence among other nations, who did not know the principle by which the Egyptians went, arose divination by the flight of birds.[1]

210. *The Blazing Star.*—The representation of a

---

[1] Hamlet says, "I am but mad north-north-west; when the wind is southerly I know a hawk from a hand-saw." Thomas Capell, the editor of the Oxford edition of Shakespeare, changes "hand-saw" to "hernshaw," which renders the passage intelligible; for hernshaw is only another name for the heron; and Hamlet, though feigning madness, yet claims sufficient sanity to distinguish a hawk from a hernshaw, when the wind is southerly—that is, in the time of the migration of the latter to the north—and when the former is not to be seen.

blazing star found in every masonic lodge, and which Masons declare to signify prudence—though why a star should have such a meaning they would be at a loss to tell—is the star Sirius, the dog-star, mentioned above, the inundation of the Nile occurring when the sun was under the stars of the Lion. Near the stars of the Cancer, though pretty far from the band of the Zodiac towards the south, and a few weeks after their rising, the Egyptians saw in the morning one of the most brilliant stars in the whole heavens ascending the horizon. It appeared a little before the rising of the sun; they therefore pitched upon this star as the infallible sign of the sun's passing under the stars of Leo, and the beginning of the inundation. As it thus seemed to be on the watch and give warning, they called it "Barker," "Anubis," "Thot," all meaning the "dog." Its Hebrew name "Sihor" in Greek became "Seirios," and in Latin "Sirius." It taught the Egyptians the prudence of retiring into the higher grounds; and thus Masons, ignorant of the origin of the symbols, yet give it its original emblematic signification.

VII.

THE HOLY ROYAL ARCH.

211.

FFICERS.—The members of this degree are denominated "companions." There are nine officers, the chief of whom (in England) is Zerubbabel, a compound word, meaning "the bright lord, the sun." He rebuilds the temple, and therefore represents the sun risen again. The next officer is Jeshua, the high priest; the third, Haggai, the prophet. These three compose the grand council. Principals and senior and junior sojourners form the base; Ezra and Nehemiah, senior and junior scribes, one on each side; janitor or tyler without the door. The companions assembled make up the sides of the arch, representing the pillars Jachin and Boaz. In front of the principals stands an altar, inscribed with the names of Solomon, Hiram, King of Tyre, and Hiram Abiff.

210. *Ceremonies.*—On entering the chapter, the

companions give the sign of sorrow, in imitation of the ancients mourning for the loss of Osiris. Nine companions must be present at the opening of a royal arch chapter; not more nor less than three are permitted to take this degree at the same time, the two numbers making up the twelve, the number of zodiacal signs. The candidates are prepared by tying a bandage over their eyes, and coiling a rope seven times round the body of each, which unites them together, with three feet of slack rope between them. They then pass under the living arch, which is made by the companions either joining their hands and holding them up, or by holding their rods or swords so as to resemble a gothic arch. This part of the ceremony used to be attended in some lodges with a deal of tomfoolery and rough horse-play. The companions would drop down on the candidates, who were obliged to support themselves on their hands and knees; and if they went too slowly, it was not unusual for one or more of the companions to apply a sharp point to their bodies to urge them on. Trials, such as the candidates for initiation into the ancient mysteries had to go through, were also imitated in the royal arch. But few if any lodges now practise these tricks, fit only for Christmas pantomimes. The candidates, after taking the oath, declare that they come in order to assist at the rebuilding of Solomon's temple, whereupon they are furnished with pickaxes, shovels, and crowbars, and retire. After a while, during which they are supposed to have been at work and to have made a discovery, they return, and state that on digging for the new foundation they discovered an underground vault, into which one of them was let down, and found a scroll, which on examination turns out to be the long-lost book of the law. They set to work again, and discover another vault, and under that a third. The sun having now gained his meridian height, darts his rays to the centre, and shines on a white marble pedestal, on which is a plate of gold. On this plate is a double triangle, and within the triangles some words they cannot understand; they therefore take the plate to Zerubbabel. There the whole mystery of Masonry—as far as known to Masons—is unveiled; what the Masons had long been in search of is found, for the mysterious writing in a triangular form is the long lost sacred word of the Master Mason which Solomon and King Hiram deposited there, as we have seen in the master's degree (207). This word is the *logos* of Plato and St. John, the omnific word; but another compound name, intended to bear the same import, is substituted by modern Masons. It is communicated to the candidates in this way:—The three principals and each three companions form the triangles, and each of the three takes his left-hand companion by the right-hand wrist, and his right-hand companion by the left-hand wrist, forming two distinct triangles with the hands, and a triangle with their right feet, amounting to a triple triangle, and then pronounce the following words, each taking a line in turn :—

> As we three did agree,
> In peace, love, and unity,
> The sacred word to keep,
> So we three do agree,
> In peace, love, and unity,
> The sacred word to search,
> Until we three,
> Or three such as we, shall agree
> This royal arch chapter to close.

The right hands, still joined as a triangle, are raised as high as possible, and the word given at low breath in syllables, so that each companion has to pronounce the whole word. It is not permitted to utter this omnific word above the breath; like the name "Jehovah" or "Oum," it would shake heaven and earth if pronounced aloud. Zerubbabel next makes the new companions acquainted with the five signs used in this degree, and invests them with the badges of Royal Arch Masonry—the apron, sash, and jewel. The character on the apron is the triple Tau, one of the most ancient of emblems, and Masons call it the emblem of emblems, "with a depth that reaches to the creation of the world and all that is therein." This triple Tau is a compound figure of three T's, called Tau in Greek. Now this Tau or T is the figure of the old Egyptian Nilometer, used to ascertain the height of the inundation. It was a pole crossed with one or more transverse pieces. As on the inundation depended the subsistence, the life of the inhabitants, the Nilometer became the symbol of life, health, and prosperity, and was thought to have the power of averting evil. It thence became an amulet, and in this manner was introduced among masonic symbols.

213. *Passing the Veils.*—In some chapters the ceremony called "passing the veils" is omitted, but to make the account of Royal Arch Masonry complete I append it here. The candidate is introduced blindfold, his knees bare, and his feet slipshod, with a cable-tow round his waist. The high-priest reads Exod. iii. 1-6, and 13, 14, and the candidate is informed that "I am that I am" is the pass-word from the first to the second veil. He is also shown a bush on fire. He is then led to the second veil, which, on giving the pass-word, he passes, and beholds the figure of a serpent and Aaron's rod. The high-priest reads Exod. iv. 1-5, and the candidate is told to pick up the rod cast down before him, that the act is the sign of passing the second veil, and that the pass-words are "Moses, Aaron, and Eleazar." He then passes the guard of the third veil. The high-priest reads Exod. iv. 6-9, and the candidate is informed that the leprous hand and the pouring out of the water are the signs of the third veil, and that "Holiness to the Lord" are the pass-words to the sanctum sanctorum. He is shown the ark of the covenant, the table of shew-bread, the burning incense, and the candlestick with seven branches. Then follow

long lectures to explain the words and symbols, but their puerility may be inferred from the following specimen:—" This triangle is also an emblem of geometry. And here we find the most perfect emblem of the science of agriculture; not a partial one like the Basilidean, calculated for one particular clime, but universal; pointed out by a pair of compasses issuing from the centre of the sun, and suspending a globe denoting the earth, and thereby representing the influence of that luminary over the creation, admonishing us to be careful to perform every operation in its proper season, that we lose not the fruits of our labour." What a farmer would say to, or what profit he could derive from, this " universal science of agriculture," or whether he needs the " admonishing" symbol, I am at a loss to imagine. The triple Tau, according to the lecture, means *templum Hierosolymæ*, also *clavis ad thesaurum, res ipsa pretiosa*, and several other things equally *true*. "But," continues the lecturer, " these are all symbolical definitions of the symbol, which is to be simply solved into an emblem of science in the human mind, and is the most ancient symbol of that kind, the prototype of the cross, and the first object in every religion or human system of worship. This is the grand secret of Masonry, which passes by symbols from superstition to science." How far all this is from the true meaning of the cross and triple Tau may be seen by reference to (49).

VIII.

GRAND ELECT KNIGHT OF KADOSH.

214.

The Term Kadosh.—This degree, the thirtieth of the ancient and accepted Scotch rite, contains a beautiful astronomical allegory, and is probably derived from Egypt. The term *Kadosh* means "holy" or "elect." (Every person in the East, preferred to a post of honour, carried a staff, to indicate that he was *Kadosh*, or elect, or that his person was sacred; whence eventually the name came to be applied to the staff itself, and hence the derivation of *caduceus*, the staff of Mercury, the messenger of the gods.)

215. *Reception into the Degree.*—There are four apartments; the initiation takes place in the fourth. They symbolize the seasons. The first apartment is hung with black, lit up by a solitary lamp of triangular form and suspended to the vaulted ceiling. It communicates with a kind of cave or closet

of reflection, containing symbols of destruction and death. The candidate, after having been left there some time, passes into the second apartment, which is draped with white; two altars occupy the centre; on one is an urn filled with burning spirits of wine, on the other a brazier with live coal and incense beside it. The candidate now faces the sacrificing priest, who addresses some words of admonition to him, and having burnt some incense, directs him to the third apartment. It is hung with blue, and the vaulted ceiling covered with stars. Three yellow tapers light up this room. This is the areopagus. The candidate, having here given the requisite explanation as to the sincerity of his intentions and promises of secrecy, is introduced into the fourth apartment, hung with red. At the east is a throne surmounted by a double eagle, crowned, with outspread wings and holding a sword in his claw. In this room, lighted up with twelve yellow tapers, the chapter takes the title of "senate;" the brethren are called "knights." In this room also stands the mysterious ladder.

216. *The Mysterious Ladder.*—It has seven steps, which symbolize the sun's progress through the seven signs of the zodiac from *Aries* to *Libra* both inclusive. This the candidate ascends, receiving at every step the explanation of its meaning from a hierophant, who remains invisible to the candidate, just as in the ancient mysteries the initiating priest

remained concealed, and as Pythagoras delivered his instructions from behind a veil. When the candidate has ascended the ladder, and is on the last step, the ladder is lowered and he passes over it, because he cannot retire the same way, as the sun does not retrograde. He then reads the words at the bottom of the ladder, *Ne plus ultra*. The last degree manufactured is always the *ne plus ultra*, till somebody concocts one still more sublime, which then is the *ne plus ultra*, till it is superseded by another. What sublimity masonic degrees will yet attain, and where they will stop, no one can tell.

217. *The Seven Steps.*—The name of the first step is *Isedakah*, which is defined "righteousness," alluding to the sun in the vernal equinox in the month of March, when the days and nights are equal all over the world, and the sun dispenses his favours equally to all.

The second step is *Shor-laban*, "white ox" figuratively. This is the only step the definition of which is literally true, which, as it might lead to a clue to the meaning of the mysterious ladder, is thus falsely denominated figurative. Taurus, the bull, is the second sign of the zodiac, into which the sun enters on the 21st April. His entry into this sign is marked by the setting of Orion, who in mythological language is said to be in love with the Pleiades; and by the rising of the latter.

The third step is called *Mathok,* "sweetness." The third sign is *Gemini,* into which the sun enters in the pleasant month of May. "Canst thou hinder the sweet influences of the Pleiades, or loose the bands of Orion?" (Job.) Now, the Pleiades were denominated by the Romans *Vergiliæ,* from their formerly rising when the spring commenced, and their sweet influences blessed the year by the beginning of spring.

The fourth step is *Emunah,* "truth in disguise." The fourth sign is *Cancer,* into which the sun enters in June. Egypt at this period is enveloped in clouds and dust, by which means the sun, which figuratively may be called truth, is obscured or disguised.

The fifth step is *Hamal saggi,* "great labour." The fifth sign is *Leo.* The great labour and difficulties to which the sun was supposed to be subject in passing this sign have already been alluded to (209).

The sixth step is *Sabbal,* "burden or patience." The sixth sign through which the sun passes is *Virgo,* marked by the total disappearance of the celestial Hydra, called the Hydra of Lerna, from whose head spring up the Great Dog and the Crab. Hercules destroys the Hydra of Lerna, but is annoyed by a sea-crab, which bites him in the foot. Whenever Hercules lopped off one of the monster's heads two others sprang up, so that his labour would have been endless, had he not ordered his companion Iolas to sear the blood with fire.

The seventh step is named *Gemunah, Binah, Jebunah,* "retribution, intelligence, prudence." The seventh sign is *Libra,* into which the sun enters at the commencement of autumn, indicated by the rising of the celestial Centaur, the same that treated Hercules with hospitality. This constellation is represented in the heavens with a flask full of wine and a thyrsus, ornamented with leaves and grapes, the symbols of the products of the seasons. The sun has now arrived at the autumnal equinox, bringing in his train the fruits of the earth; and recompense is made to the husbandman in proportion to his prudence and intelligence.

The ladder will remind the reader of the ladder of the Indian mysteries; of the ladder seen by Jacob in his dream; the pyramids with seven steps; and the seven caverns of various nations.

IX.

PRINCE OF ROSE-CROIX.

218.

DISTINCT from Rosicrucian, and has various Names.—This, the eighteenth degree of the ancient and accepted Scotch rite, is one of the most generally diffused of the higher degrees of Masonry. It is often confounded with the cabalistic and alchemistic sect of the Rosicrucians; but there is a great distinction between the two. The name is derived from the rose and the cross, and has no connection with alchemy; the import of the rose has been given in another place. The origin of the degree is involved in the greatest mystery, as already pointed out. The degree is known by various names, such as " Sovereign Princes of Rose-Croix," " Princes of Rose-Croix de Heroden," and sometimes " Knights of the Eagle and Pelican." It is considered the *ne plus ultra* of Masonry, which however is the case with several other degrees.

219. *Officers and Lodges.*—The presiding officer is called the " Ever Most Perfect Sovereign," and the two wardens are styled " Most Excellent and Perfect Brothers." The degree is conferred by a body called a " Chapter of the Sovereign Princes of Rose-Croix," and in three apartments, the first representing Mount Calvary, the second the site and scene of the Resurrection, and the third Hell. It will therefore be seen that it is a purely Christian degree, and therefore not genuine Masonry, but an attempt to christianize Freemasonry. The first apartment is hung with black, and lighted with thirty-three lights upon three candlesticks of eleven branches. Each light is enclosed in a small tin box, and issues its light through a hole of an inch diameter. These lights denote the age of Christ. In three angles of the room, north-east, south-east, and south-west, are three pillars of the height of a man, on the several chapiters of which are inscribed the names of Faith, Hope, and Charity. Every lodge has its picture descriptive of its form, and of the proper place of its officers and emblems. On the east, at the south and north angles, the sun and moon and a sky studded with stars are painted; the clouds very dark. An eagle is seen beating the air with his wings, as an emblem of the supreme power. Besides other allegorical paintings, there is also one of a cubic stone, sweating blood and water. On the stone is a rose, and the letter J,

which means the expiring Word. The space round the picture, representing the square of the lodge, is filled with darkness, to represent what happened at the crucifixion. Below it are all the ancient tools of masonry, with the columns divided and broken into many parts. Lower down is the veil of the temple rent in twain. Before the master is a little table, lighted by three lights, upon which the Gospel, compasses, square, and triangle are placed. All the brethren are clothed in black, with a black scarf from the left shoulder to the right side. An apron, white, bordered with black; on the flap are a skull and cross-bones, between three red roses; on the apron is a globe surmounted by a serpent, and above the letter J. The master and the other officers wear on the neck a wide ribbon of black mohair, from which hangs the jewel, a golden compass, surmounted by a triple crown, with a cross between the legs, its centre being occupied by a full-blown rose; at the foot of the cross is a pelican feeding its young from its breast; on the other side is an eagle with wings displayed. The eagle is the emblem of the sun, the "sun of righteousness;" the pelican of course alludes to Christ shedding His blood for the human race; the cross and the rose explain themselves.

220. *Reception in the First Apartment.*—The candidate is clothed in black, decorated with a red ribbon, an apron doubled with the same colour, and

a sword and scarf. After much preliminary ceremony, he is introduced into the apartment, and told by the master that the word that is lost and which he seeks cannot be given, because confusion reigns among them, the veil of the temple is rent, darkness covers the earth, the tools are broken, &c.; but that he need not despair, as they will find out the new law, that thereby they may recover the word. He is then told to travel for thirty-three years. The junior warden thereupon conducts him thirty-three times round the lodge, pointing out to him the three columns, telling him their names, Faith, Hope, and Charity, and bidding him remember them, as henceforth they must be his guides. After a little more talk, he is made to kneel with his right knee upon the Gospel and take the following oath: " I promise by the same obligations I have taken in the former degrees of Masonry never to reveal the secrets of the Knight of the Eagle, under the penalty of being for ever deprived of the true word; that a river of blood and water shall issue continually from my body, and under the penalty of suffering anguish of soul, of being steeped in vinegar and gall, of having on my head the most piercing thorns, and of dying upon the cross; so help me the Grand Architect of the Universe." The candidate then receives the apron and sash, both symbols of sorrow for the loss of the word. A dialogue ensues, wherein the hope of finding the word is foreshadowed; whereupon the master and brethren proceed to the second apartment, where they exchange their black aprons and sashes to take red ones.

221. *Second Apartment.*—This apartment is hung with tapestry; three chandeliers, with thirty-three lights, but without the boxes, illuminate it. In the east there is a cross surrounded with a glory and a cloud; upon the cross is a rose of paradise, in the middle of which is the letter G. Below are three squares, in which are three circles, having three triangles, to form the summit, which is allegorical of Mount Calvary, upon which the Grand Architect of the Universe expired. Upon this summit is a blazing star with seven rays, and in the middle of it the letter G again. The eagle and pelican also re-appear here. Below is the tomb. In the lower part of the square are the compasses, drawing-board, crow, trowel, and square. The cubic stone, hammer, and other tools are also represented.

222. *Reception in the Third Apartment.*—But the second point of reception takes place in a third apartment, which is made as terrifying as possible, to represent the torments of hell. It has seven chandeliers with grey burning flambeaux, whose mouths represent death's heads and cross-bones. The walls are hung with tapestry, painted with flames and figures of the damned. The candidate,

on presenting himself as a searcher of the lost word, has his sash and apron taken from him, as not humble enough to qualify him for the task, and is covered with a black cloth strewn with dirty ashes, so that he can see nothing, and informed that he will be led to the darkest of places, from which the word must come forth triumphant to the glory and advantage of Masonry. In this condition he is led to a steep descent, up and down which he is directed to travel, after which he is conducted to the door, and has the black cloth removed. Before him stand three figures dressed as devils. He then parades the room three times, without pronouncing a word, in memory of the descent into the dark places, which lasted three days. He is then led to the door of the apartment, covered with black cloth, and told that the horrors through which he has passed are as nothing in comparison with those through which he has yet to pass; therefore he is cautioned to summon all his fortitude. But in reality all the terrible trials are over, for he is presently brought before the master, who asks: "Whence come you?" "From Judæa."—"Which way did you come?" "By Nazareth."—"Of what tribe are you descended?" "Judah."—"Give me the four initials?" "I.N.R.I." —"What do these letters signify?" "Jesus of Nazareth, King of the Jews."—"Brother, the word is found; let him be restored to light."

The junior warden quickly takes off the cloth, and at the signal of the master all the brethren clap their hands three times and give three huzzas. The candidate is then taught the signs, grips, and pass-word. The master then proceeds to the instruction of the newly made Knight of the Eagle or Prince Rose-Croix, which amounts to this, that after the erection of Solomon's temple masons began to neglect their labours, that then the cubical stone, the corner-stone, began to sweat blood and water, and was torn from the building and thrown among the ruins of the decaying temple, and the mystic rose sacrificed on a cross. Then masonry was destroyed, the earth covered with darkness, the tools of masonry broken. Then the blazing star disappeared, and the word was lost. But masons having learnt the three words, Faith, Hope, and Charity, and following the new law, masonry was restored, though masons no longer built material edifices, but occupied themselves in spiritual buildings. The mystic rose and blazing star were restored to their former beauty and splendour.

X.

THE RITES OF MISRAIM AND MEMPHIS.

223.

ANOMALIES of the Rite of Misraim.— Another of those diversities, which may be called the constant attendants of the life of vast associations, is the rite of "Misraim." What chiefly distinguishes it from other rites, and renders it totally different from masonic institutions, is the supreme power given to the heads, whose irremovability we have seen abolished, in order to open the lodges to the forms of genuine democracy. This rite is essentially autocratic. One man, with the title of "Absolute Sovereign Grand Master," rules the lodges, and is irresponsible — an extraordinary anomaly in the bosom of a liberal society to behold a member claiming that very absolute power against which Freemasonry has been fighting for centuries!

224. *Organization.*—The rite of Misraim was founded at a time when there was already a question of reducing the number of the Scotch rite of thirty-three degrees, practically reduced to five. Then arose the rite of Misraim with ninety degrees, arranged in four sections, viz. 1. Symbolic, 2. Philosophic, 3. Mystical, 4. Cabalistic; which were divided into seventeen classes. The rites are a medley of Scotch rites, Martinism, and Templarism, and the absolute grand masters arrogate to themselves the right of governing all masonic lodges throughout the world. The foundations of this system were laid at Milan in 1805, by several Masons who had been refused admission into the Supreme Grand Council. During the first year and for some time after postulants were only admitted as far as the eighty-seventh degree; the other three, complementing the system, embraced the *unknown* superiors. Thus masonic degrees often served as a mask for the most opposed individualities, and unconsciously favoured the views and schemes of astute diplomatists and ambitious princes.

225. *History and Constitution.*—From Milan the order spread into Dalmatia, the Ionian Islands, and the Neapolitan territory, where it produced a total reform in a chapter of Rosicrucians, the "Concordia," established in the Abruzzi. It was not till 1814 that the rite of Misraim was introduced

into France, where the pompous denominations of its endless hierarchy met with no slight success. Never had such titles been heard of in Masonry: Supreme Commander of the Stars, Sovereign of Sovereigns, Most High and Most Powerful Knight of the Rainbow, Sovereign Grand Prince Hiram, Sovereign Grand Princes, &c., these were some of the titles assumed by the members. The trials of initiation were long and difficult, and founded on what is recorded of the Egyptian and Eleusinian mysteries. In the first two sections the founders of the rite seem to have attempted to bring together all the creeds and practices of Scotch Masonry combined with the mysteries of Egypt; and in the last two sections all the chemical and cabalistic knowledge professed by the priests of that country, reserving for the last three degrees the supreme direction of the Order. Attempts were made to introduce it into Belgium, Sweden, and Switzerland, and also into Ireland, and latterly into England; but everywhere it is in a languishing condition. The Grand Orient of France has never recognized the rite as a part of Masonry, though it has three lodges in Paris.

226. *Rites and Ceremonies.*—The Order celebrates two equinoctial festivals, the one called "The Reawakening of Nature," and the other, "The Repose of Nature." In the sixty-ninth degree, designated as "Knight of Khanuka, called Hynaroth," particular

instructions are given as to man's relation to the Deity, and the cabalistic mediation of angels. In the ninetieth and last degree, the lodge is opened with the words "Peace to Men," and the wish that all men might become proselytes of reason and true light. In this rite, altogether modern, we meet with gnostic and cabalistic words and conceits —a phenomenon which were impossible did not gnostic ideas permeate all the veins of the masonic body.

227. *Rite of Memphis.*—It is a copy of the rite of Misraim, and was founded at Paris in 1839, and afterwards extended to Brussels and Marseilles. It was composed of ninety-one degrees, arranged in three sections and seven classes. A large volume printed at Paris, with the ambitious title of "The Sanctuary," gives an account of all the sections and their scope. The first section teaches morality and explains the symbols; the second instructs in physical science, the philosophy of history, and explains the poetical myths of antiquity, its scope being to promote the study of causes and origins. The third and last section exhausts the story of the Order, and is occupied with high philosophy, studying the religious myth at the different epochs of mankind.

XI.

MODERN KNIGHTS TEMPLARS.

228.

ORIGIN.—We read that several lords of the Court of Louis XIV., including the Duke de Gramont, the Marquis of Biran, and Count Tallard, formed a secret society, whose object was pleasure. The society increased. Louis XIV., having been made acquainted with its statutes, banished the members of the Order, whose denomination was, "A slight Resurrection of the Templars."

229. *Supposititious List of Grand Masters.*—In 1705, Philip Duke of Orleans collected the remaining members of the society that had renounced its first scope to cultivate politics. A Jesuit father, Bonanni, a learned rogue, fabricated the famous list of supposititious Grand Masters of the Temple since Molay, beginning with his immediate successor, Larmenius. No imposture was ever sus-

tained with greater sagacity. The document offered all the requisite characteristics of authenticity, and was calculated to deceive the most experienced palæologist. Its object was to connect the new institution with the ancient Templars. To render the deception more perfect, the volume containing the false list was filled with minutes of deliberations at fictitious meetings under false dates. Two members were even sent to Lisbon, to obtain if possible a document of legitimacy from the "Knights of Christ," an Order supposed to have been founded on the ruins of the Order of the Temple. But the deputies were unmasked and very badly received: one had to take refuge in England, the other was transported to Africa, where he died.

230. *Revival of the Order.*—But the society was not discouraged; it grew, and was probably the same that concealed itself before the outbreak of the revolution under the vulgar name of the Society of the Bull's Head, and whose members were dispersed in 1792. At that period the Duke of Cosse-Brissac was grand master. When on his way to Versailles with other prisoners, there to undergo their trial, he was massacred, and Ledru, his physician, obtained possession of the charter of Larmenius and the MS. statutes of 1705. These documents suggested to him the idea of reviving the order; Fabré-Palaprat, a Freemason, was chosen

grand master. Every effort was made to create a belief in the genuineness of the Order. The brothers Fabré, Arnal, and Leblond hunted up relics. The shops of antiquaries supplied the sword, mitre, and helmet of Molay, and the faithful were shown his bones withdrawn from the funeral pyre on which he had been burned. As in the middle ages, the society exacted that aspirants should be of noble birth; such as were not were ennobled by the society. Fourteen honest citizens of Troyes on one occasion received patents of nobility and convincing coats of arms.

231. *The Leviticon.* — The society was at first catholic, apostolic, Roman, and rejected Protestants; but Fabré suddenly gave it an opposite tendency. Having acquired a Greek MS. of the fifteenth century, containing the Gospel of St. John, with readings somewhat differing from the received version, preceded by a kind of introduction or commentary, called " Leviticon," he determined, towards 1815, to apply its doctrines to the society governed by him, and thus to transform an association, hitherto quite orthodox, into a schismatic sect. This Leviticon is nothing but the well-known work with the same title by the Greek monk, Nicephorus. He, having been initiated into the mysteries of the Sufites, who to this day, in the bosom of Mohamedanism preserve the dismal doctrines of the Ishmaelites of the lodge of Cairo (133), attempted

to introduce these ideas into Christianity, and for that purpose wrote the "Leviticon," which became the Bible of a small number of sectaries; but persecution put an end to them. This singular MS was translated into French in 1822, and printed, with modifications and interpolations, by Palaprat himself. This publication was the cause of a schism in the Order of the Temple. Those knights that adopted its doctrines made them the basis of a new liturgy, which they rendered public in 1833 in a kind of Johannite church; but people only laughed at it.

232. *Ceremonies of Initiation.*—The lodges in this degree are called encampments, and the officers take their names from those that managed the original institution of the Knights Templars. The penal signs are the chin and beard sign and the saw sign. The grand sign is indicative of the death of Christ on the cross. There is a word, a grip, and pass-words, which vary. The knights, who are always addressed as "Sir Knights," wear knightly costume, not omitting the sword. The candidate for installation is "got up" as a pilgrim, with sandals, mantle, staff, cross, scrip, and wallet, a belt or cord round his waist, and in some encampments a burden on his back, which is made to fall off at the sight of the cross. On his approach, an alarm is sounded with a trumpet, and after a deal of pseudo-military parley he is admitted, and a saw is applied

to his forehead by the second captain, whilst all the Sir Knights are under arms. The candidate, being prompted by the master of the ceremonies, declares that he is a weary pilgrim, prepared to devote his life to the service of the poor and sick, and to protect the holy sepulchre. After perambulating the encampment seven times he repeats the oath, having first put away the pilgrim's staff and cross and taken up a sword. In this oath he swears to defend the sepulchre of our Lord Jesus Christ against all Jews, Turks, infidels, heathens, and other opposers of the Gospel. "If ever I wilfully violate this my solemn compact," he continues, "as a Brother Knight Templar, may my skull be sawn asunder with a rough saw, my brains taken out and put in a charger to be consumed by the scorching sun, and my skull in another charger, in commemoration of St. John of Jerusalem, that first faithful soldier and martyr of our Lord and Saviour. Furthermore, may the soul that once inhabited this skull appear against me in the day of judgment. So help me God." A lighted taper is afterwards put into his hand, and he circumambulates the encampment five times "in solemn meditation;" and then kneeling down is dubbed knight by the grand commander, who says, "I hereby instal you a masonic knight hospitaller of St. John of Jerusalem, Palestine, Rhodes, and Malta, and also a Knight Templar." The grand commander next clothes him with the mantle, and invests him with the apron, sash, and jewel, and presents him with sword and shield. He then teaches him the so-called Mediterranean password and sign. The motto of the Knight Templar is, *In hoc signo vinces*. In some of the encampments the following is the concluding part of the ceremony:—One of the equerries dressed as a cook, with a white nightcap and apron and a large kitchen knife in his hand, suddenly rushes in, and, kneeling on one knee before the new Sir Knight, says, "Sir Knight, I admonish you to be just, honourable, and faithful to the Order, or I, the cook, will hack your spurs from off your heels with my kitchen knife." He then retires. Sometimes the spurs are hacked off by another personage, namely the Commissioner in Bankruptcy. Some few years ago an unfortunate encampment pitched in Bedford Row, London. Though the knights, no doubt, were very brave against Turks, infidels, and all that sort of gentry, they could not face their creditors, who thereupon compelled the Order to make its last stand in Basinghall Street—rather an inglorious end; but, as one of the counsel observed, the Sir Knights were probably all away in the Holy Land fighting for the recovery of the Holy Sepulchre, and so their affairs at home fell slightly into disorder.

XII.

FREEMASONRY IN ENGLAND AND SCOTLAND.

233.

FREEMASONRY *in England.*—The authentic history of Freemasonry, *i.e.* operative Masonry, in England dates from Athelstan, from whom his brother Edwin obtained a royal charter for the Masons, by which they were empowered to meet annually in a general assembly, and to have the right to regulate their own Order. And, according to this charter, the first Grand Lodge of England met at York in 926, when all the writings and records extant, in Greek, Latin, French, and other languages, were collected; and constitutions and charges in conformity with ancient usages, so far as they could be gathered therefrom, were drawn up and adopted. The Old York Masons were on that account held in especial respect, and Blue or genuine Masonry is still distinguished by the title of the York Rite.

After the decease of Edwin, Athelstan himself presided over the lodges; and after his death, the Masons in England were governed by Dunstan, Archbishop of Canterbury in 960, and Edward the Confessor in 1041. Down to the present time the grand masters have been persons of royal blood, sometimes the king himself. Till the beginning of the last century, as already stated (194), they were operative masons, and the monuments of their activity are still found all over the land in abbeys, monasteries, cathedrals, hospitals, and other buildings of note. There were, indeed, periods when the Order was persecuted by the state, but these were neither so frequent nor so long as in other countries.

234. *Freemasonry in Scotland.*—Tradition says that on the destruction of the Order of Templars, many of its members took refuge in Scotland, where they incorporated themselves with the Freemasons, under the protection of Robert Bruce, who established the chief seat of the order at Kilwinning. There is a degree of Prince of Rose-Croix de Heroden, or Hérédom, as it is called in French. This Heroden, says an old MS. of the ancient Scotch Rite, is a mountain situated in the north-west of Scotland, where the fugitive Knights Templars found a safe retreat; and the modern Order of Rose-Croix claims the kingdom of Scotland and Abbey of Kilwinning as having once been its chief seat of govern-

ment. By some writers, however, it is asserted that the word Hérédom is simply a corruption of the Latin expression *hæredium*, signifying "an heritage," and alludes to the castle of St. Germain, the residence of Charles Stuart the Pretender, to further whose restoration the Order of Rose-Croix was invented. The subject is in a state of inextricable confusion, but scarcely worth the trouble of elucidation. King Robert Bruce endeavoured, like other princes before and after him, to secure for himself the supreme direction of those associations, which, though not hostile to the reigning power, could by their organization become the *foci* of danger. It is the common opinion that this king reserved for himself and his successors the rank of grand master of the whole Order, and especially of the lodge of Hérédom, which was afterwards transferred to Edinburgh.

235. *Modern Freemasonry*.—At the beginning of the last century the operative period of Masonry may be said to have come to an end. In 1716, there being then only four lodges existing in London, a proposition was made and agreed to that the privilege of Masonry should no longer be restricted to operative masons—we have seen that it had ere then been broken through (194)—but should extend to men of various professions, provided they were regularly initiated into the Order. Thus began the present era of Masonry, retaining the original constitutions, the

ancient landmarks, symbols, and ceremonies. The society, proclaiming *brotherly love, relief,* and *truth* as their guiding principles, obtained a wider field for their operations, and more freedom in their mode of action. But to what does this action amount? To eating, drinking, and mummery. There is nothing in the history of modern Masonry, in this country at least, that deserves to be recorded. The petty squabbles between Lodges and Orders may help to fill masonic newspapers, but for the world at large they have no interest; and as to any useful knowledge to be propagated by Masons, that is pure delusion. Yet, considering that the Order reckons its members by hundreds of thousands, its pretensions and present condition and prospects merit some consideration; and it must be admitted that its charities are administered on a somewhat munificent scale. In that respect honour is due to the craft.

XIII.

FREEMASONRY IN FRANCE.

236.

INTRODUCTION *into France.*—Freemasonry was introduced into France, by the partisans of James and the Pretender, as a possible means of re-seating the Stuart family on the English throne. Not satisfied with turning masonic rites to unforeseen and illegitimate uses, new degrees were added to those already existing, such as those of "Irish Master," "Perfect Irish Master," and "Puissant Irish Master," and by promises of the revelation of great secrets and leading them to believe that Freemasons were the successors of the Knights Templars, the nobility of the kingdom were attracted towards the Order and liberally supported it with their means and influence. The first lodge established in France was that of Dunkirk (1721), under the title of "Friendship and Fraternity." The second, whose name has not been handed down, was founded in Paris in 1725 by Lord Derwentwater. Other followers of the Pretender established other lodges, of all which Lord Derwentwater was the grand master, until that nobleman lost his life for his devotion to the cause of the Stuarts.

237. *Chevalier Ramsay.*—The Chevalier Ramsay, also a devoted adherent of the house of Stuart, endeavoured more effectually to carry out the views of his predecessors, and in 1728 attempted in London to lay the basis of a masonic reform, according to which the masonic legend referred to the violent death of Charles I., while Cromwell and his partisans represented the assassins to be condemned in the lodge. He therefore proposed to the Grand Lodge of England to substitute in the place of the first three degrees those of Scotch Mason, Novice, and Knight of the Temple, which he pretended to be the only true and ancient ones, having their administrative centre in the Lodge of St. Andrew at Edinburgh. But the Grand Lodge at once rejected his views, whose objects it perceived. Ramsay went to Paris, where he met with great success. His system gave rise to those higher degrees which have since then been known by the name of the Ancient Scotch Rite. Many of these innovations made up for their want of consistency with masonic traditions by splendour of external decorations and gorgeousness of ceremonies. But the *hautes grades* of the

French, and the philosophic degrees of the Ancient Scotch Rite, are not innovations, but illustrations of pure symbolic Masonry.

238. *Philosophical Rites.* — Philosophy indeed began to insinuate itself into Masonry, simplifying the rites and purifying its doctrines. Among the philosophic degrees then introduced, that of the " Knights of the Sun" is noteworthy. Its declared scope was to advocate natural, in opposition to revealed, religion. There is but one light in the lodge, which shines from behind a globe of water, to represent the sun. It has some resemblance to the " Sublime Knight Elected." But on the other hand, by these innovations systems multiplied, and the Order served as a pretext and defence of institutions having no connection with Masonry. Cabala, magic, conjuration, divination, alchemy, and demonology, were taught in the lodges. These abuses led to the establishment of an administrative centre at Arras in 1747. Another was founded at Marseilles in 1751. Three years afterwards the Chevalier de Bonneville founded in Paris a chapter of the high degrees, with the title, afterwards become famous, of the " Chapter of Clermont," and lodged it in a sumptuous palace built by him in a suburb of Paris. The system adopted was to some extent that of Ramsay. Another chapter, in opposition to his, was founded in 1762, with the title of " Council of the Knights of the East." In 1766, the Baron

Tschudy founded the Order of the "Blazing Star," in which ideas derived from the Temple and the Jesuits were strangely intermingled.

239. *The Duke de Chartres.*—Freemasonry in France was not without influence on the Revolution. The Duke de Chartres having been elected grand master, all the lodges were united under the Grand Orient; hence the immense influence he afterwards wielded. The mode of his initiation is thus related :—Before becoming grand master he was received into the degree of Knight of Kadosh. Five brethren introduced him into a hall, representing a grotto strewn with human bones, and lighted up with sepulchral lamps. In one of the angles was a lay figure covered with royal insignia. The introducers bade him lie down on the ground like one dead, naming the degrees through which he had already passed, and repeating the former oaths. Afterwards, they extolled the degree into which he was about to be received. Having bidden him to rise, he was made to ascend a high ladder, and to throw himself from the top. Having then armed him with a dagger, they commanded him to strike the crowned figure, and a liquid, resembling blood, spurted from the wound over his hands and clothes. He was then told to cut off the head of the figure. Finally, he was informed that the bones with which the cave was strewn came from the body of James Molay, Grand Master of the Order of the Temple,

and that the man whom he had stabbed was Philip the Fair, King of France. The Grand Orient was established in a mansion formerly belonging to the Jesuits in Paris, and became a revolutionary centre. The share the Grand Orient, the tool of the Duke de Chartres, took in the events of the French Revolution is matter of history.

XIV.

THE CHAPTER OF CLERMONT AND THE STRICT OBSERVANCE.

240.

ESUITICAL *Influence.*—Catholic ceremonies, unknown in ancient Freemasonry, were introduced from 1735 to 1740, in the Chapter of Clermont, so called in honour of Louis of Bourbon, Prince of Clermont, at the time grand master of the Order in France. From that time, the influence of the Jesuits on the fraternity made itself more and more felt. The candidate was no longer received in a lodge, but in the city of Jerusalem; not the ideal Jerusalem, but a clerical Jerusalem, typifying Rome. The meetings were called *Capitula Canonicorum,* and a monkish language and asceticism prevailed therein. In the statutes is seen the hand of James Lainez, the second general of the Jesuits, and the aim at universal empire betrays itself, for at the

reception of the sublime knights the last two chapters of the Apocalypse are read to the candidate—a glowing picture of that universal monarchy which the Jesuits hoped to establish. The sect spread very rapidly, for when Baron Hunde came to Paris in 1742, and was received into the highest Jesuit degrees, he found on his return to Germany that those degrees were already established in Saxony and Thuringia, under the government of Marshall, whose labours he undertook to promote.

241. *The Strict Observance.*—From the exertions of these two men arose the "Rite of Strict Observance," which seemed also for a time intended to favour the tragic hopes of the House of Stuart; for Marshall, having visited Paris in 1741, there entered into close connection with Ramsay and the other adherents of the exiled family. To further this object, Hunde mixed up with the rites of Clermont what was known or supposed to be known of the statutes of the Templars, and acting in concert with Marshall, overran Germany with a sect of new Templars, not to be confounded with the Templars that afterwards joined the masonic fraternity. But Hunde seems after all to have rendered no real services to the Stuarts; though when Charles Edward visited Germany, the sectaries received him in the most gallant manner, promising him the most extensive support, and asking of him titles and estates in a kingdom which he had yet to conquer.

Thus he was brought to that state of mental intoxication which afterwards led him to make an absurd entry into Rome, preceded by heralds who proclaimed him king. Hunde seems, in the sad story of the Stuarts, to have acted the part of a speculator; and the rite of the Strict Observance, permeated by the Jesuitical leaven, had probably an aim very different from the re-establishment of the proscribed dynasty. It is certain that at one time the power of the New Templars was very great, and prepared the way for the Illuminati.

XV.

THE RELAXED OBSERVANCE.

242.

ORGANIZATION *of Relaxed Observance.*—In 1767, there arose at Vienna a schism of the Strict Observance; the dissentients, who called themselves "Clerks of the Relaxed Observance," declaring that they alone possessed the secrets of the association, and knew the place where were deposited the splendid treasures of the Templars. They also claimed precedence not only over the rite of Strict Observance, but also over all Masonry. Their promises and instructions revolved around the philosopher's stone, the government of spirits, and the millennium. To be initiated it was necessary to be a Roman Catholic, and to have passed through all the degrees of the Strict Observance. The members knew only their immediate heads; but Doctor Stark, of Königsberg, a famous preacher, and Baron Raven, of Mecklenburg, were well-known chiefs of the association.

243. *Disputes in German Lodges.*—Before the establishment of the Strict Observance various German lodges had already introduced the Templar system; hence disputes of all kinds arose, and a convention was held at Brunswick on May 22nd, 1775, to arrange the differences. Dr. Stark presented himself; he was a disciple of Schrœpfer and of Gugumos, who called himself high priest, knight, prince, possessor of the philosopher's stone, of the secret to evoke the spirits of the dead, &c. Stark declared to the members of the convention that he was called *Archimedes ab aquila fulva*, that he was chancellor of the Grand Chapter of Scotland, and had been invited by the brethren of that supreme body to instruct them in the true principles of the order. But when he was asked to produce his credentials, he refused. The Brunswickers, however, thinking that the brethren of Aberdeen might possess some secrets, sent a deputation thither; but the good folks of Aberdeen knew even less than their German friends, for they knew only the first three degrees. Stark, though found out, was not to be put down, but wrote a book, entitled "The Coping Stone," in which he represented the Strict Observance as hostile to religion, society, and the state.

244. *Rite of Zinnendorf.*—This was not the first

attack made on the system of Hunde. In 1766, Count Zinnendorf, chief physician in the Prussian army, who had been received into the Strict Observance, was struck from the list of members of the lodge of the Three Globes. In revenge, he founded at Berlin and Potsdam lodges on the Templar system, which, however, he soon abandoned, and composed a new rite, invented by himself, and consisting of seven degrees, which was protected by Frederick the Great. The new order made fierce and successful war both on the Strict and the Relaxed Observance.

245. *African Architects.*—About 1765, Brother Von Kopper instituted in Prussia, under the auspices of Frederick II., the order of "African Architects," who occupied themselves with historical researches, mixing up therewith masonry and chivalry. The order was divided into eleven degrees. They erected a vast building, which contained a large library, a museum of natural history, and a chemical laboratory. Until 1786, when it was dissolved, the society awarded every year a gold medal with fifty ducats to the author of the best memoir on the history of Masonry. This was one of the few rational masonic societies. The African Architects did not esteem decorations, aprons, collars, jewels, &c. In their assemblies they read essays, and communicated the results of their researches. At their simple and decorous banquets

instructive and scientific discourses were delivered. While their initiations were gratuitous, they gave liberal assistance to zealous but needy brethren. They published many important works on Freemasonry.

XVI.

THE CONGRESS OF WILHELMSBAD.

246.

VARIOUS Congresses.—To put an end to the numerous disputes raging among masonic bodies, various congresses were held. In 1778, a congress was convened at Lyons; it lasted a month, but was without result. In 1785, another was held at Paris, but the time was wasted in idle disputes with Cagliostro. The last and most important was that which assembled at Wilhelmsbad in 1782, under the presidency of the Duke of Brunswick, who was anxious to end the discord reigning among German Freemasons. It was attended by masons from Europe, America, and Asia. From an approximative estimate it appears that there were then upwards of three millions of masons in the different parts of the globe.

247. *Discussions at Wilhelmsbad.*—The statements contained in Dr. Stark's book, " The Coping

Stone" (241), concerning the influence of the Jesuits in the masonic body, formed one of the chief topics discussed. Some of the chiefs of the Strict Observance produced considerable confusion by being unable to give information concerning the secrets of the high degrees, which they had professed to know; or to render an account of large sums they had received on behalf of the order. The main point was to settle whether Masonry was to be considered as a continuation of the order of the Templars, and whether the secrets of the sect were to be sought for in the modern Templar degrees. After thirty sittings, the answer was in the negative; the chiefs of the Strict Observance were defeated, and the Duke of Brunswick suspended the order for three years, from which blow it never recovered. The Swedes professed to possess all the secrets; the Duke of Brunswick hastened to Upsala to learn them, but found that the Swedes knew no more than the Germans; whence new dissensions arose between the masons of the two nations.

248. *Result of Convention.*—The only result of the convention of Wilhelmsbad was the retention of the three symbolical degrees, with the addition of a new degree, that of the "Knight of Beneficence." The Duke of Brunswick represented the aristocratic element, and was thus opposed to Masonry, which in its spirit is democratic. The result of the congress strengthened the influence

of the duke; hence the opposition of Germany to the principles of the French Revolution, which broke out soon after—an opposition which was like discharging a rocket against a thunderbolt, but which was carried to its height by the manifesto of the Duke of Brunswick, so loudly praised by courtly historians, and of which the German princes made such good use as to induce the German confederacy to surround France with a fiery line of deluded patriotism. Freemasonry had been made the tool and fool of prince- and priest-craft.

XVII.

MASONRY AND NAPOLEONISM.

249.

Masonry protected by Napoleon.—With renewed court frivolities and military pomp, the theatrical spirit of Masonry revived. The institution, so active before and during the Revolution, because it was governed by men who rightly understood and worthily represented its principles, during the empire fell into academic puerilities, servile compliance, and endless squabbles. That period, which masonic writers, attached to the latter and pleased with its apparent splendour, call the most flourishing of French Masonry, in the eyes of independent judges appears as the least important and the least honourable for the masonic order. Napoleon at first intended to suppress Freemasonry, in which the dreaded *ideologists* might easily find a refuge. The representative system of the Grand Orient clashed with his monarchical principles, and the oligarchy of the Scotch rite aroused his suspicions. The Parisian lodges, however, practised in the art of flattery, prostrated themselves before the First Consul, prostrated themselves before the Emperor, and sued for grace. The suspicions of Napoleon were not dissipated; but he perceived the policy of avoiding violent measures, and of disciplining a body that might turn against him. After considerable hesitation, he declared in favour of the Grand Orient, and the Scotch rite had to assume the second place. A single word of Napoleon had done more to establish peace between them than all former machinations. The Grand Orient became a court office, and Masonry an army of *employés*. The Grand Mastership was offered to Joseph Napoleon, who accepted it, though never initiated into Freemasonry, with the consent of his brother, who, however, for greater security, insisted on having his trusty arch-chancellor Cambacérès appointed Grand Master Adjunct, to be in reality the only head of the order. Gradually all the rites existing in France gave in their adhesion to the imperial policy, electing Cambacérès as their chief dignitary, so that he eventually possessed more masonic titles than any other man before or after him. In 1805, he was made Grand Master Adjunct of the Grand Orient; in 1806, Sovereign Grand Master of the Supreme Grand Council; in the same year, Grand Master of the rite of Heroden of Kilwinning; in 1807, Supréme Head of the

French rite; in the same year, Grand Master of the Philosophic Scotch rite; in 1808, Grand Master of the order of Christ; in 1809, National Grand Master of the Knights of the Holy City; in the same year, Protector of the High Philosophic Degrees.

250. *Spread of Freemasonry.*—But masonic disputes soon again ran high. The arch-chancellor, accustomed and attached to the usages and pomps of courts, secretly gave the preference to the Scotch rite with its high-sounding titles and gorgeous ceremonies. The Grand Orient carried its complaints even to Napoleon, who grew weary of these paltry farces—he who planned grand dramas; and at one time he had determined on abolishing the order altogether, but Cambacérès succeeded in arresting his purpose, showing him the dangers that might ensue from its suppression—dangers which must have appeared great, since Napoleon, who never hesitated, hesitated then, and allowed another to alter his views. Perhaps he recognized the necessity in French society of a body of men who were free at least in appearance, of a kind of political safety-valve. The French had taken a liking to their lodges, where they found a phantom of independence, and might consider themselves on neutral ground, so that a masonic writer could say: "In the bosom of Masonry there circulates a little of that vital air so necessary to generous minds." The Scotch rite, secretly protected, spread through-

out the French departments and foreign countries, and whilst the Grand Orient tried to suppress it, and, to prevent innovations, elected a "Director of Rites," the Supreme Grand Council established itself at Milan, and elected Prince Eugene Grand Master of the Grand Orient of Italy. The two highest masonic authorities, which yet had the same master in Cambacérès, and the same patron in Napoleon, continued to combat each other with as much fury as was shown in the struggle between France and England. But having no public life, no parliamentary debates, no opposition journals, the greater part of the population took refuge in the lodges, and every small town had its own. In 1812, there existed one thousand and eighty-nine lodges, all depending on the Grand Orient; the army had sixty-nine, and the lodge was opened and closed with the cry, *Vive l'Empereur!*

251. *Obsequiousness of Freemasonry.*—Napoleon, unable and unwilling to suppress Freemasonry, employed it in the army, in the newly-occupied territories, and in such as he intended to occupy. Imperial proselytism turned the lodges into schools of Napoleonism. But one section of Masonry, under the shadow of that protection, became the very contrary, anti-Napoleonic; and not *all* the lodges closed their accustomed labours with the cry of *Vive l'Empereur!* It is, however, quite certain that Napoleon by means of the masonic society facili-

tated or secured his conquests. Spain, Germany, and Italy were covered with lodges—antechambers, more than any others, of prefectures and military command—presided over and governed by soldiers. The highest dignitaries of masonry at that period were marshals, knights of the Legion of Honour, nobles of ancient descent, senators, councillors, all safe and trusty persons; a state that obeyed the orders of Cambacérès, as he obeyed the orders of Napoleon. Obsequiousness came near to the ridiculous. The half-yearly words of command of the Grand Orient retrace the history of Napoleonic progress. In 1800, " Science and Peace;" in 1802, after Marengo, " Unity and Success;" in 1804, after the coronation, " Contentment and Greatness;" after the battle of Friedland, " Emperor and Confidence;" after the suppression of the tribune, " Fidelity;" at the birth of the King of Rome, " Posterity and Joy;" at the departure of the army of Russia, " Victory and Return."— Terrible victory and unfortunate return !

252. *Anti-Napoleonic Freemasonry.*—Napoleon, we have seen, made a league with Freemasonry, to obtain its support. He is also said to have made certain promises to it; but, as he failed to keep them, the masons turned against him, and had a large share in his fall. This, however, is not very probable, and is attributing too much influence to an order which had only recently recovered itself. Still

the anti-Napoleonic leaven fermented in the masonic society. Savary, the minister of police, was aware of it in 1810, and wanted to apply to the secret meetings of Freemasons the article of the penal code, forbidding them; but Cambacérès once more saved the institution, which saved neither him nor his patron. Freemasonry, if not by overt acts, at least by its indifference, helped on the downfall of Napoleon. But it was not altogether inactive, for even whilst the Napoleonic star illumined almost alone the political heavens of Europe, a masonic lodge was formed whose object was the restoration of the Bourbons, whose action may be proved by official documents to have extended through the French army, and led to the seditious movements of 1813.

XVIII.

FREEMASONRY, THE RESTORATION AND THE SECOND EMPIRE.

253.

THE *Society of " France Regenerated."*—The Restoration, whose blindness was only equalled by its mediocrity—which, unable to create, proposed to itself to destroy what even time respects, the memories and glories of a people—could not please Freemasonry much. Hostile to Napoleon in his last years, it could not approve of the conduct of the new government. At all events, the Freemasons held aloof, though cynics might suggest that this was done with a view of exacting better terms. In the meanwhile, a society was formed in Paris, which, assuming masonic forms and the title of "France Regenerated," became an instrument of espionage and revenge in the hands of the new despot. But the very government in whose favour it acted, found it necessary within a year from its foundation silently to suppress it; for it found the rabid zeal of these adherents to be more injurious to its interests than the open opposition of its avowed enemies.

254. *Priestly Opposition to Masonry.*—The masonic propaganda, however, was actively carried on. The priests, on their part, considered the moment come for inaugurating an anti-masonic crusade. Under Napoleon the priesthood could not breathe; the court was closed against it, except on grand occasions, when its presence was needed to add outward pomp to imperial successes. As the masters of ceremonies, the priests had ceased in France to be the councillors and confessors of its rulers; but now they re-assumed those functions, and the masons were at once recommended to the hatred of the king and the mistrust of the public. They were represented as abettors of rationalism and regicide; the consequence was, that a great many lodges were closed, though on the other hand the rite of Misraim was established in Paris in 1816, whose mother lodge was called the "Rainbow," a presage of serenity and calm, which, however, did not save the society from police persecution. In 1821, this lodge was closed, and not re-opened till 1830. Towards the same time was founded the lodge of "Trinosophists." In 1821, the Supreme Grand Council rose to the surface again, and with it the disputes between it and the Grand Orient. To enter into

their squabbles would be a sad waste of time, and I therefore pass them over.

255. *Political Insignificance of Masonry.*—The Freemasons are said to have brought about the July revolution of 1830, but proofs are wanting, and I think they may be absolved from that charge. Modern Freemasonry is a very tame affair; and, though very fond of being dressed up as knights, masons, as a rule, are mere carpet-knights. Louis-Philippe, who was placed on the throne by that revolution, took the order under his protection and appointed his son, the Duke of Orleans, Grand Master. On the duke's death, in 1842, his brother, the Duke de Nemours, succeeded him in the dignity. In this latter year, the disputes between the Grand Orient and the Supreme Grand Council were amicably settled. Again we are told that at a masonic congress held at Strasburg the foundations of the revolution of 1848 were laid. It is certain that Cavaignac, Lamartine, Ledru-Rollin, Prudhon, Louis Blanc, Marrast, Vilain, Pyat, and a great number of German republicans, attended that congress; but for this reason it cannot strictly be called a masonic, it was rather a republican, meeting. On the establishment of the Provisional Government after the revolution of 1848, the Freemasons gave in their adhesion to that government; on which occasion some high-flown speeches about liberty, equality, and fraternity were made, and everybody

congratulated his neighbour that now the reign of universal brotherhood had begun. But the restoration of the empire, which followed soon after, showed how idle all this oratory had been, and how the influence of Masonry in the great affairs of the world really is *nil*.

256. *Freemasonry and Napoleon III.*—Again the Napoleonic air waves around the Grand Orient. The nephew showed himself from the first as hostile to Freemasonry as his uncle had been; but the decree prohibiting the French lodges from occupying themselves with political questions, under pain of the dissolution of the order, did not appear until the 7th Sept., 1850. In January, 1852, some superior members of the order proposed to offer the dignity of Grand Master to Lucien Murat, the President's cousin. The proposal was unanimously agreed to; and on the 19th of the same month the new Grand Master was acknowledged by all the lodges. He held the office till 1861, when he was obliged to resign, in consequence of the masonic body having passed a vote of censure upon him for his expressions in favour of the temporal power of the pope, uttered in the stormy discussion of the French senate in the month of June of that year. The Grand Orient was again all in confusion. Napoleon III. now interfered, especially as Prince Napoleon was proposed for the office of Grand Master; which excited the jealousy of the Mu-

ratists, who published pamphlets of the most vituperative character against their adversaries, who on their side replied with corresponding bitterness. Napoleon imposed silence on the litigants, prohibited attendance at lodges, promised that he himself would appoint a Grand Master, and advised his cousin to undertake a long voyage to the United States. Deprived of the right of electing its own chief, the autonomy of Freemasonry became an illusion, its programme useless, and its mystery a farce. In the meanwhile, the quarrels of the partizans of the different candidates calmed down; Prince Napoleon returned from America; Murat resigned himself to this defeat, as to others, and the emperor forgot all about Freemasonry. At last, in January, 1862, there appeared a decree, appointing Marshal Magnan to be Grand Master. A Marshal! The nephew, in this instance, as in many others, had taken a leaf out of his uncle's book.

257. *Jesuitical Manœuvres.*—Napoleonic Freemasonry, not entirely to lose its peculiar physiognomy, ventured to change its institutions. Jesuitism cast loving eyes on it, and drew it towards itself, as in the days of the Strict Observance. Murat threw out his net, but was removed just when it was most important for the interest of the Jesuits that he should have remained. He proposed to transform the French lodges—of which in 1852 there were 325, whilst in 1861, only 269 could be found—

into societies of mutual succour, and to abandon or submit the higher masonic sphere of morality and humanity to the society, which in these last sixty years has already overcome and incorporated the whole Roman clergy, once its rivals, and by oblique paths also many of the conservative sects of other creeds. Murat did not succeed, but others may; and though the masons say that Jesuitism shall not succeed, yet, how is Freemasonry, that professes to meddle neither with politics nor religion, to counteract the political and religious machinations of the Jesuits? And even if Freemasonry had the same weapons, are there men among the order able to wield them with the ability and fearlessness that distinguish the followers of Loyola? I fear not.

XIX.

FREEMASONRY IN ITALY.

258.

WHIMSICAL Masonic Societies.—We have but few notices of the early state of Freemasonry in Italy. We are told that in 1512 there was founded at Florence a Society under the name of "The Trowel," composed of learned and literary men, who indulged in all kinds of whimsical freaks, and who may have served as prototypes to the order of "The Monks of the Screw," established towards the end of the last century in Ireland. Thus at one time they would meet in the lodge, dressed as masons and labourers, and begin to erect an edifice with trays full of macaroni and cheese, using spices and bonbons for mortar, and rolls and cakes for stones, and building up the whole with all kinds of comestibles. And thus they went on, until a pretended rain put an end to their labours. At another time it was Ceres, who, in search of Proserpine, invited the Brethren of the Trowel to accompany her to the infernal regions. They followed her through the mouth of a serpent into a dark room, and on Pluto inviting them to the feast, lights appeared, and the table was seen to be covered with black, whilst the dishes on it were foul and obscene animals, and bones of dead men, served by devils carrying shovels. Finally all this vanished, and a choice banquet followed. This Society of the Trowel was in existence in 1737. The clergy endeavoured to suppress it; and would no doubt have succeeded, but for the accession of Francis, Duke of Tuscany, who, as we have seen, had been initiated in Holland, and who set free all the Freemasons that had been incarcerated, and protected the order. But the remembrance of that persecution is preserved in the rituals, and in the degree of "Magus," the costume is that of the Holy Office, as other degrees commemorate the inquisitors of Portugal and Spain.

259. *Illuminati in Italy.*—The sect of the Illuminati, of whom Count Filippo Strozzi was a warm partisan, soon after spread through Italy, as well as another order, affiliated with the Illuminati, mystical and alchymistical, and in opposition to the Rosicrucians, called the "Initiated Brethren of Asia," which had been founded at Vienna. It only accepted candidates who had passed through the first three degrees of the York rite. Like Egyptian

Masonry, it worshipped the Tetragrammaton, and combined the deepest and most philosophical ideas with the most childish superstitions.

260. *Freemasonry at Naples.*—In the kingdom of Naples the masons amounted to many thousands. An edict of Charles III. (1751), and another of Ferdinand IV. (1759), closed the lodges, but in a short time they became a dead letter, and in vain did the minister, Tanucci, hostile to the institution, seek to revive them. The incident of a neophyte dying a few days after his initiation gave a pretext for fresh persecution. The masons, assembled at a banquet, were arrested; and in vain did Lévy, a lawyer, undertake their defence. He was expelled the kingdom; his book in favour of the order was publicly burnt by the executioner. But Queen Caroline, having dismissed Tanucci, again sanctioned masonic meetings, for which she received the thanks of the Grand Orient of France. It would seem, however, that in a very few years, Freemasonry again had to hide its head, for in 1767 we hear of it as a "secret" society, whose existence has just been discovered. The document which records this discovery puts the number of Freemasons at 64,000, which probably is an exaggeration; still, among so excitable a population as that of southern Italy, secret societies at all times found plenty of proselytes.

261. *Details of Document.*—The document re-

ferred to says:—At last the great mine of the Freemasons of Naples is discovered, of whom the name, but not the secret, was known. Two circumstances are alleged by which the discovery was brought about:—a dying man revealed all to his confessor, that he should inform the king thereof; a knight, who had been kept in great state by the society, having had his pension withheld, betrayed the Grand Master of the order to the king. This Grand Master was the Duke of San Severo. The king secretly sent a confidential officer with three dragoons to the duke's mansion, with orders to seize him before he had time to speak to any one, and bring him to the palace. The order was carried out; but a few minutes after a fire broke out in the duke's mansion, destroying his library, the real object being, as is supposed, to burn all writings having reference to Freemasonry. The fire was extinguished, and the house guarded by troops. The duke having been brought before the king, openly declared the objects, system, seals, government, and possessions of the order. He was sent back to his palace, and there guarded by troops, lest he should be killed by his former colleagues. Freemasons have also been discovered at Florence, and the Pope and the Emperor have sent thither twenty-four theologians to put a stop to the disorder. The king acts with the greatest mercy towards all implicated, to avoid the great dangers that might ensue from a contrary course. He has also appointed four persons of great standing to use the best means to destroy so abominable a sect; and has given notice to all the other sovereigns of Europe of his discovery, and the abominable maxims of the sect, calling upon them to assist in its suppression, which it will be folly in them to refuse to do. For the order does not count its members by thousands, but by millions, especially among Jews and Protestants. Their frightful maxims are only known to the members of the fifth, sixth, and seventh lodges, whilst those of the first three know nothing, and those of the fourth act without knowing what they do. They derive their origin from England, and the founder of the sect was that infamous Cromwell, first bishop, and then lover of Anne Boleyn, and then beheaded for his crimes, called in his day " the scourge of rulers." He left the order an annual income of £10,000 sterling. It is divided into seven lodges: the members of the seventh are called Assessors; of the sixth, Grand Masters; of the fifth, Architects; of the fourth, Executors (here the secret ends); of the third, Ruricori(!); of the second and first, Novices and Proselytes. Their infamous idea is based on the allegory of the temple of Solomon, considered in its first splendour, and then overthrown by the tyranny of the Assyrians, and finally restored—thereby to signify the liberty of man after the creation of the world, the tyranny of the priesthood, kings, and laws, and the re-establishment of that liberty. Then follow twelve maxims, in which these opinions and aims are more fully expounded, from which it appears that they were not very different from those of all other republican and advanced politicians.

262. *Freemasonry at Venice.*—The Freemasons were at first tolerated at Venice, but in 1686 the government suddenly took the alarm, and ordered the closing of all lodges, and banished the members; but the decree was very leniently executed, and a lodge of nobles having refused to obey, the magistrates entered it at a time when they knew no one to be there. The furniture, ornaments, and jewels were carried out and publicly burnt or dispersed, but none of the brethren were in any way molested. A lodge was re-established afterwards, which was discovered in 1785, when all its contents were again burnt or otherwise destroyed. From the ritual, which was found among the other effects, it appears that the candidate for initiation was led, his eyes being bandaged, from street to street, or canal to canal, so as to prevent his tracing the locality, to the Rio Marino, where he was first conducted into a room hung with black, and illumined by a single light; there he was clothed in a long garment like a winding sheet, but black; he put on a cap something like a turban, and his hair was drawn over his face, and in this elegant figure he was placed

before a looking-glass, covered with a black curtain, under which were written the words, " If thou hast true courage, and an honest desire to enter into the order, draw aside the curtain, and learn to know thyself." He might then remove the bandage and look at himself. He was then again blindfolded, and placed in the middle of the room, while thirty or forty members entered and began to fight with swords. This was to try the candidate's courage, who was himself slightly wounded. The bandage was once more removed, and the wound dressed. Then it was replaced, and the candidate taken to a second apartment, hung with black and white, and having in the middle a bed covered with a black cloth, on the centre of which was a white cross, whilst on either side was represented a white skeleton. The candidate was laid on the bed, the bandage being removed, and he was there left with two tapers, the one white, the other yellow. After having been left there for some time, the brethren entered in a boisterous manner beating discordant drums. The candidate was to show no sign of trepidation amidst all these solemn (?) ceremonies; and then the members embraced him as a brother, and gave him the name by which he was henceforth to be known in the society.

263. *Abatement under Napoleon.*—During the reign of Napoleon I., numerous lodges were founded throughout Italy; and it cannot be denied by the

greatest friends of the order that during that period Freemasonry cut a most pitiful figure. For a society that always boasted of its independence of, and superiority to, all other earthly governments, to forward addresses such as the following to Napoleon, seems something like self-abasement and self-stultification:—" O Napoleon! thy philosophy guarantees the toleration of our natural and divine religion. We render thee honour worthy of thee for it, and thou shalt find in us nothing but faithful subjects, ever devoted to thy august person!"

264. *The Freemasonry of the Present in Italy.*— Very little need or can be said as regards the active proceedings of Italian Masonic lodges of the present day, though they have been reconstituted and united under one or two heads. But their programme deserves attention, as pointing out those reforms, needed not only in Italy, but everywhere where Freemasonry exists. The declared object, then, of Italian Freemasonry is, the highest development of universal philanthropy; the independence and unity of single nations, and fraternity among each other; the toleration of every religion, and absolute equality of worship; the moral and material progress of the masses. It moreover declares itself independent of every government, affirming that Italian Freemasonry will not recognize any other sovereign power on earth but right reason and universal conscience. It further declares—and this deserves

particular attention—that Freemasonry is not to consist in a mysterious symbolism, vain ceremonies, or indefinite aspirations, which cover the order with ridicule. Again, Masonry being universal, essentially human, it does not occupy itself with forms of government, nor with transitory questions, but with such as are permanent and general. In social reforms abstract theories, founded on mystical aspirations, are to be avoided. The duty of labour being the most essential in civil society, Freemasonry is opposed to idleness. Religious questions are beyond the pale of Freemasonry. Human conscience is in itself inviolable; it has no concern with any positive religion, but represents religion itself in its essence. Devoted to the principle of fraternity, it preaches universal toleration; comprehends in its ritual many of the symbols of various religions, as in its syncretism it chooses the purest truths. Its creed consists in the worship of the Divine, whose highest conception, withdrawn from every priestly speculation, is that of the Great Architect of the Universe; and in faith in humanity, the sole interpreter of the Divine in the world. As to extrinsic modes of worship, Freemasonry neither imposes nor recommends any, leaving to everyone his free choice, until the day, perhaps not far distant, when all men will be capable of worshipping the Infinite in spirit and in truth, without intermediaries and outward forms. And whilst man in his secret relations to the Infinite fecundates the religious thought, he in his relations to the Universe fecundates the scientific thought. Science is truth, and the most ancient cultus of Freemasonry.

In determining the relations of the individual to his equals, Freemasonry does not restrict itself to recommending to do unto others what we wish others would do unto us; but inculcates to do good, oppose evil, and not to submit to injustice in whatsoever form it presents itself. Freemasonry looks forward to the day when the iron plates of the "Monitor" and the "Merrimac" will be beaten into steam-ploughs; when man, redeemed by liberty and science, shall enjoy the pure pleasures of intelligence; when peace, fertilised by the wealth and strength now devoted to war, shall bring forth the most beautiful fruit of the tree of life.

265. *Reform needed.*—Greatly therefore is the academic puerility of rites to be regretted, which drags back into the past an institution that ought to launch forward into the future. It is self-evident that Freemasonry in this state cannot last—that a reform is necessary; and as De Castro, from whom the above is taken, thinks that it would be an honour to Italy to be the leader in such a reform, it would be an honour to any country that initiated it. Masonry ought not to be an ambulance, but a vanguard. It is embarrassed by its excessive bag-

gage, its superfluous symbols. Guarding secrets universally known, it cannot entertain secrets of greater account. Forcing itself to believe itself to be the sole depositary of widely-spread truths, it deprives itself and the world of other truths. In this perplexity and alternative of committing suicide or being born anew, what will Masonry decide on?

XX.

CAGLIOSTRO AND EGYPTIAN MASONRY.

266.

LIFE *of Cagliostro.*—Joseph Balsamo, the disciple and successor of St. Germain, who pretended at the court of Louis XV. to have been the contemporary of Charles V., Francis I., and Christ, and to possess the elixir of life and many other secrets, had vaster designs and a loftier ambition than his teacher, and was one of the most active agents of Freemasonry in France and the rest of Europe. He was born at Palermo in 1743, and educated at two convents in that city, where he acquired some chemical knowledge. As a young man, he fell in with an Armenian, or Greek, or Spaniard, called Althotas, a kind of adventurer, who professed to possess the philosopher's stone, with whom he led a roving life for a number of years. What became of Althotas at last is not positively known. Balsamo at last found his way to Rome, where he married the beautiful

Lorenza Feliciani, whom he treated so badly, that she escaped from him; but he recovered her, and acquired great influence over her by magnetically operating upon her. There is no doubt that he was a powerful magnetizer. Visiting Germany, he was initiated into Freemasonry, in which he soon began to take a prominent part. He also assumed different titles, such as that of Marquis of Pellegrini, but the one he is best known by is that of Count Cagliostro; and by his astuteness, impudence, and some lucky hits at prophesying, he acquired a European notoriety and made many dupes, including persons of the highest rank, especially in France, where he founded many new Masonic lodges. He was the author of a book called "The Rite of Egyptian Masonry," which rite he established first in Courland, and afterwards in Germany, France, and England. After having been banished from France, in consequence of his implication in the affair of the queen's necklace, and driven from England by his creditors, he was induced by his wife, who was weary of her wandering life, and anxious once more to see her relations, to visit Rome, where he was arrested on the charge of attempting to found a Masonic lodge, against which a papal bull had recently been promulgated, and thrown into the castle of St. Angelo, in 1789. He was condemned to death, but the punishment was commuted to perpetual imprisonment. His wife was shut up in a convent, and died soon after. Having been transferred to the Castle of San Leo, he attempted to strangle the monk sent to confess him, in the hope of escaping in his gown; but the attempt failed, and it is supposed that he died, a prisoner, in 1795.

267. *The Egyptian Rite.*—The Egyptian rite invented by Cagliostro is a mixture of the sacred and profane, of the serious and laughable; charlatanism is its prevailing feature. Having discovered a MS. of George Cofton, in which was propounded a singular scheme for the reform of Freemasonry in an alchymistic and fantastic sense, Cagliostro founded thereon the bases of his masonic system, taking advantage of human credulity, enriching himself, and at the same time seconding the action of other secret societies. If there were not now believers in spirit-rapping and table-turning, it would be difficult to understand how Cagliostro succeeded in gaining so many followers and so much wealth, considering his vulgar tricks and shallow pretences. He gave his dupes to understand that the scope of Egyptian Masonry was to conduct men to perfection by means of physical and moral regeneration; asserting that the former was infallible through the *prima materia* and the philosopher's stone, which assured to man the strength of youth and immortality, and that the second was to be achieved by the discovery of a pentagon that would restore man to his primitive innocence. This rite indeed is a tissue of fa-

tuities it would not be worth while to allude to, did it not offer matter for study to the philosopher and moralist. Cagliostro pretended that the rite had been first founded by Enoch, remodelled by Elias, and finally restored by the Grand Copt. Both men and women were admitted into the lodges, though the ceremonies for each were slightly different, and the lodges for their reception entirely distinct. In the reception of women, among other formalities there was that of breathing into the face of the neophyte, saying, "I breathe upon you this breath to cause to germinate in you and grow in your heart the truth we possess; I breathe it into you to strengthen in you good intentions, and to confirm you in the faith of your brothers and sisters. We constitute you a legitimate daughter of true Egyptian adoption and of this worshipful lodge." One of the lodges was called "Sinai," where the most secret rites were performed; another "Ararat," to symbolize the rest reserved for masons only. Concerning the pentagon, Cagliostro taught that it would be given to the masters after forty days of intercourse with the seven primitive angels, and that its possessors would enjoy a physical regeneration for 5557 years, after which they would through gentle sleep pass into heaven. The pentagon had as much success with the upper ten thousand of London, Paris, and St. Petersburg, as the philosopher's stone ever enjoyed; and large sums were given for a few grains of the rejuvenating *prima materia*. There exists yet between Basle and Strasburg a sumptuous Chinese temple, where the famous pentagon was worshipped; and the lodge " Sinai" at Lyons was as gorgeous as a palace.

268. *Cagliostro's Hydromancy.*—But beside masonic delusions, Cagliostro made use of the then little understood wonders of magnetism to attract adherents; and as many persons are seduced by the wine-cup, so he made dupes of many by means of the water-bottle, which trick, as might be shown, was very ancient, and consisted in divination by hydromancy. A child, generally a little girl, was made to look into a bottle of water, and see therein events, past, present, and to come, the child having of course been well tutored beforehand; and as Cagliostro was really a man of observation, he made many shrewd guesses as to the future, and sometimes fortune favoured him—as in the case of Schieffort, one of the leaders of the Illuminati, who refused to join the Egyptian rite, at which Cagliostro was so incensed, that he caused the little girl to see in the decanter the exterminating angel, who declared that in less than a month Schieffort would be punished. Now it so happened that within that period Schieffort committed suicide, which of course gave an immense lift to Cagliostro and his bottle. In this respect indeed Cagliostro was a forerunner of our modern spiritualists; and as he did not keep his

Cagliostro and Egyptian Masonry. 355

occult power a secret from all, but freely communicated it, magical practices were thus introduced into the lodges, which well served the purposes of the astute, but brought discredit on the institution. And all this occurred at the period of the Encyclopedists, and on the eve of mighty events!

XXI.

ADOPTIVE MASONRY.

269.

HISTORICAL Notice.—According to one of the fundamental laws of Masonry—and a rule prevailing in the greater mysteries of antiquity—women cannot be received into the order. Women cannot keep secrets, at least so Milton says, through the mouth of Dalila:—

> "Granting, as I do, it was a weakness
> In me, but incident to all our sex,
> Curiosity, inquisitive, importune
> Of secrets; then with like infirmity
> To publish them; both common female faults."

But we have already seen that Cagliostro admitted women to the Egyptian rite; and when at the beginning of the eighteenth century several associations sprang up in France, which in their external aspect resembled Freemasonry, but did not exclude women, the ladies naturally were loud in their praise of such institutions, so that the masonic brotherhood, seeing it was becoming unpopular, had recourse to the stratagem of establishing "adoptive" lodges of women, so called because every such lodge had finally to be adopted by some regular masonic lodge. The Grand Orient of France framed laws for their government, and the first lodge of adoption was opened in Paris in 1775, in which the Duchess of Bourbon presided, and was initiated as Grand Mistress of the rite. The Revolution checked the progress of this rite, but it was revived in 1805, when the Empress Josephine presided over the "Loge Impériale d'Adoption des Francs-Chevaliers" at Strasburg. Similar lodges spread over Europe, Great Britain excepted; but they soon declined, and are at present confined to the place of their origin.

270. *Organisation.*—The rite consists of the same degrees as those of genuine Masonry. Every sister, being a dignitary, has beside her a masonic brother holding the corresponding rank. Hence the officers are a Grand Master and a Grand Mistress, an Inspector and an Inspectress, a Depositor and a Depositrix, a Conductor and a Conductress. The business of the lodge is conducted by the sisterhood, the brethren only acting as their assistants; but the Grand Mistress has very little to say or to do, she being only an honorary companion to the Grand Master. The first, or apprentice's degree, is only

introductory; in the second, or companion, the scene of the temptation in Eden is emblematically represented; the building of the tower of Babel is the subject of the mistress's degree; and in the fourth, or that of perfect mistress, the officers represent Moses, Aaron, and their wives, and the ceremonies refer to the passage of the Israelites through the wilderness, as a symbol of the passage of men and women through this to another and better life. The lodge room is tastefully decorated, and divided by curtains into four compartments, each representing one of the four quarters of the globe, the eastern, or furthermost, representing Asia, where there are two splendid thrones, decorated with gold fringe, for the Grand Master and the Grand Mistress. The members sit on each side in straight lines, the sisters in front and the brothers behind them, the latter having swords in their hands. All this pretty playing at masonry is naturally followed by a banquet, and on many occasions by a ball. And a very proper sequel to private theatricals! At the banquets the members use a symbolical language; thus the lodge-room is called "Eden," the doors "barriers," a glass is called a "lamp," water "white oil," wine "red oil;" to fill your glass is "to trim your lamp," &c.

271. *Jesuit Degrees.*—The Jesuits, *qui vont passer leur nez partout*, soon poked it into Adoptive Masonry—for to get hold of the women is to get hold

of the better half of mankind—and founded new lodges, or modified existing ones of that rite to further their own purposes. Thus it is that a truly monkish asceticism was introduced into some of them, by the Jesuits divided into ten degrees; and we find such passages in the catechism as these: "Are you prepared, sister, to sacrifice life for the good of the catholic, apostolic Roman Church?" The tenth or last degree was called the "Princess of the Crown," and a great portion of the ritual treats of the Queen of Sheba. This rite was established in Saxony in 1779.

XXII.

ANDROGYNOUS MASONRY.

272.

ORIGIN and Tendency. — Gallantry already makes its appearance in Adoptive Masonry; and this gallantry, which for so many ages was the study of France, and was there reduced to an ingenious art, manufactured on its own account rites and degrees that were masonic in name only. Politics were dethroned by amorous intrigues; and the enumerators of great effects sprung from trifling causes might in this chapter of history find proofs of what a superficial and accidental thing politics are, when not governed by motives of high morality, nor watched by the incorruptible national conscience. And Androgynous Masonry did not always confine itself to an interchange of compliments and the pursuit of pleasure; still, as a rule, its lodges for the initiation of males and females—defended by some of their advocates as founded on Exod. xxxviii. 8—are a whimsical form of that court life which in France and Italy had its poets and romancers; and which rose to such a degree of impudence and scandal as to outrage the modesty of citizens and popular virtue. It is a page of that history of princely corruption, which the French people at first read of with laughter, then with astonishment, finally with indignation; and which inspired it with those feelings which at last found their vent in the excesses of the great Revolution. Every Revolution is a puritanical movement, and the simple and neglected virtue of the lowly-born avenges itself upon the pompous vices of their superiors.

273. *Earliest Androgynous Societies.*—Some of these were founded in France and elsewhere by an idle, daring, and conquering soldiery. As their type we may take the order of the " Knights and Ladies of Joy," founded with extraordinary success at Paris in 1696, under the protection of Bacchus and Venus, and whose printed statutes are still in existence; and that of the " Ladies of St. John of Jerusalem," and the " Ladies of St. James of the Sword and Calatrava." They, as it were, served as models to the canonesses who till the end of the last century brought courtly pomp and mundane pleasures into the very cloisters of France, and compelled austere moralists to excuse it by saying that it was *dans le goût de la nation.*

274. *Other Androgynous Societies.*—In the order

of the " Companions of Penelope, or the Palladium of Ladies," whose statutes are said to have been drawn up by Fénélon (with how much truth is easily imagined), the trials consist in showing the candidate that work is the palladium of women; whence we may assume the pursuits of this society to have been very different from the equivocal occupations of other orders. The order of the " Mopses" owed its origin to a religious scruple. Pope Clement XII. having issued, in 1738, a Bull, condemning Freemasonry, the Roman Catholics, not wishing to deprive themselves of their fraternal meetings, instituted, under the above name (derived from the German word *Mops*, a young mastiff, the symbol of mutual fidelity), what was pretended to be a new association, but what was in fact only Freemasonry under another name. In 1776 the " Mopses" became an androgynous order, admitting females to all the offices, except that of Grand Master. There was, however, a Grand Mistress also. In 1777 there was established in Denmark the androgynous order of the " Society of the Chain," to which belongs the honour of having founded and of maintaining at its own expense the Asylum for the Blind at Copenhagen, the largest and best managed of similar institutions in Europe. The order of " Perseverance," the date of whose foundation is unknown, but which existed in Paris in 1777, and was supported by the most distinguished persons, had a laudable custom, which might be imitated by other societies, viz., to inscribe in a book, one of which is still extant, the praiseworthy actions of the male and female members of the association. But one of the most deserving masonic androgynous institutions was that of the " Sovereign Chapter of the Scotch Ladies of France," founded in 1810, and divided into lesser and greater mysteries, and whose instructions aimed chiefly at leading the neophyte back to the occupations to which the state of society called him or her. To provide food and work for those wanting either, to afford them advice and help, and save them from the cruel alternative of crime—such was the scope of this society, which lasted till the year 1828.

275. *Vicious Androgynous Societies.*—The Society of the "Wood-store of the Globe and Glory" was founded in 1747 by the Chevalier de Beauchêne, a lively boon companion, who was generally to be found at an inn, where for very little money he conferred all the masonic degrees of that time; a man whose worship would have shone by the great tun of Heidelberg, or at the drinking bouts of German students. The Wood-store was supposed to be in a forest, and the meetings, which were much in vogue, took place in a garden outside Paris, called "New France," where assembled lords and clowns, ladies and grisettes, indulging in the easy costumes and manners of the country. Towards the middle of

the eighteenth century, there was established in Britanny the order of the "Defoliators."

In the order of "Felicity," instituted in Paris in 1742, and divided into the four degrees of midshipman, captain, chief of a squadron, and vice-admiral, the emblems and terms were nautical: sailors were its founders, and it excited so much attention, that in 1746 a satire, entitled, "The Means of reaching the highest Rank in the Navy without getting Wet," was published against it. Its field of action was the field of love. A Grand Orient was called the offing, the lodge the squadron, and the sisters performed the fictitious voyage to the island of Felicity *sous la voile des frères et pilotées par eux;* and the candidate promised "never to receive a foreign ship into her port as long as a ship of the order was anchored there."

The order of the "Lovers of Pleasure" was a military institution, a pale revival of the ceremonies of chivalry and the courts of love, improvised in the French camp in Gallicia. From the discourse of one of the orators we select the following passage: "Our scope is to embellish our existence, always taking for our guide the words: 'Honour, Joy, and Delicacy.' Our scope, moreover, is to be faithful to our country and the august sovereign who fills the universe with his glorious name, to serve a cause which ought to be grateful to every gentle soul, that of protecting youth and innocence, and of establishing between the ladies and ourselves an eternal alliance, cemented by the purest friendship." This society, it is said, was much favoured by Napoleon I., and hence we may infer that its aim was not purely pleasure; at all events it is remarkable, that a society, having masonic rites, should have given its services to the "august sovereign" who had just withdrawn his support from genuine Freemasonry.

276. *Knights and Nymphs of the Rose.*—This order was founded in Paris in 1778 by Chaumont, private secretary to Louis-Philippe d'Orléans, to please that prince. The chief lodge was held in one of the famous *petites maisons* of that epoch. The great lords had lodges in their own houses. The Hierophant, assisted by a deacon called " Sentiment," initiated the men, and the Grand Priestess, assisted by the deaconess called " Discretion," initiated the women. The age of admission for knights was " the age to love," that of ladies, " the age to please and to be loved." Love and mystery were the programme of the order; the lodge was called the Temple of Love, which was beautifully adorned with garlands of flowers and amorous emblems and devices. The knights wore a crown of myrtle, the nymphs a crown of roses. During the time of initiation a dark lantern, held by the nymph of Discretion, shed a dim light, but afterwards the lodge was illuminated with numerous

wax candles. The aspirants, laden with chains, to symbolize the prejudices that kept them prisoners, were asked, "What seek you here?" To which they replied, "Happiness." They were then questioned as to their private opinion and conduct in matters of gallantry, and made twice to traverse the lodge over a path covered with love-knots, whereupon the iron chains were taken off, and garlands of flowers, called "chains of love," substituted. The candidates were then conducted to the altar, where they took the oath of secresy; and thence to the mysterious groves in the neighbourhood of the Temple of Love, where incense was offered up to Venus and her son. If it was a knight who had been initiated, he exchanged his crown of myrtle for the rose of the last initiated nymph; and if a nymph, she exchanged her rose for the myrtle crown of Brother Sentiment. The horrors of the Revolution scattered these knights and nymphs, who, like thoughtless children, were playing on a volcano.

277. *Mason's Daughter.*— This is an androgynous degree invented in the Western States of America, and given to master masons, their wives, and unmarried sisters and daughters. It refers to circumstances recorded in chapters xi. and xii. of St. John's Gospel.

XXIII.

PERSECUTIONS OF FREEMASONRY.

278.

CAUSES of Persecution. — The secresy with which the masonic brotherhood has always surrounded its proceedings is no doubt highly grateful to the members, but it has its drawbacks. The outside world, who cannot believe that masonic meetings, which are so jealously guarded against the intrusion of non-masons, have no other purpose than the rehearsal of a now totally useless and pointless ritual, followed by conviviality, naturally assume that there must be something more behind; and what seems to fear the light is usually supposed to be evil. Hence all governments, as long as they did not know what modern Freemasonry really is, persecuted and endeavoured to suppress it. But as soon as they discovered its real scope and character, they gave it their support, feeling quite convinced that men who could find entertainment in the doings of the lodges, would never, as it is popularly called, set the Thames on fire. Thus one of the first persecutions against Freemasonry arose in Holland in 1734. A crowd of ignorant fanatics, incited thereto by the clergy, broke into a lodge at Amsterdam and destroyed all its furniture and ornaments; but the town clerk having at the suggestion of the order been initiated, the States-General, upon his report, sanctioned the society, many of the chief persons becoming members. Of course when lodges were turned into political clubs, and the real business of Masonry was cast aside for something more serious, the matter assumed a very different aspect. The persecutions here to be mentioned will therefore be such only as took place against Freemasonry, legitimately so called.

279. *Instances of Persecution.*—Pope Clement XII., in 1737, issued a decree against the order, which was followed by a more severe edict next year, the punishment therein awarded for being found guilty of practising Freemasonry being confiscation and death, without hope of mercy. This was a signal of persecution in the countries connected with Rome. The parliament of Paris, however, refused to register the papal Bull; and an apology for the order was published at Dublin. But Philip V. of Spain declared the galleys for life, or punishment of death with torture to be the doom of Freemasons; a very large number of whom he caused to be arrested

and sentenced. Peter Torrubia, Grand Inquisitor of Spain, having first made confession and received absolution, entered the order for the express purpose of betraying it. He joined in 1751, and made himself acquainted with the entire ramifications of the craft; and in consequence members of ninety-seven lodges were seized and tortured on the rack. Ferdinand VI. declared Freemasonry to be high treason, and punishable with death. When the French became masters of Spain, Freemasonry was revived and openly practised, the members of the Grand Lodge of Madrid meeting in the hall previously occupied by their arch-enemy the Inquisition. With the return of Ferdinand VII., who re-established the Inquisition, the exterminating process recommenced. In 1814, twenty-five persons suspected of Freemasonry were dragged in chains to confinement; but the subsequent arrests were so numerous that no correct account is obtainable, nor can the ultimate fate of the accused be recorded. In 1824, a law was promulgated, commanding all masons to declare themselves, and deliver up all their papers and documents, under the penalty of being declared traitors. The Minister of War, in the same year, issued a proclamation, outlawing every member of the craft, and in 1827 seven members of a lodge in Granada were executed; while in 1828, the tribunals of the same city condemned the Marquis of Lavrillana and Captain Alvarez to be beheaded for having founded a lodge.

In 1735, several noble Portuguese instituted a lodge at Lisbon, under the Grand Lodge of England, of which George Gordon was Master; but the priests immediately determined on putting it down. One of the best known victims of the Inquisition was John Coustos, a native of Switzerland, who was arrested in 1743, and thrown into a subterranean dungeon, where he was racked nine times in three months for not revealing the secrets of Masonry. He had, however, to appear in an *auto-da-fe*, and was sentenced to five years' work as a galley slave; but the British Government claiming him as a subject, he was released before the term of his punishment expired. Thirty-three years passed without anything more being heard of Freemasonry in Portugal; but in 1776, two members of the craft were arrested, and remained upwards of fourteen months in prison. In 1792, Queen Elizabeth ordered all Freemasons to be delivered over to the Inquisition; a very few families escaped to New York, where they landed with the words, *Asylum quærimus*. Among their American brethren they found not only an asylum, but a new home. The French empire ushered in better days; but with the restoration of the old *régime* came the former prejudices and persecutions. In 1818, John VI. promulgated from the Brazils an edict against all secret societies, including Freemasonry; and again in 1823, a similar though more stringent proclamation appeared in Lisbon. The punishment of death therein awarded has been reduced to fine and transportation to Africa.

In Austria, the papal bulls provoked persecutions and seizures; hence arose the order of the Mopses (274), which spread through Holland, Belgium, and France. In 1747, thirty masons were arrested and imprisoned at Vienna. Maria Theresa, having been unable to discover the secrets of the order, issued a decree to arrest all masons, but the measure was frustrated by the good sense of the Emperor Joseph I., who was himself a mason, and therefore knew that the pursuits of the order were innocent enough. Francis II., at the Diet of Ratisbon in 1794, demanded the suppression of all masonic societies throughout Germany; but Hanover, Brunswick, and Prussia united with the smaller states in refusing their assent.

The history of Freemasonry in Central Italy during the last century and this, as may be supposed, is a mere repetition of sufferings, persecutions, and misfortunes; the members of the craft being continually under punishment, through the intolerance of the priesthood and the interference of the civil power.

But persecution was not confined to Catholic countries. Even in Switzerland, the masons at one time were persecuted. The Council of Berne, in 1745, passed a law with certain degrees of punishment for members of lodges; which law was renewed in 1782. It is now abrogated. Frederick I., King of Sweden, a very few years after the introduction (1736) of Freemasonry, forbade it under penalty of death. At present the king is at the head of the Swedish craft. The King Frederick Augustus III. of Poland caused, in 1739, enactments to be published, forbidding, under pain of severe punishment, the practice of Freemasonry in his kingdom. In 1757, the Synod of Stirling adopted a resolution debarring all Freemasons from the ordinances of religion. In 1799, Lord Radnor proposed in the English Parliament a bill against secret societies, and especially against Freemasonry; and a similar but equally fruitless attempt against the order was made in 1814 by Lord Liverpool. The Society is now acknowledged by law; the Prince of Wales is one of its members, and is now one of its Past Grand Masters.

280. *Anti-Masonic Publications.*—One of the earliest English publications against Freemasonry is "The Freemasons; an Hudibrastic Poem," London, 1723. It is written in the coarsest style of invective, describing the masons as a drunken set of revellers, practising all kinds of filthy rites. Several works of no literary merit appeared at various intervals between 1726 and 1760, professing to reveal the masonic secrets, but their authors

evidently knew nothing of the craft. In 1768, a rabid parson published a sermon, entitled "Masonry, the Way to Hell." It is beneath criticism. Numerous works of a similar tendency, or professing to reveal what masonry was, thenceforth appeared at short intervals in England, France, Germany, and Italy, such as "Les Plus Secrets Mystères de la Maçonnerie;" "Le Maschere Strappate" (The Masks torn off); "The Veil Removed, or the Secret of the Revolutions fostered by Freemasonry;" Robison's "Proofs of a Conspiracy against all the Religions and Governments of Europe carried on in the Secret Meetings of Freemasons, Illuminati, and Reading Societies," a work which must have astonished the masons not a little, and for which they were no doubt in their hearts very grateful to the author, for he makes the masons out to be very terrible fellows indeed. Good easy men, who only thought of enjoying their "beer and 'baccy," and of going through a little mummery, to find that they were, "unbeknown" to themselves, very near upsetting all the thrones of Europe! The work of the Abbé Barruel is of the same stamp; it is entitled: "Mémoires pour servir à l'Histoire du Jacobinisme," and is noteworthy for nothing but absence of critical power and honesty of statement. A great deal is now written against Freemasonry; but the writers in most instances know neither what Freemasonry is, nor what it pretends to be.

XXIV.

SCHISMATIC RITES AND SECTS.

281.

CHISMATIC *Rites and Sects.*—The pretended derivation of Freemasonry from the Knights Templars has already been referred to; but Masonry, the system, not the name, existed before the Order of the Temple, and the Templars themselves had masonic rites and degrees three hundred years before their downfall. Those who, however, maintain the above view say that the three assassins symbolize the three betrayers of the order, and Hiram the Grand Master Molay; and according to the ritual of the Grand Lodge of the Three Globes, a German degree, the lights around the coffin signify the flames of the pile on which Molay was burnt. To the Rosicrucians and to certain German lodges Hiram is Christ, and the three assassins, Judas that betrays, Peter that denies Him, and Thomas that disbelieves His resurrection. The ancient Scotch rite had its origin in other false accounts of the

rise of the order. In the last century schisms without number arose in the masonic body. It would be impossible in a work like this to name them all; a few only can be referred to. Out of the non-masonic society of the Rosicrucians was formed in 1777 an association, calling itself the "Brothers of the Golden Rosy Cross." It was very numerous in Germany, the Netherlands, and Sweden. A second schism from the Rosicrucians was the "Society of the Initiated Brothers of Asia," which was originated in 1780, and whose pursuits were those of alchemy. Its existence was but brief. Rolling, a member, in 1787 published in print its laughable secrets. A lodge was founded in 1768 by one Schrœpfer in his own house, where he conjured up ghosts! The King of Saxony, being incredulous, had him flogged as an impostor. The charlatan disguised himself, assumed the title of Count de Steinville, went to the Court of Dresden and frightened the king with horrible apparitions. This was his revenge, but the French ambassador discovered the cheat. Schrœpfer escaped to Leipsic and began afresh his mummeries. But having promised his dupes more than he could accomplish, he shot himself in the wood of Rosenthal, near Leipzig. The "Moravian Brothers of the Order of Religious Freemasons, or Order of the Mustard-Seed," was another German rite, founded in 1739. Its mysteries were founded on the passage in St. Mark iv., in which Christ compares the kingdom of heaven to a grain of mustard-seed. The brethren recognized each other by a ring inscribed with the words:—" No one of us lives for himself." The jewel was a cross of gold, surmounted by a mustard-plant with the words:—" What was it before? Nothing." Nearly all the degrees of the Scotch rite are schismatic. In like manner all the English and American orders of chivalry, and their conclaves and encampments, are ridiculous parodies of ancient chivalry.

In 1758, Lacorne, a dancing master, and Pirlet, a tailor, invented the degree of the " Council of the Emperors of the East and West," whose members assumed the titles of " Sovereign Prince Masons, Substitutes General of the Royal Art, Grand Superintendents and Officers of the Grand and Sovereign Lodge of St. John of Jerusalem." The ritual consisted of twenty-five degrees, and as it was calculated by its sounding titles and splendour of ritual to flatter the vanity of the frivolous, it was at first very successful; and Lacorne conferred on one of his creatures, a Hebrew, the degree of Inspector, and sent him to America to spread the order there. In 1797, other Jews added eight new degrees, giving to this agglomeration of thirty-three pompous degrees, the title of " Ancient and Accepted Scotch Rite." The Grand Orient of France, seeing its own influence declining, proposed advantageous and honourable terms to the Supreme Grand Council, which was at the head of the Scotch rite, and an agreement was come to in 1804. The Grand Orient retaining the first name, received into its bosom the Supreme Grand Council and the rich American symbolism. But the connection did not prosper, and was dissolved in 1805. Again, what is called Mark-Masonry in England is considered spurious; whilst in Scotland and Ireland it is held to be an essential portion of Freemasonry. These are curious anomalies.

282. *Ludicrous Degree.*—The following lodge was actually established about 1717. Some joyous companions, having passed the degree of craft, resolved to form a lodge for themselves. As none of them knew the Master's part, they at once invented and adopted a ritual which suited every man's humour. Hence it was ordered that every person during initiation should wear boots, spurs, a sword, and spectacles. The apron was turned upside down. To simplify the work of the lodge, they abolished the practice of studying geometry—which was sheer pretence, for the only geometry a mason studies in the lodge is that mentioned by Hudibras:

> " For he, by geometric scale,
> Could take the size of pots of ale;
> Resolve by sines and tangents straight,
> If bread or butter wanted weight."

Some of the members proved that a good knife

and fork in the hands of a dexterous brother, over proper materials, would give greater satisfaction and add more to the rotundity of the lodge than the best scale and compass in Europe; adding that a line, a square, a parallelogram, a rhombus, a rhomboid, a triangle, a trapezium, a circle, a semi-circle, a quadrant, a parabola, a hyperbola, a cube, a parallelepipedon, a prism, a prismoid, a pyramid, a cylinder, a curve, a cylindroid, a sphere, a spheroid, a paraboloid, a cycloid, a paracentric, frustums, segments, sectors, gnomons, pentagons, hexagons, polygons, ellipses, and irregular figures of all sorts, might be drawn and represented upon bread, beef, mutton, ham, fowls, pies, etc., as demonstratively as upon sheets of paper or the tracing board, and that the use of the globes might be taught and explained as clearly and briefly upon two bottles as upon any twenty-eight inch spheres.

XXV.

DIFFUSION OF THE ORDER.

283.

FREEMASONRY *in Spain and Portugal.*—In 1726, the Grand Lodge of England granted a patent for the establishment of a lodge at Gibraltar; another was founded in the following year at Madrid, which, declaring itself independent of foreign supervision, established lodges at Cadiz, Barcelona, Valladolid, and other places. The Inquisition, seeing the danger that threatened the Church, persecuted the order; hence the mystery that surrounds the labours of the brotherhood in the Iberian peninsula.

In Portugal, the first lodges were founded, not under English, but under French auspices; but English influence soon made itself felt in the establishment of additional lodges, though in great secrecy; which, however, did not save many Freemasons from becoming the victims of the Inquisition.

284. *Freemasonry in Russia.*—In 1731, Freemasonry dared to oppose itself to Russian despotism, which, not fearing and probably despising it, did not molest it. The times were unpropitious. The sanguinary Biren ruled the Empress Anne, whom by means of the amorous fascination he exercised upon her, he easily persuaded to commit all kinds of folly and cruelty; and Masonry, though it knew itself to be tolerated, yet did not feel secure, and cautiously kept itself in the background. In 1740 England founded a lodge at St. Petersburg, and sent thither a Grand Master. The order spread in the provinces, and in 1763 the lodge "Clio" was opened at Moscow. Catherine II. wished to know its statutes, perceiving the advantage or injury they might bring to her government as she either promoted or persecuted the association. In the end she determined to protect the order; and in a country where the court leads opinion, lodges soon become the fashion. But Masonry thus becoming the amusement of a wealthy nobility, it soon lost sight of its primitive objects. In no other country probably did the brotherhood possess such gorgeous temples; but, deprived of the vivifying and invigorating air of liberty, its splendour could not save it from a death of inanition.

285. *Freemasonry in Switzerland.*—English pro

selytism, always the most active, established a lodge at Geneva in 1737, whose first Grand Master was George Hamilton. Two years afterwards, the foreigners dwelling at Lausanne united and founded the lodge called the "Perfect Union of Foreigners." Lodges were also opened at Berne; but the manœuvres of the Grand Lodges of the states surrounding Switzerland introduced long and fierce dissensions. In 1765, the Strict Observance founded at Basle the lodge "Liberty," which became the mother-lodge of many others, and, calling itself the "German Helvetic Directory," chose for its chief the celebrated Lavater. Then followed suppressions; but the order revived, and in 1844 the different territorial Grand Lodges united into one federal Grand Lodge, called "Alpina," which revised the ancient statutes. The Swiss Freemasons intend to erect a grand temple, which perhaps could nowhere find a more fitting site than in a country where four nations of diverse languages and races dwell in perfect liberty.

286. *Freemasonry in Sweden and Poland.*—In 1748, Sweden already had many and flourishing lodges. In 1754, was instituted the Grand Lodge of Sweden, under a patent from the Grand Lodge of Scotland; it afterwards declared its autonomy, which has been recognized by all the masonic bodies of Europe.

Freemasonry, at first suppressed in Poland, was

revived under Stanislaus Augustus, and the auspices of the Grand Orient of France, who established lodges in various towns of that country. These united in 1784 to form a Grand Orient, having its seat at Warsaw.

287. *Freemasonry in Holland and Germany.*—In Holland the Freemasons opened a lodge in 1731, under the warrant of the Grand Lodge of England; it was, however, only what is called a lodge of emergency, having been called to initiate the Duke of Tuscany, afterwards Francis I., Emperor of Germany. The first regular lodge was established at the Hague in 1734, which, five years after, took the name of " Mother-lodge." Numerous lodges were opened throughout the country, and also in the Dutch colonies; and the Freemasons founded many schools, with the avowed object of withdrawing instruction from clerical influence.

In Germany lodges were numerous as early as the middle of last century, so that in the present one we have witnessed the centenaries of many of them—as for instance, in 1837, of that of Hamburg; in 1840, of that of Berlin; in 1841, of those of Breslau, Baireuth, Leipzig, and many more.

288. *Freemasonry in Turkey, Asia, Africa, and Oceania.*—The order also spread into Turkey, where, however, as may be supposed, for a long time it led but a harassed existence. Lodges were established at Constantinople, Smyrna, and Aleppo; and

it may be mentioned, as a fact in favour of Freemasonry, that the Turkish Freemasons are in a more advanced state of civilization than is usual among Orientals generally. They reject polygamy, and at the Masonic banquets the women appear unveiled; so that whatever their western sisters may have to say against Masonry, the women of the East certainly are gainers by the introduction of the order.

The most important masonic lodges of Asia are in India; they are under the jurisdiction of the Grand Lodges of England and Scotland.

Freemasonry was introduced into Africa by the establishment of a lodge at Cape Coast Castle in 1735. There are now lodges at the Cape of Good Hope; in the islands of Mauritius, Madagascar and St. Helena; and at Algiers, Tunis, Morocco, Cairo, and Alexandria.

Lodges have existed since 1828 at Sydney, Melbourne, Paramatta, and other places; in all about two hundred.

289. *Freemasonry in America.*—The first lodge established in Canada was at Cape Breton, in the year 1745. Lodges existed from as early a period in the West Indian Islands. On the establishment of the Brazilian empire, a Grand Lodge was initiated; and in 1825 Don Pedro I. was elected its Grand Master. In 1825, the Grand Lodge of Mexico was instituted, where the Liberals and Federalists joined

the York rite, whilst the Clerics, Monarchists, and Centralizers adopted the Scotch rite; the two parties carrying on a relentless war. Texas, Venezuela, and the turbulent republics of South America, all had their masonic lodges, which were in many cases political clubs in disguise.

The lodges in the territory now forming the United States date as far back as 1729. Until the close of the revolutionary war these were under the jurisdiction of the Grand Lodge of England; but almost every state of the Union now has its own Grand Lodge, independent of all foreign power.

XXVI.

FUTILITY OF MODERN FREEMASONRY.

290.

VAIN Pretensions of Modern Freemasonry.—After this necessarily brief account of Freemasonry, past and present, the question naturally suggests itself, What is its present use? Is it not an institution that has outlived the object of its foundation? Are its pretensions not groundless, and its existence a delusion and anachronism? The answers to all these questions must be unfavourable to Freemasonry. Its present use is confined to that of any other benefit society. It was founded in ages when the possession of true religious and scientific knowledge was the privilege of the few, who made the cultivation and propagation of such knowledge the occupation of their lives. But now that knowledge is the birthright of all, and may openly raise its head, a society that professes to keep science for the few is but a retrograde institution.

291. *Vanity of Masonic Ceremonial.*—There are thousands of excellent men who have never seen the inside of a lodge, and yet are genuine Freemasons, *i. e.* liberal-minded and enlightened men, devoted to the study of nature and the progress of mankind, moral and intellectual; men devoid of all political and religious prejudices, true cosmopolitans. And there are thousands who have passed through every masonic degree, and yet are not masons; men who take appearances for realities, the means for the end, the ceremonies of the lodge for Freemasonry. But the lodge with all its symbols is only the *form* of the masonic *thought*. In the present age, however, this form, which was very suitable, nay, necessary, for the time when it was instituted, becomes an anachronism. The affectation of possessing a secret is a childish and mischievous weakness. The objects modern masons profess to pursue are brotherly love, relief, and truth; surely the pursuit of these objects cannot need any secret rites, traditions, and ceremonies. In spite of the great parade made in masonic publications about the science and learning peculiar to the craft, what discovery of new scientific facts or principles can masons claim for the order? Nay, are well-known and long-established truths familiar to them, and

made the objects of study in the lodges? Nothing of the kind.

292. *Masonry diffuses no knowledge.*—We get neither science nor learning from a mason, *as a mason*. The order, in fact, abjures religious and political discussion, and yet it pretends that to it mankind is indebted for its progress, and that, were it abolished, mental darkness would again overshadow the world. But how is this progress to be effected, if the chronic diseases in the existing religious and political systems of the world are not to be meddled with? As well might an association for the advancement of learning abjure inquiry into chemical and mechanical problems, and then boast of the benefits it conferred on science! It is Hamlet with the part of Hamlet omitted. If then Masonry wishes to live on, and be something more than a society of Odd Fellows or Druids, new lodges must be formed by educated men—not by the mere publicans and other tradesmen that now found lodges to create a market for their goods—who might do some good by teaching moral and natural philosophy from a deeper ground than the scholastic and grossly material basis on which all teaching at present is founded, and by rescuing science from the degraded position of handmaiden to mere physical comfort, into which modern materialism has forced it. They might found Masonic Colleges, where the

night-side of physics and metaphysics, which is the very mother of all *lux e tenebris,* as the Masonic motto has it, would be revealed to the properly qualified student, who would thus be enabled to see not only *how* a thing is, but *why* it is so.

293. *Masonry is unfitted for the task.*—That is to say, let such masonic societies be formed, if Masonry can be shown to be a necessary institution, and societies the best means for promoting the discovery of truth, and the spread of knowledge.

But are societies the most suitable means for the discovery of scientific or any other truths? Learned societies as a rule are merely mutual admiration societies, diversified by occasional junketings under pretence of the pursuit of knowledge. Discoveries are made by private individuals, whilst societies simply seek to guide all the rills of knowledge into their reservoir, to proclaim themselves the possessors of the treasures, the search after which, had they been consulted beforehand, they would probably have condemned or ridiculed. No invention or discovery of any note can be named that owes its existence to any society. Hence masonic societies would do very little good. Besides the Freemasons who are men of talent, are not such because they belong to the brotherhood, but in spite of it. If the highest knowledge now possessed by men were taught in the lodge, it would still be knowledge not confined to masons, but diffused among all studious men. Of course, if Masonry had the practical meaning which I theoretically ascribe to it, then the case would be altered; but modern Masonry will never reach that standard needed to make it really the instructor of mankind.

294. *Decay of Freemasonry.*—Selfishness, an eye to business, vanity, frivolity, gluttony, and a love of mystery-mongering, concealed under the specious pretence of brotherly love and a longing for instruction—these are the motives that lead men into the lodge. The facility and frequency with which worthless characters are received into the order; the manner in which all its statutes are disregarded; the dislike with which every brother who insists on reform is looked upon by the rest; the difficulty of expelling obnoxious members; the introduction of many spurious rites, and the deceptiveness of the rites themselves, designed to excite curiosity without ever satisfying it; the puerility of the symbolism; the paltriness of the secret when revealed to the candidate, and his ill-concealed disgust when at last he gets behind the scenes and sees through the rotten canvas that forms so beautiful a landscape in front—all these too plainly show that the lodge has banished Freemasonry. And like monasticism or chivalry, it is no longer wanted. Having no political influence and no political aspirations, or, when it has such aspirations revealing them by insane

excesses, such as the late citation before masonic tribunals of Napoleon III., the Emperor of Germany, the Crown Prince, the Pope, and Marshal Prim, by French, Italian, and Spanish masons respectively, and under the Grand Masterships of Crémieux, Garibaldi, and others of the same revolutionary and violent principles, and after a farcical sham trial, condemning the accused so cited—to which summons of course they paid no attention—to death, or in plain English, to assassination, a crime really perpetrated on the person of Marshal Prim; being no longer even a secret society—for a society sanctioned by the State, as Freemasonry is, cannot be called a secret society; having no industrial or intellectual rallying-point—it must eventually die from sheer inanition. It may prolong its existence by getting rid of all the rites and ceremonies which are neither simple nor grand, nor founded on any authority or symbolic meaning, and by renouncing the silly pretence of secrets, and undertaking to teach what I have sketched in various portions of this work, concerning the origin and meaning of Masonry and its symbols, illustrating its teaching by the ornaments and practice of the lodges. This seems to be the only ground on which Freemasonry could claim to have its lease of existence, *as* Freemasonry, renewed.

295. *Masonic Literature.*—It is almost absurd to talk of masonic literature; it scarcely exists.

Except the works written by Oliver, Mackay, Findel, and Ragon, there is scarcely anything worth reading about Freemasonry, of which a Freemason is the author. The countless lectures by brethren, with a few exceptions, consist of mere truisms and platitudes, very much like twaddling sermons, published by request. Its periodical literature—in this country at all events—is essentially of the Grub Street kind, consisting of mere trade-circulars, supported by puffing masonic tradesmen and vain officials, who like to have their working in the lodge trumpeted forth in this fashion: "The way in which he had worked the ceremonies that evening was a great treat to the lodge." "The W. M. proceeded to instal him in that fluent and impressive manner for which he is known," &c. &c.—or by brethren who like to have their speeches or attempted speeches recorded, in this style: "Brother W. felt a little nervous, but hoped to be an ornament to the lodge" (!) "Brother D. had presided at a dish, and it had afforded him much satisfaction, inasmuch as he had had it in his power to make some brethren comfortable," &c. I am not inventing, but actually copying from a masonic newspaper, and might fill pages with similar stuff. All attempts permanently to establish masonic periodicals of a higher order have hitherto failed from want of encouragement. The fact is, men of education take very little interest in Masonry, for it has nothing to offer them in an intellectual point of view; because even masons who have attained to every *ne plus ultra* of the institution, know nothing of its origin and meaning. As to masonic poetry, the poet laureate to Moses and the Profits would not acknowledge one line of it; the bard Close would indignantly repudiate it.

END OF VOL. I.

About the Author

Charles William Heckethorn was born in Switzerland, around 1826. His early years appear to have been spent in Basel but he later moved to Britain and became a naturalised British citizen. In 1850 he was "Professor of French and German in Mr. Bass's School Ryde, Isle of Wight". He married Sarah Forsyth in 1851. When his wife Sarah died, in 1895, he married Jane Baker and they had a daughter, Wilhelmine J. Heckethorn (born around 1879).

Heckethorn's first book was *Exercises in French orthography*, published in 1850 while he was working at Mr. Bass's School Ryde, Isle of Wight. He then produced a translation of *The Frithjof Saga by Esaias Tegnér* in 1856. He did not produce another book until 1875 (foreword dated 1874) when his two volume history, *The secret societies of all ages and countries*, was published. A second edition was published in 1897 and a German language edition in 1900.

In 1875, Heckethorn produced *Roba d'Italia, or, Italian lights and shadows*, an account of a journey through Italy, which was criticised by *The Literary Review* for plagiarising *Roba di Roma*. The journal then alternately criticised and praised the book for its eccentric nature and digressions before heartily recommending it to its readers. The papal anecdotes were found to be amusing but a strong antithesis to the church was noted throughout the work that condemned the waste of teaching the dimensions of Solomon's temple while the *"laws of nature and scientific truths"* were neglected.

Heckethorn then produced books at regular intervals including poetry and children's stories, and a history of the Lincoln's Inn Fields area. His last work, *London memories*, was published in 1900 and contained a chapter on the history of South Lambeth Road. The book was criticised in *The Spectator* for its arrogant view of the past which condemned earlier generations as *"barbarians in manners, and in morals reprobates"* and contained the claim that *"nothing will elevate man but science"*.

Heckethorn died on 13 January 1902 at his home in South Lambeth Road, London.

Selected publications

- *Exercises in French orthography, on a plan entirely new &c.* Relfe & Fletcher, London, 1850.
- *The Frithjof Saga ... Translated into English in the original metres.* Trübner & Co., London, 1856.
- *The secret societies of all ages and countries.* Richard Bentley, London, 1875 (2 vols.)

- *Roba d'Italia, or, Italian lights and shadows: A record of travel.* Samuel Tinsley, London, 1875.
- *Roses and thorns: Poems.* B. Dobell, London, 1888.
- *The windmill and its secrets. A Dove Dale romance.* Trübner & Co., London, 1888.
- *The wondrous tale of Cocky, Clucky, and Cackle. Freely translated from the German of Brentano by C.W. Heckethorn.* J. Hogg, London, 1889.
- *Lincoln's Inn Fields and the localities adjacent: Their historical and topographical associations.* Elliott Stock. London, 1896.
- *The printers of Basle in the XV & XVI centuries: Their biographies, printed books and devices.* Unwin, London, 1897.
- *London souvenirs.* Chatto & Windus, London, 1899.
- *London memories, social, historical, and topographical.* Chatto and Windus, London, 1900.